WHEN THE HANDS ARE MANY

When the Hands Are Many

COMMUNITY ORGANIZATION AND SOCIAL

CHANGE IN RURAL HAITI

Jennie M. Smith

Cornell University Press   ITHACA AND LONDON

First published 2001 by Cornell University Press
First printing, Cornell Paperbacks, 2001

Printed in the United States of America

Library of Congress Cataloging-in-Publication Data

Smith, Jennie Marcelle.
   When the hands are many : community organization and social change in rural Haiti / Jennie Marcelle Smith.
     p. cm.
   Includes bibliographical references (p.   ) and index.
   ISBN 0-8014-3797-0—ISBN 0-8014-8673-4 (pbk.)
   1. Peasantry—Haiti—Grand'Anse (Dept.)—Political activity. 2. Peasantry—Haiti—Grand'Anse (Dept.)—Societies, etc. 3. Community organization—Haiti—Grand'Anse (Dept.) 4. Social values—Haiti—Grand'Anse (Dept.) 5. Folk songs, Creole—Social aspects—Haiti—Grand'Anse (Dept.) I. Title.
   HD1531.H2 S55 2001
   303.4'097294'66—dc21   00-012448

Cloth printing   10 9 8 7 6 5 4 3 2 1

Paperback printing   10 9 8 7 6 5 4 3 2

Dedicated to

my grandfather, Lawrence D. Smith,

in celebration of his contagious love of learning, and his

lived commitment to community,

&

to "outsiders" everywhere.

Contents

Acknowledgments

This text rests on research funded by a Fulbright Student Fellowship from the Institute of International Education, an Inter-American Foundation Dissertation Field Research Fellowship, and a University of North Carolina Off-Campus Research Fellowship. I am indebted as well to Caroline H. and Thomas S. Royster Jr. for the Carolina Society of Fellows Dissertation Fellowship.

During the course of doing fieldwork in Bamòn and Tisous, I was the recipient of innumerable gestures of hospitality and kindness from those with whom I lived and worked. The steaming rounds of freshly baked cassava bread delivered to my door by Djouli's children; the late afternoon chats on Madan Mèsidye's porch; the impromptu advising sessions from market women; the tall sticks of sugar cane cut near the path during long, thirsty journeys; the spontaneous dancing lessons; Tant Elena's fussing care; the overly generous portions of the season's first harvests; the always-open doors of "Eskot's" home in Jeremie and Nini's home in Nazon; Santina's offerings of corossol fruit; the many ears of roasted corn and freshly picked coconuts; Madan Bèna's tin cups of sweet morning coffee, always carefully covered with a white cotton cloth; cool glasses of water; stories, riddles and proverbs told by candlelight and laughter—these are gestures that have redefined for me what hospitality means, and have left me eternally grateful. I am most grateful of all for the generous friendship, companionship, and assistance of my research associate, Benwa.

I am also indebted to numerous coworkers, friends, neighbors, teachers and mentors in other areas of Haiti—from Port-au-Prince, to Kalfounò, to Papay, to Koladè. Invaluable, too, have been the support, critique, advice, and encouragement of many indiv'duals on "this side of the water." Many thanks to my tirelessly brilliant adviser, Dorothy Holland at the University of North Carolina-Chapel Hill, and the other members of an encouraging, challenging, and supportive Ph.D. committee: James Peacock, Carla Freeman, Donald Nonini, and Judith Farquar. I am thankful as well to Alison Greene, Donna Davin, Alisa Ray, Randy Reeves, and Fran Benson and Candace Akins at Cornell University Press, for their careful and insightful critiques and suggestions. For friendship, encouragement, and support, I owe many thanks to Suphronia Cheeks, Karen Ebey-Tessendorf, Alicia Wise, Gina Ulysse, Florence and Sophie Peacock, John McGowan and the Carolina Society of Fellows group, Bryant "Tonton Liben" Freeman, Bob Maguire, Bob Corbett and the "Corbett list" community, Scott Campbell, the Beyond Borders crew, the Mennonite Central Committee, Elaine Nocks, Susan Shaw, Diane Levy, Tricia Samford, Leslie Bartlett, Carla Jones, and Alice Wiener. I am most wordlessly grateful to my family.

Acronyms

CDC	Center for Disease Control
CHA	Council on Hemispheric Affairs
CIVPOL	UN Civilian Police Force
CNG	National Governing Council (ruled Haiti 1986–88)
CRS	Community Relations Service (U.S. Department of State)
EERP	Emergency Economic Recovery Plan
FRAPH	Front Révolutionnaire Armé pour l'Avancement et le Progrès Haïtien
GP	*gwoupman peyizan* (peasant group[ing])
GDP	Gross Domestic Product
GFV	*gwoupman fanm vanyan* (strong women's group[ing])
GNP	Gross National Product
GT	*gwoupman tètansanm* (heads-together group[ing])
IDB	Inter-American Development Bank
IGO	intergovernmental organization
IHERC	Inter-Hemispheric Education Resource Center
IMF	International Monetary Fund
INS	U.S. Immigration and Naturalization Service
IOM	International Organization for Migration
MICIVIH	UN/OAS International Civilian Mission to Haiti
MSPP	Ministry of Public Health and Sanitation (of the Haitian government)
NED	National Endowment for Democracy
NGO	nongovernmental organization
OAS	Organization of American States
ODA	Office of Overseas Development Assistance (Great Britain)

OTI	Office of Transition Initiatives (USAID)
PEPPADEP	Programme pou l'Eradication de la Peste Porcine Africaine et pour le Développement de l'Elvage Porcin
PNH	Haitian National Police
PSC	Project for Social Change
PVC	polyvinyl chloride
SAP	structural adjustment program
TKL	*ti kominote legliz* (little church communities)
TNC	transnational corporation
UN	United Nations
USAID	United States Agency for International Development
USDA	United States Department of Agriculture
VSN	Volontaires de la Sécurité Nationale
WB	World Bank

WHEN THE HANDS ARE MANY

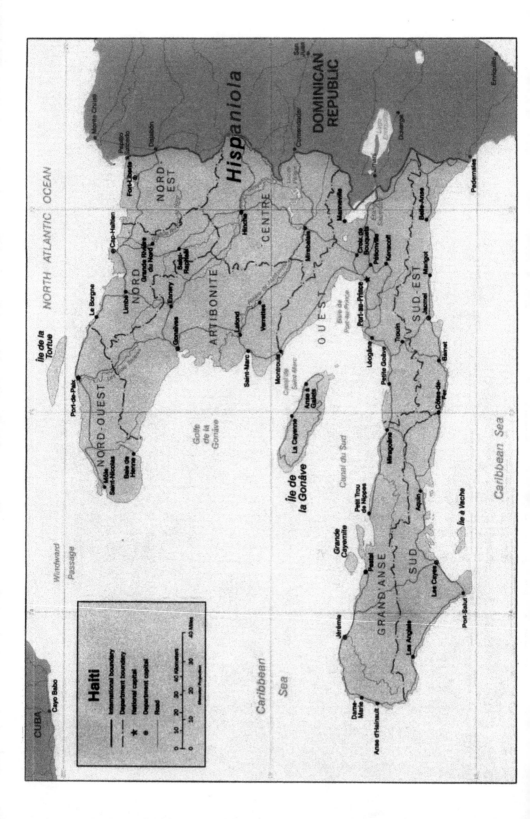

1

Introduction

All nations have varying degrees of associational culture which feed into organisational life,
which in turn constitutes civil society. Civil society is therefore not an entity which can be
created or imposed from above, depending on the needs of the state or international agencies.
(McIlwaine 1998, 667)

"Formerly the things which happened in the world had no connection
among themselves. . . . But since then all events are united in a common
bundle" (Polybius, as quoted in Robertson 1990, 21). Penned in the second
century B.C. this declaration seems tailored precisely for our own times. As
the twenty-first century begins we are truly becoming an intricately interconnected world. Yet just as dramatic as the pace of global integration is the
growing rate of inequity between the world's citizens. Despite several
decades of ambitious international aid initiatives, the post–World War II vision of closing the "First World"–"Third World" divide is more distant from
our grasp than ever. Even as North-Western governments and nongovernmental agencies respond by developing new and improved agendas, gaps
in wealth and power expand.[1] It is time for radically new ways of thinking
and acting globally and locally.

The country of Haiti provides a superb case study of the limitations of
the post–World War II attempts of North-Western powers to develop and
democratize the rest of the world. Founded in 1804 by former slaves following one of the most extraordinary revolutions of modern history, Haiti
once stood as a beacon of hope and inspiration for colonized peoples
throughout the New World. Today, despite the innumerable development
and democratization programs implemented there, it is famous instead
for the desperate poverty of its people and the violent instability of its
state.

But the deficiencies of aid are not all we stand to learn from Haiti. It also
offers us unique guidance in how the problems and challenges presented
by the inequalities that plague our contemporary world might be ad-

dressed more effectively. This book looks specifically at lessons we stand to learn from the country's poorest citizens—its rural peasantry.

Haitian peasants are some of the most politically disempowered, malnourished, and illiterate people of the world. It is not surprising, then, that they are consistently viewed by others as victims in need of rescue or social problems in need of reform. Their eroded fields, their exhausted bodies, their undernourished children, their collapsing schoolhouses—all of these make them potential targets for material and technological aid. I argue that they also are potential teachers and guides.

Escobar has pointed out that

> One must then resist the desire to formulate alternatives at an abstract, macro level; one must also resist the idea that the articulation of alternatives will take place in intellectual and academic circles, without meaning by this that academic knowledge has no role in the politics of alternative thinking.
>
> Where, then, lies "the alternative"? . . . A first approach is to look for alternative practices in the resistance of grassroots groups present to dominant interventions. (1995, 222)

In the context of Haiti, this necessarily involves looking toward the peasantry. Anthropologist Michel-Rolph Trouillot urged us to do just that more than a decade ago: "Any solution to the Haitian crisis must find its roots in the resources of the peasantry. . . . And to do this, . . . intellectuals, politicians and planners—foreign and Haitian alike—[must] talk less about (or 'for') the peasantry and begin listening more attentively to what its diverse subgroups have said in the past and have to say now about their own future" (1990, 229–30).

This book may be seen in part as an answer to that call.

By taking as my primary theoretical and methodological point of departure the words and practices of Haitian peasants themselves rather than either scholarly constructions of them or a particular theoretical framework. I part ways with traditional anthropological work. In this text it is Haitian peasants who are "doing theory," who are debating the meanings of social progress, development, democracy, and modernity. In highlighting the poor's own models for positive social, economic, and political change, this book also departs from dominant patterns in development literature. Neither does it follow the path taken by most analysts of Haiti itself. While often bemoaning the state of Haiti's most populous sector Haitianists have rarely provided accounts of what these internal "outsiders" (*moun andeyò*, or "the people out there," as they are called by their fellow citizens) have said and done about their situation (A superb exception to this pattern is Drexel Woodson's 1990 work).

This attempt to re-present the Haitian peasantry should not be seen as an exercise in glorifying "the voices of the voiceless" or ennobling the downtrodden. It is, rather, a portrayal of an uneven struggle of a few groups of ordinary people to survive the harsh realities of the world in which they live—and in the process, to find meaning, protect their dignity, build community, and work toward a more decent tomorrow. In documenting this struggle, I trace the historical roots of the peasantry's current situation, document its experiences with foreign development and democratization agendas, describe the collective strategies its members have developed, and reveal the spiritual and cultural resources they have called on for help.

I focus specifically on an in-depth ethnographic study of a song tradition called *chante pwen* and rural civic organizations called "peasant groups." Representing a large variety of organizational structures and objectives (some focus on agricultural labor exchange, others on mutual economic assistance, community development, or political advocacy), contemporary peasant groups draw on a history of community-based organization predating the Saint Domingue Revolution. Still reflective of this past, they also are actively engaged in the globalizing, transnationalizing, developing, and democratizing world in which the peasantry is immersed.

A Haitian priest once told me that peasant groups have been for his country an "underground spring." My research bears out this metaphor. I found not only that these groups have long provided sustenance to rural Haitian communities but also that they have important contributions to make in the formulation of Haiti's future, as well as in larger endeavors aimed at challenging some of the disparities, injustices, and divisions characterizing our contemporary human community.

Such a view of civil society in rural Haiti will undoubtedly be met with skepticism. It is not uncommon for analysts to claim that the country has no real civil society. (This argument has been used to assert that Haiti is not ready for democracy and to explain why it seems unable to develop.) Again, like Haiti's disappearing springs, peasant groups have remained largely invisible to outside observers. Although certain types of groups—namely, those associated with externally based development and democratization initiatives—have gained more attention in recent years, even discussions of grass-roots organization in Haiti have virtually ignored those groups initiated and directed exclusively by peasants.[2] Most analyses that do exist are grounded in the development-oriented ideologies and the modernist scholarly classifications of the North–West. By evaluating these groups on the basis of foreign concepts of success and progress, such standards leave us with a myopic lens through which to view them—a lens that compels us to see Haitian peasant groups primarily in terms of what they are not, do not have, and do not do. As a result, they are generally portrayed as either counterprogressive or irrelevant remnants of a backward traditional culture, remnants whose survival, while hitherto remarkable, is inevitably doomed by the pressures of contemporary economic, environmental, and social pressures.[3]

Unfortunately, this myopic viewpoint has closed the door to understanding the diverse objectives of Haitian peasant groups and appreciating the multilayered and heavily nuanced value they have for those who participate in them. Using a number of case studies from my work with peasant groups in Haiti's Northeast, Central Plateau, and Grand'Anse regions, I seek to paint a quite different portrait, grounded instead in what group members say about their lives, their communities, their society, and about what social change can and should mean. From this account there emerges a coherent, if "partial and halting" (Haraway 1988, 590), vision of a "good society" and of how that society might be brought about. Contained in this vision are a number of provocative critiques of dominant North-Western understandings of concepts such as progress, development, democracy, and civil society, as well as suggestions about changes that need to be made in the ways we attempt to understand and contribute to the struggles for survival and social change instigated by those identified as poor and disempowered.

"Americans Don't Have Democracy!"

Walking along the mountainous footpath toward the northeastern community of Kayayo, I thought about the community-group meeting I was going to.[4] It was the fall of 1990, and as December 16—the date for what would be Haiti's first democratic elections—quickly approached, civic education campaigns were being carried out all over the country. In the rural area where I lived, the primary forum for this voter education was the local peasant group. Today, the Kayayo group would be discussing the concept of democracy. As I walked, I considered how the Haitian people had never before been ruled by a democratically elected government, and contemplated how I might contribute to the meeting by sharing my more cultivated understanding of democratic philosophies and procedures.

When I arrived at the one-room schoolhouse where the group would be meeting, I took a seat by the educator, Ton Gi, a farmer and preacher from a neighboring village.[5] As we chatted, people began to arrive. Although it was barely eight o'clock in the morning, most of the group members had already spent a few hours in the fields, and walked in wiping their brows and placing their machetes on the dirt floor by their bare feet. Once we all greeted one another, prayed, and sang a group song, Ton Gi opened the meeting with a question: "What is democracy?" After a long pause, one man tentatively offered a definition. "Democracy," he said slowly and thought-fully, "is when every person is able to have enough food to eat—and good food—not just corn meal mush with no bean sauce." A woman with a child nursing at her breast added, "It's when everybody has the chance to give their children an education, instead of having to keep them out of school because we can't afford shoes or books, or need them to work in the fields." "It's when the 'little people,'" her brother chimed in, "not just the 'big men' in town, or those folks in Port-au-Prince, have a right to say what they think without getting beaten up by the section chief [the local military commander]. Everybody ought to have that right." Several other people continued: "Democracy is having a bed to sleep on, instead of a pile of straw or rags heaped on the floor." "Some people shouldn't have to walk miles to get cruddy water while other people get *ice* in their glasses every day." "I hear that folks in La Gonâve are boiling green mangoes to stay alive these days. That's not democracy."

As the discussion continued, Ton Gi challenged those present to reflect on factors inhibiting democratic change in Haiti. Several members de-scribed the traditional power structures of their local community, and shared stories of corruption and abuse. A woman finally suggested, "Well . . . I have heard that some people have *too* much food to eat, so much that they can't even eat it all! Maybe *they've* been getting some of *ours*." The group agreed that in order for democracy to be established in Haiti, a re-distribution of wealth as well as of political power would have to occur. They ended the meeting by talking about the upcoming elections as one opportunity to work toward their vision of democracy.

This was not the first time I had gone into a meeting of Haitian peasants thinking I had something to teach, only to be presented with compelling lessons—many of which forced me to reexamine my own notions of how things are and how they should be. Among the most dynamic and provoca-tive community-group meetings I attended were those centered on democ-racy. A number of those have closely resembled the Kayayo discussion. The following two excerpts are from a meeting that took place six years later, in the mountains of Haiti's southwestern peninsula:

> "The Americans, they come here to tell us what democracy is, but as for me, I don't see that they truly understand the thing."
>
> "American democracy, that's not real democracy! How can you have democracy if you don't have respect?" "Hmmph." . . . "*Demokrasi? Se pa demokrasi sa, sa se demokrache!*" [Democracy? That's not democra-*cy*.
> That's democra-*spit!*][6]

What is going on here? From media and scholarly accounts, one could easily surmise that few Haitian peasants have thought at much length about the concept of democracy. My reflections prior to the Kayayo meeting reveal the common assumption that because the Haitian population had never lived under a democratic form of government, they have had no real access to this realm of inquiry. This position was summarized well in a conversation I had in 1996 with an expatriate human rights worker:

> People [Haitians] have a very good idea of what's right and what's wrong, but as for grasping the theory of democracy, they are nowhere close. I learned it because I studied that stuff in textbooks, but they don't get taught any of this in school. . . . My right to sling my fist ends where the other man's nose begins; they don't have this concept at all. . . . They don't have a social contract with each other. . . . They don't really know how to deal with one another.

Some have explained rural Haitians' presumed ignorance on issues like democratic governance by appealing to the peasantry's reputation as an isolated, illiterate, chronically undernourished, and desperately poor population. These are people who simply cannot afford to expend their mental energies on very much besides surviving from day to day. The peasants quoted above beg to differ. Not only do they reveal that they have thought carefully about what democracy is; they also reveal that they have formulated careful critiques of what democracy is *not.*

Comments such as those declaring that Americans don't know what "real democracy" is were not just spur-of-the-moment outbursts of anti-American sentiment. At one meeting, I was told that the problem with American democracy is that it "has no respect. . . . You can see it in the way Americans dress and act." People sometimes added to such criticisms a concern that "American democracy" was threatening to undermine the establishment of a "true democracy" in Haiti. They talked about how the U.S. government was trying to push the Haitian government to implement structural adjustment programs and other policies sure to increase disparities in wealth and power. They also expressed skepticism of the foreign-sponsored, civic-education campaigns that had recently appeared in the region.[7] Among the influences considered especially threatening were television, popular music, and movies from the United States, all of which seemed to be undermining the morals of Haiti's young people (especially those in urban areas), and hence the rest of the society. *"Demokra-che!"*

Where have these judgments about the nature of democracy come from? Analysis of their content reveals that they are not simply regurgitations of facts from social studies books, newscasts on the radio, or the "democracy-enhancement" initiatives promoted by international organizations. They are primarily grounded, rather, in their speakers' own experiences in regulating community life, organizing work, engaging with the past, and grappling with their place in the world. They are grounded in peasants' own understandings of the way things are and the way things ought to be.

While these understandings are often markedly distinct from those reflected in contemporary efforts to develop and democratize the Haitian population, they are strikingly similar to the ideas and visions of many others who find themselves in similar political, social, and economic circumstances. Even though the discourses and practices highlighted in the following chapters are full of historical and cultural particularities, they share much in common with those documented in literatures on community-based movements elsewhere in the South—particularly in the larger Latin American and Caribbean region. Haynes suggests that such movements, "wittingly or unwittingly . . . , are contributing to the slow emergence of the democratic process by strengthening and enlarging civil society," and are thus "at the cutting edge of a democratic revolution whose central themes are liberty, equality and autonomy." (1997, 15, 5). Other scholars are less optimistic and warn that these movements and the civil societies they compose can also be "the seat of numerous relations of oppression" (Laclau and Mouffe 1985, 179).

Regardless of the disagreements about the potentialities of these movements, they clearly merit much more attention than they have previously received. This is particularly true for those movements based in rural areas. As Starn notes,

> Peasant mobilization has received little attention in the literature on new social movements. One obvious reason for the oversight rests with the greater visibility of urban politics, which unfold in the backyards of the leading scholars in debates on contemporary social activism. More deeply, it is easy to ignore or dismiss peasant organizing as outdated class politics. Movements like those for human rights, racial and sexual liberation, and the environment appear to mesh with a postmodern condition of shifting, plural, and nonessential subjectivities. Peasant protest, by contrast, brings to mind modernist images of class struggle and Socialist revolution. The word *peasant* sounds not even modern but medieval. (1992, 91, italics in the original)

By thus ignoring peasants, Starn adds, "most scholarship on new social movements . . . misses some of the most vital new politics on the planet" (1992, 90).

Background and Approach

> The starting-point of critical elaboration is consciousness of what one really is, and is "knowing thyself" as a product of the historical processes to date,

which have deposited in you an infinity of traces, without leaving an inventory. (Gramsci 1991)

Plenty of anthropology has been done here [in Haiti], but *for what, for whom?* (a Haitian priest, during a February 1995 interview)

Recollections of Kayayo were in the back of my mind when I began graduate study in anthropology less than a year after the meeting, which fell near the end of my first stay in Haiti (1988–91). During those three years, I had worked with a U.S.-based nongovernmental organization (NGO) as the health education and women's concerns coordinator of a community-based development project. This project was based in Kalfounò, a remote rural district of Haiti's northeastern mountains. While in Kalfounò, I had become deeply troubled by portrayals of peasants I found in popular media and scholarly accounts of Haiti, in conversations with wealthier Haitians, and in interactions with other foreign aid workers. My frustration grew out of the stark contrast between these portrayals and my perceptions of what local coworkers, friends, and neighbors were doing and saying about their lives. I began to suspect that this gap might be a key to understanding why outside interventions had so miserably failed to effect lasting positive changes in Haiti. I suspected that the same gap and similar results were evident in other areas of the South.

Further pursuing these issues was at the forefront of my agenda when I entered graduate school in sociocultural anthropology at the University of North Carolina, Chapel Hill, in the fall of 1991.[8] I returned to Haiti in January 1995 and stayed until May 1996, conducting dissertation research. I spent most of that year and a half in a rural community located in the mountains of Haiti's southwestern Grand'Anse department.

I was the recipient of innumerable gestures of hospitality and kindness during the course of my fieldwork—from neighbors, friends, coworkers, and strangers alike. Just as touching, meaningful, and inspirational as the assistance and gestures of these individuals were the ways I was received by the community organizations with which I studied. Nothing, however, enhanced either my everyday life or the nature and results of my research as much as the tirelessly insightful, good-natured, energetic, and creative assistance of Benwa, the peasant-group leader and local resident who became my research associate soon after I moved to Tisous. He walked endless miles with me through rough terrain, showing me the way to the dozens of neighborhoods we visited throughout the Grand'Anse. He helped me gain entrée into many meetings, ceremonies, and homes. He tutored me on local agricultural cycles, on class stratification among peasants, on herbal remedies and magical cures, on the nature and histories of the groups we visited, on religion, and on life. Although he had never been able to com-

Landscape of Kalfounò.

plete his secondary-school education, in many ways he was a practicing anthropologist long before I began my fieldwork and had informally studied
rural organization for years. Already deeply involved in the peasant-group
movement there, his commitment to the well-being of the groups and their
members continually kept in check our research objectives and strategies.
He was unimaginably patient and forgiving with my own frailties and failures, and was equally as kind and generous of heart to those with whom we
worked. He cared about our work and believed in its objectives, and
thereby kept me from getting discouraged on more than a few occasions.

Benwa and I conceptualized the modus operandi in which we aspired to
work as that of *onè-respe* (honor-respect). In the countryside, it is customary
to call out before entering someone's yard, *"Onè!"* (Honor!). One then hes-
itates until hearing the welcome, *"Respè!"* (Respect!) before entering.
Demonstrations of honor and respect between hosts and guests regardless
of social standing is a code of etiquette held in high esteem by rural
Haitians. It is important that visitors be especially attentive to and obser-

The author with neighbors in Tisous.

vant of such codes, not only because of their inherent value as mutually bestowed acknowledgments of the dignity of the other but also because they
can clear paths to greater acceptance. As Haitians sometimes put it, *"Bèl
bonjou se paspò ou"* (A lovely greeting is your passport). In practicing ethnog-
raphy, Benwa and I tried to be as true as possible to this code of approaching with honor, hesitating with a listening ear, and engaging in a dialogue
characterized by mutual respect.

This approach has been unwieldy at times and, on occasion, downright
impossible to follow. In more than a few instances, the desires of those with
whom we worked and their expectations of what I ought to offer them
(often, a certain sort of material aid) simply could not be reconciled with
my research objectives, ethical codes, or financial resources. Such dilem-
mas were joined by those presented by the field of anthropology. At the
close of the twentieth century, North-Western ethnographers are increasingly confronted with postmodernist critiques that portray our endeavors
as "spy work," which, though perhaps more sophisticatedly disguised, is just
as vulnerable to being used as a tool with which the powerful can more effectively exploit the powerless, as were the accounts of certain colonial and

World War II-era anthropologists. Such critiques directly influenced me to become more sensitive to the complex intellectual and ethical contradictions involved in ethnographic work. Yet this book also represents a refusal to take postmodernist critiques to their logical end—that is, silence. "You write this down, Djeni!" I was told more than a few times in the field. "You go tell them what I'm saying." More than any theoretical counterargument, this insistence convinced me of my responsibility to tell their stories as well as I can and as awkwardly and insufficiently as I must.

The Haitian "Peasantry"

> Peasantry means something different when referring to the Senegal River Valley, the equatorial forest, central Zimbabwe, highland Ethiopia, and the oasis on the Sahara. And it may mean something different when referring to quite different labor processes even within the same area, as in the case of the Central Sudan. (Isaacman 1993, 228)

> Debates about who peasants are, or how best to define peasantries . . . promise to be unending. (Mintz 1973, 92)

What do I mean when I refer to Haitian "peasants"? As the above quotations suggest, defining *peasant* and *peasantry* has long been a problematic task that has generated much more controversy than consensus. *Peasant* seems to be "one of those words whose meaning everyone knows yet whose definition is never precise" (Leyburn 1941, 74; see also Starn 1992, 96). In facing this dilemma, many scholars have concluded that the term is meaningless and have altogether given up on using it. Others have simply used it without defining its meaning. I have chosen to use the term (*peyizan*, or *abitan*, in Haitian Creole), first, because it is meaningful to Haitians; it is what they use to talk about the people who are the focal point of this book. Second, I agree with Nonini that alternative terms, such as *simple commodity procedures* and *petty commodity procedures*, too readily characterize the groups they denote as differentiated by economic factors alone (1992, 166–67).[9]

My understanding of what the Haitian peasantry is (and is not) both integrates and rejects elements of definitions developed by other students of Haiti in accordance with my field research.[10] Haitian peasants, first of all, are agriculturalists who cultivate small plots of land. They are not subsistence farmers but produce cash crops as well as domestic foodstuffs and are dependent on a variety of imported goods. Perhaps the most distinctive characteristic of Haitian peasants is that they commonly own at least part of the land they work.[11] Landlessness is a growing problem in rural Haitian communities. But this access to land has markedly distinguished them from rural dwellers in most other areas of the Caribbean and Latin America, and has had a profound impact on many aspects of their culture, from local economic and political systems to community organizations, religious traditions, and the content of day-to-day life. Besides farming, another economic activity central to Haitian peasant life is the buying and selling of produce and other goods in rural and urban markets.[12] This industry is largely dominated by women, although women also are active in agricultural production and are responsible for most domestic chores.[13]

In describing Haitian peasant culture, many scholars have focused primarily on how the peasantry differs politically and economically from the Haitian elite (see especially Leyburn 1941; Mintz 1974; Trouillot 1990). This is not surprising, for despite the many gradations of wealth that may be identified among Haiti's population, the differences and distances that exist between its (most powerful) urban rich and its (most populous) rural poor are striking.[14] Leyburn concludes that these two classes are actually "castes" and characterizes them as "different as day from night . . . and as separate as oil and water" (Leyburn 1941, 4). Whereas members of Haiti's tiny upper crust boast levels of affluence that would humble many U.S. millionaires, most Haitian peasants live in grinding poverty. Whereas the elite have reaped the benefits of the best educational institutions in Europe and the Americas, the majority of peasants are unable to read and write. Whereas the wealthy fly to Paris, Montreal, and Miami to shop for clothes and receive high-tech medical care, the poor suffer from chronic hunger and malnutrition, and die from diseases that have long been easily treatable. Whereas many elites pride themselves on their light complexions, peasants are assumed to be (and most are) dark. Whereas the elite sector is concentrated in the capital city of Port-au-Prince, peasants tend to reside in the scattered rural settlements of the mountainous countryside. That the former are commonly referred to as *moun andeyò-s*, "the people out there," or "the outsiders," reflects the two groups' understandings of their relative positionalities in the nation they call home.

Yet in reality, Haiti's rural poor have never constituted an isolated population, nor have they been removed from larger political, economic, social, and cultural spheres. Rather, they have always been "fully integrated into the Haitian economy, which itself [has been] fully integrated into the larger capitalist world-economy"[15] (Dupuy 1989, 103; see also Vander Zaag 1999, 68). Each day, thousands of rural market women travel long distances on donkeys, on foot, or in public transportation vehicles to buy and sell their wares in towns, villages, and cities throughout the country. A significant number of them also travel back and forth to Jamaica, the Bahamas, the Dominican Republic, and other Caribbean countries. Many peasants have relatives in the United States, Canada, or Europe. Nearly everyone claims relatives in Port-au-Prince. Every October, large numbers of teenagers move from their homes in the countryside to provincial cities where they finish their secondary-school education. Wage-labor opportunities draw young women and men to *chèche lavi* (search for a living) in Port-au-Prince. And with every new era of political turmoil, another incalculable number of activists and community leaders flee their homes and go into hiding, living transient lives for days, months, or sometimes years at a time. Their constant engagement in commerce, labor migration, dispersed family networks, and a host of other systems reveals that rural Haitians, far from being "out there," are right in the midst of processes that increasingly characterize our thoroughly transboundaried world.

Bamòn and Tisous

Most of the fieldwork cited here, as I have noted, was carried out in a mountainous rural community of the Grand'Anse department. Located on the tip of Haiti's southwestern peninsula, the Grand'Anse is one of the most geographically rugged and remote regions of the country (with peaks reaching more than 2,300 meters) and is even more neglected than most other departments in terms of infrastructure. It is also among the most beautiful of Haiti's territories, the unending mountainscapes being less thoroughly stripped of trees than many areas.

Tisous, the settlement where I resided, is one of more than thirty *abita-syon*-s[16] within the "rural section" or "zone"[17] of Bamòn, which covers nearly 120 square kilometers of territory and hosts between nine and twelve thousand people.[18] Bamòn claims one small village, Nazon. Although located toward one edge of the zone, this village is considered the "center" of the Bamòn rural section, largely because it is the local headquarters of the Catholic church. As such, it also has been the headquarters for the numerous priests, brothers, and sisters (most of them foreigners) who have served the parish. With substantial amounts of foreign-aid money, numerous visits by engineers and builders from abroad, and the manual labor of local residents, these missionaries have "developed" Nazon over the past few decades—by adding physical structures that dwarf those found in any other area of the zone. Besides their own multistoried offices and homes, the clergy have orchestrated the construction of the area's largest Catholic church, Bamòn's most well-equipped and well-funded primary school, its only fully functioning secondary school, and the zone's sole North-Western medical clinic.

Its location also places Nazon's residents close to the only road through the Bamòn rural section and in fairly close proximity (around a one- to one-and-a-half hour walk) to the departmental capital, Jérémie.[19] These advantages, plus the fact that the Haitian and foreign clergy who have resided there have provided employment opportunities unparalleled in other areas of the zone, have resulted in substantial demographic changes in Nazon during the past few generations. Unlike the communities clustered around it, a substantial portion of Nazon's residents are no longer *ti peyizan*-s (small peasants) and have greater access to wealth, formal education, professional training, and nonagricultural jobs than the majority of people in the zone. They work as domestics or drive vehicles for the clergy, teach school, oversee large landholdings, run small businesses, trade large quantities of merchandise, work as skilled carpenters and builders, and staff the local clinic or the Jérémie hospital. Here many residents enjoy roofs of corrugated tin, floors of concrete, glassware, pens and pencils, mirrors, leather sneakers, radios, store-bought clothes (as opposed to secondhand *rad pepe* purchased in the area's outdoor markets),[20] and other luxuries much more rare in other areas. Nazon also has the greatest degree of class stratification in the rural section, meaning that many of its poorest citizens are worse off than the poorest of other Bamon neighborhoods. Still, simply being from this community, often called "town," carries with it a certain sort of social capital. My neighbors in Tisous often referred to Nazon residents in general as "big shots."

Most Bamòn residents live in one of many abitasyon-s, or "hamlets," such as Tisous. Abitasyon-s generally consist of anywhere from a dozen to more than a hundred residences scattered throughout the abitasyon's land area. Approximately twenty-six households claimed Tisous as their home abitasyon during my time there. Like those of most abitasyon-s, its boundaries are loosely and inconsistently defined by locals. Geographically, Tisous is at the other end of the zone from Nazon and, therefore, considered one of Bamòn's more out-of-the-way communities. Tisous also is commonly described by residents and outsiders in terms of how far it lies from "the city." In terms meaningful to residents, Tisous is a nearly four-hour walk from Jérémie.

The vast majority of Bamòn residents, like most rural Haitians, are small farmers and traders. The major crops raised in the area include many varieties of beans, corn, millet, plantains, yams, and breadfruit ("Here breadfruit is our mama and our papa"). Other crops are tropical sweet potatoes, pumpkins, manioc, sugar cane, highland rice, chayote squash, taro, malanga, coffee, and cocoa. Bamòn peasants cultivate a large variety of fruits (including but not limited to mangos, oranges, grapefruits, corossol, bananas, avocados, passion fruit, pomegranates, coconuts, guavas, papayas, and shaddock) as well. Most households own several chickens, a rooster, a goat or two, and possibly a pig. Those with more economic security may own several goats or pigs, along with a head or two of cattle.

The area generally experiences two rainy seasons (meaning rain may fall on most days for a few hours, generally during the afternoon). These tend to occur in April and May, and again beginning in October or November and lasting through most of December. Unfortunately, many recent years have been plagued with longer than usual dry (also known as "hungry") seasons, a situation that has aggravated the already diminishing ability of the peasants there to support themselves with their work.

While nearly all the women in Bamòn work in the fields, care for small livestock, and conduct most domestic and child-rearing tasks, most also work as *timachann-s* or small commercantes. This generally involves selling portions of their families' produce at nearby markets and buying other items (either local produce or imported products) to sell at a slightly higher price in their home communities or at markets elsewhere. They may also prepare and sell foodstuffs, such as homemade candies, cookies, beverages, or fried foods, alongside heavily traveled pathways or at events such as cockfights, or in the marketplaces, or around the grounds of churches or schools. Only a handful of Bamòn residents have been able to amass enough capital to open small storefront businesses. Those who have, commonly sell kerosene for lamps, shortening, rice, flour, tomato paste, cooking oil, and radio batteries. (Most of these products are carried from Jérémie by family members, either on foot or with the assistance of a mule or donkey.)

Other entrepreneurial pursuits taken up by Bamòn residents with more economic capital than most include the making and selling of sugar cane syrup. Often, these same individuals (usually men) produce the area's unrefined white rum, called *kleren, tafya,* or *gwòg*. Others run small bakeries that make the nationally popular white rolls, known in Bamòn as *pen vensenk* or *pen senkant*. The technologies employed in the production of these items are no more (and sometimes less) developed than those available during much of the colonial era. Cane syrup, for example, is made with simple oxen-driven presses, while rolls are shaped by hand and baked in large clay ovens. This is not surprising, given that the zone, like most areas of rural Haiti, lacks electricity and running water.

Besides the Catholic elementary and secondary schools in Nazon, there are more than a dozen much smaller and more modest schools scattered throughout Bamòn. Each of these offers a few years of primary-school education. Tisous hosts one of them. Like nearly all of the rest, it is housed in a single-room structure, which also serves as a place for church services and community meetings. The Bamòn area has many small churches (Protestant and Pentecostal), as well as several Catholic chapels affiliated with the Nazon church. Temples for serving the *lwa*-s[21] also populate the area, and Bamón is home to numerous *manbo*-s, *ougan*-s, and *bòkò*-s. Some of these priestesses, priests, and priest-sorcerers are known throughout the Grand'Anse department for their extraordinary powers.

Linguistic Issues

If there is something of value in this book, it is primarily to the credit of Benwa and to the groups and individuals I met in Tisous, in Bamòn, in the greater Grand'Anse, in Port-au-Prince, in Kalfounò, and in the many other communities I have visited during my involvement with Haiti over the past twelve years. Because the tables could turn in Haiti's political landscape at any time and, once again, make peasant groups and their empathizers the targets of brutality, I am unable to give these people and places the acknowledgment they deserve. Instead, I have masked their identities. The only names that have not been changed are the names of nationally known figures and organizations, the capital city of Port-au-Prince, and major provincial towns (e.g., Jérémie), most of which are written in French for easy identification.

All translations are my own unless noted otherwise. I have drawn from a number of texts in translating terms from Haitian Creole to English. Most prominent among these is the Freeman-Laguerre *Haitian-English Dictionary* (1996). Others include Vilsaint's *Diksyonè-Anglè-Kreyòl/English-Kreyòl Dictionary* (1991), Targète and Urciolo's *Haitian Creole-English Dictionary* (1993), and the *Haitian Creole-English-French Dictionary* of the Indiana University Creole Institute (Valdman 1981).

The Creole spelling system used here is the phonemic system approved by the Haitian government in 1979. In the interest of clarity, I have adopted Gage Averill's system for signifying the pluralization of Creole terms within English text by substituting an "-s" for the Creole ending *yo* which (because it is also an article) would not always be appropriate to use (Averill 1997). When a term consists of a noun and a modifier, I tack the plural ending onto the end of compound term (as one would with the Creole *yo*), rather than to the noun in particular. (In translating pointing songs, for example, I write *chante pwen*-s instead of *chante-s pwen*.) I do not use the "-s" for terms that are immersed in Creole-language passages or quotations.

I have struggled throughout the writing of this text with the dilemma of whether to use the past or present tense in my descriptions. Following the circulation of Fabien's *Time and the Other* (1983) and a number of other works, the general trend in anthropology has been to move away from using the present tense in ethnographic description. Present-tense description, it is argued, makes the subjects of a work appear timeless and unchanging by implying that they are doing now what they have always done and what they will continue to do evermore. Moreover, as Robinson points out, it has allowed anthropologists

> to avoid describing the phenomenal reality encountered—the social relations actually observed during field work—by reconstructing an alleged reality through filtering out, using criteria which are not made explicit, all that is deemed modern or new, all those changes arising from the expansion of capitalist markets and the capitalist mode of production. (1986, 6)

Because of such problems, most ethnographers now use the past tense in writing about their observations.

My dilemma is that many of the organizations and practices discussed here have often been portrayed as obsolete, as if they are either dead or are dying. Because I hope to emphasize instead their contemporary relevance, I use the present tense when making statements about the general characteristics of organizations, styles of discourse, habitual practices, locations, genres of music, and so forth. When communicating the specific things I observed people doing and saying during my research, I generally use the past tense. My desire is to demonstrate both that the observations discussed here occurred in particular, historically located moments, and that their subjects—though grounded in time—are neither frozen in time nor things of the past.

2

Persistent Legacies

They are all gone now—the ones who did these things—gone to their reward. But the afterbirth is lodged in the woman's body and will not be expelled. All the waste of birth. Foul-smelling and past its use. (Mrs. Stevens, in Michelle Cliff's novel, *Abeng* [1984, 165])

The administration of the colony of Saint Domingue by the French is widely acknowledged as one of the most ruthless and bloody legacies of the colonial era. Numerous historical accounts have documented the cruelties practiced against Africans enslaved there. Carolyn Fick offers this assessment:

> Punishment, often surpassing the human imagination in its grotesque refinements of barbarism and torture, was often the order of the day.
>
> The barbarism of some masters left little to the imagination. While administering the whip, they would stop, place a burning piece of wood on the slave's buttocks, and then continue, rendering the subsequent blows all the more painful. Common was the practice of pouring pepper, salt, lemon, ashes or quicklime on the slave's open and bleeding wounds, under the pretext of cauterizing the skin, while at the same time increasing the torture. . . . Other examples exist of slaves being thrown into hot ovens and consumed by fire; or of being tied to a skewer about an open fire, there to roast to death; or of having white-hot slats applied to their ankles and soles of their feet, this being repeated hour after hour. There were masters who would stuff a slave with gunpowder—like a cannon—and blow him to pieces. Women had their sexual parts burned by a smoldering log; others had hot wax splattered over hands, arms, and backs, or boiling cane syrup poured over their heads.
>
> Some preferred the art of direct mutilation. They would hang a slave by the ears, mutilate a leg, pull teeth out, gash open one's side and pour melted lard into the incision, or mutilate genital organs. Still others used the torture of live burial, whereby the slave, in the presence of the rest of the slaves who were forced to bear witness, was made to dig his own grave. Some would have a slave buried up to the neck and the head coated with sugar, leaving it to be devoured by flies, while others managed to invent insidious variations. Less

refined cruelties, but none the less horrible, included locking slaves up in barrels, dragging them by horses, making them eat their own excrement and drink their urine.

. . . in colonial Saint Domingue there seemed to be an indeterminate line between economic interest on the one hand, and pure self-indulgent sadism, on the other. (1990, 34–36)

In his classic account of the first days of the Saint Domingue revolution and its leader, Toussaint L'Ouverture, C.L.R. James concludes that "on such a soil as San Domingo slavery, only a vicious society could flourish" (1989 [1963], 27). Indeed, the legacies entrenched on this western third of the island of Hispañola during the seventeenth and eighteenth centuries continue to reverberate in Haiti today.

Predatory Parasitism

On January 1, 1804, when hundreds of thousands of formerly enslaved women and men celebrated the death of the Saint Domingue colony, they hoped to put its horrors behind them. As free citizens of the newly liberated country of Haiti, they looked toward a society where they could enjoy the fruits of economic sovereignty and political liberty.

Instead, during the ensuing two centuries, they and their descendents have witnessed the entrenchment of policies and structures that have left them among the most impoverished and disenfranchised citizens of the world. Many say that Haiti is a land of irony and paradox. It surely hosts no paradox more absurd, and no irony more bitter, than the stark contrast between its hopes at the beginning of the nineteenth century and its realities at the beginning of the twenty-first. Though this contrast is bewildering, its causes are not mysterious. Historians attest that the ideals of the Saint Domingue revolution were subverted even in the first days of the Haitian republic, as the revolutionaries who became its first rulers sought to reinstitute many of the policies characteristic of the European colonialism they had overthrown. Jean-Jacques Dessalines[1] wasted little time, for instance, before seeking to establish what was essentially a revised plantation system: "Again, there was only a substitution of masters . . . As for the common people in whose name the creation of the principle of equality had been proclaimed . . . their situation, in a century of liberty and political independence, was that of servitude minus the presence of the *Code Noir* and the whip of the commander" (Jean Price-Mars 1983 [1928], 105).

Henry Christophe would impose similar policies during his reign (1807–16). The "Code Henri," describes Dupuy, confined all laborers to the plantations and compelled them to work under strict discipline. Work began at dawn and lasted until sunset from Monday to Friday. And, as before, the workers received one-forth of the value of the crops as wages, in addition to being given small family plots for their own food cultivation. Moreover, the laborers were bound to their respective plantations and could not willingly move to another plantation or to another part of the country. (Dupuy 1989, 87)

As Leyburn describes it, "There was actually little difference between the attitude of this ruling clique toward the mass of laborers and that of their white owners. Both looked upon them as cattle" (1941, 41). In his historical account of the relationship between the Haitian state and the Haitian nation, Trouillot (1990) describes how the campaign of Haiti's rulers to subjugate and exploit the rest of the population has continued largely unabated ever since.[2] As Mintz puts it, eventually the Haitian population grew to "expect little from their government—and they got less" (1995, 81).

Among the most enduring government strategies was the 1826 Code Rurale of Jean-Pierre Boyer, aimed primarily at establishing Boyer's own version of militarized agriculture. Like others before it, this initiative ultimately failed, owing primarily to the stubborn nonparticipation of a young peasantry, whose members were determined to own and work their own land. According to Leyburn, "The workers simply ignored [the Code Rurale]" (1941, 69). This persistent resistance, however, did not prevent the code and other policies legitimizing disciplinary state control over the labor and resources from having a profoundly negative impact on the social, economic, and political realities of rural Haiti. Indeed, they have played a central role in the peasantry's increasing impoverishment.

Other forms of subjugation have been more indirect, though no less harmful. McGowan notes that while the agricultural sector has provided the bulk of domestic production, it has received "virtually no reinvestments" (1997, 4). Whereas Haiti's wealthiest citizens have often paid little of their incomes in taxes, the government has extracted great proportions of the peasantry's earnings, acquired *senk kòb* by *senk kòb*.[3] Trouillot notes that:

Most countries impose some form of indirect taxation, but in the Haitian case indirect taxation, and in particular the various fees and duties collected at the customhouses, have been the principal source of government revenues since Pétion's regime [1806–16]. Whenever the state increased the fees and duties on coffee, the exporters . . . passed the charges on to the *spéculateurs* (licensed middlemen . . .), who in turn imposed them on the peasants by reducing the price paid them for their produce. (1990, 62)

These revenues, along with taxes collected directly from peasants' pockets, have traditionally traveled directly to the provincial capitals and, after an initial skimming, to Port-au-Prince.[4] They have rarely returned to the regions where they were generated in the form of infrastructure, schools, medical care, or other social services. In fact, though more than 80 percent of government revenues have come from peasant farmers, over 90 percent of government expenditures have been made in the capital (McGowan 1997, 4), where they have fattened Haitian rulers' bank accounts, expanded their real estate holdings, built their mansions on the hillsides above Pétionville, and amassed the magazines of weapons they have used to secure their reign against challenges by the populace. "The state," Trouillot concludes, "had chosen to live at the expense of the nation" (1990, 64). Because of this continuing tradition, many analysts have characterized the Haitian state as "predatory," and the country's small elite as "parasitic." The appropriateness of these labels is underlined by the fact that 1 percent of Haitians now control 50 percent of the country's wealth, and that more than 70 percent of the population lives in severe poverty (McGowan 1997, 4).

When Haitians use the term *leta* (literally, "state"), they are generally referring both to the government and to the economic elite, thus revealing the thorough amalgamation of the entities that have ruled them. The accuracy of this conflation is affirmed by Dupuy.

> [In Haiti's] market system and its correlative property relations, the contractual relations between owners and producers or between buyers and sellers (of labor-power or of other commodities), presuppose a political, juridical, and coercive apparatus—the state—to guarantee and legitimize the existence and reproduction of that system of production and exchange. (1988, 106)

As telling as the term *leta* itself are the adjectives rural Haitians commonly attach to it. Among the most popular references to the Haitian power structure are *leta peze souse* and *leta gwo vale piti* (the squeeze-and-suck state, and the big-devours-the-little state).[5]

Another term commonly employed by rural Haitians to describe the ruling sector is *leta mèsenè* (mercenary state). Supplementing economic legacies such as the Code Rurale and the surplus extraction system have been equally invidious traditions of political exclusion and repression. As Fanon noted, "For if you think that you can manage a country without letting the people interfere, if you think that the people upset the game by their mere presence, whether they slow it down or whether by their natural ignorance they sabotage it, then you must have no hesitation: you must keep the people out" (1963, 189).

In its efforts to minimize the participation of the majority in the political life of the country, Haiti's *leta* has developed systems and structures no less elaborate than those ensuring the population's lack of control over the formal economic sector. From institutionalizing French as the country's official language (it was not until the adoption of the 1987 Constitution that Haitian Creole, the language of the majority, was given the same status); to chronically refusing to permit free and genuine elections; to neglecting infrastructural development; to establishing a schooling system that has virtually guaranteed widespread illiteracy; to deploying repressive military and paramilitary forces (Duvaliers' infamous VSN being only one among many)—Haiti's rulers have relentlessly (and, when necessary, violently) pursued an agenda of "keeping the people out." As a result, peasants have generally found themselves excluded from "all the professions, most governmental and military offices, and the large business enterprises" (Leyburn 1941, 4), and with "no claim whatsoever" on the state (Trouillot 1991, 16).

The entrenchment of the peasantry's immiseration has been fueled and rationalized by another perennial strand running throughout Haitian history: the legacy of symbolic violence. C. L. R. James notes that the Saint Domingue colonists "took great pains that the Negro should remain the brute beast they wanted him to be" (1989 [1963], 17). He quotes a memoir published in 1789 that labels Saint Domingue blacks " 'unjust, cruel, barbarous, half-human, treacherous, deceitful, thieves, drunkards, proud, lazy, unclean, shameless, jealous to fury, and cowards.' " " 'The safety of the whites demands,' " the author (then governor of Martinique) concludes, " 'that we keep the Negroes in profound ignorance [and] treat [them] as one treats beasts' " (in James 1989 [1963], 17–18).

Just as in the case of its economic exploitation, the discursive abuses of Haiti's majority peasant population that began during the colonial era have not been challenged but, rather, elaborated by the nation's rulers. Constructed as dirt poor, barefoot, uncivilized, superstitious, and lethargic, these "outsiders" are rendered wholly incapable of contributing in a constructive way to the oversight of their country's political system or its economic resources.

Interventions from "Across the Water"

The Haitian leta has not been alone in its persistent subjugation of the Haitian nation. Another legacy dating back to the first days of Haiti's history is the self-interested manipulation of foreign powers. Following independence, "Haitians found themselves in a world entirely hostile to the idea of self-governing blacks" (Farmer 1992, 164). There, as Dupuy explains, "the presence of an independent black republic in a sea of slavery threatened white supremacy and the slave system" in other French colonies as well as in "the southern United States and the English Caribbean" (1989, 93).

Thus challenged by the very existence of this nation-state of former slaves, the leaders of Europe and North America sought to isolate Haiti both politically and economically. A decades-long multilateral blockade lasting through the middle of the nineteenth century virtually guaranteed the country's economic ruin. Perhaps the most devastating single punishment inflicted on Haiti's economy was France's demand for an indemnity of 150 million francs in return for officially recognizing Haiti's independence and resuming commercial trade. While the Boyer regime finalized this deal with France in 1825, it was not until 1862 that the U.S. government recognized Haiti as a sovereign country. Trouillot points out that this long-delayed recognition came only "when the Union's need for cotton, increased by the Civil War and the movement against slavery, emphasized the desirability of formal contracts" (1990, 53). For these reasons, Mintz claims: "It [can] be said that the freedom Haiti had won in an incredible revolution against powerful enemies came to be a punishment. The struggle brought the Haitian people justified admiration in many quarters, but its price has been isolation and virtual abandonment" (as cited in Leyburn 1941, xxxi).

Once the United States had established economic interests in Haiti, it set out to influence the country's political system. The list of initiatives launched by the U.S. government and nongovernmental U.S. agencies to "civilize" (or, to use the terminology of more recent campaigns, "democratize and develop") Haiti is long. Among the most notable of these efforts was the 1915–34 occupation of the country. The Occupation came on the heels of several decades of chaos in Haitian politics.[6] While the Occupation was ostensibly aimed at establishing political stability, once in power U.S. troops and statesmen carried out campaigns that had much more far-reaching effects. Among them were rewriting Haiti's constitution (to, among other things, abolish the law forbidding foreign ownership of Haitian land) and establishing the *gendarmerie* (*gad*) military force. Trained by U.S. Marines, this force—designed not to protect the country against external threats but, rather, to control and discipline the Haitian population itself—would endure until the early 1990s and become infamous for its ruthless anti-insurgency campaigns.

In the end, the Occupation both intensified the parasitic relationship between the state and the people, and fostered new opportunities for parasites from overseas. Trouillot explains the overall effects of the Occupation in this way:

The Occupation worsened the economic crisis by augmenting the peasantry's forced contribution to the maintenance of the State and of the urban parasites. It worsened the crisis of power by centralizing the Haitian Army and disarming [citizens in] the provinces. Of course, by putting in place the structures of military, fiscal, and commercial centralization, the Occupation postponed judgement day for thirty years; but it also guaranteed that the finale would be bloody. (quoted in Farmer 1992, 177)

Trouillot credits these domestically and externally imposed legacies as having made the rise of the totalitarian Duvalier regime all but inevitable. This regime, with the help of generous amounts of aid from the United States and other nations, found endless ways to expand upon the abuses of the dictatorships that had preceded it. The effects were devastating. During its 1957–86 reign, between twenty thousand and fifty thousand people were murdered, and tens of thousands more fled into exile.

Risking Hope

The last two decades of the twentieth century brought many political changes in Haiti. After finally forcing Jean-Claude Duvalier and his government out of the country in 1986, the Haitian population set about trying to *dechouke*, or "uproot," the traditions of corruption and abuse that had so chronically and so thoroughly permeated the country's power structure. A new constitution, widely praised for its recognition of the rights of rich and poor alike, was ratified in 1987. Public debates about the government became possible, and underground civic organizations surfaced and thrived. But the next few years also were marred by numerous coups and a number of violent crackdowns on popular organizations and pro-democracy movements.

This era of instability and uncertainty ended temporarily when, on December 16, 1990, the Haitian people participated in their country's first successful democratic elections. Monitored by the United Nations, the Organization of American States, and other foreign delegations, these elections brought a long tradition of popular nonparticipation to an end. Voting in unprecedented numbers, the Haitian people elected as their president Jean-Bertrand Aristide, the overwhelmingly popular Catholic priest. A euphoria of empowerment and hope reverberated throughout the nation, as poor Haitians again dreamed of better days to come. Finally, a society like the one described by the Kayayo peasant group and envisioned by their newly liberated ancestors at the dawn of the nineteenth century seemed to be within their grasp.

During Aristide's first few months in office, unprecedented efforts were launched to control drug trafficking, decrease government corruption, institute land reforms, provide guarantees for workers' rights, and initiate advances in the areas of public health, human rights, education, and domestic production. These initiatives came to a sudden halt only eight months after Aristide's inauguration, however, when his government was overthrown by a bloody coup d'état. Haiti would decline rapidly during the ensuing three years, as its population suffered the abuses of a brutal military dictatorship and its paramilitary cohorts. Tens of thousands of people (most of them members of the peasantry or the urban poor) were beaten, imprisoned, raped, tortured, and killed. Hundreds of thousands migrated from the countryside to the protective anonymity of the city. Others fled Port-au-Prince to hide in the mountains. Thousands more attempted to escape by crowding onto one of the rickety crafts streaming from Haiti's coastline.[7] Added to the chaos and terror experienced by Haiti's citizenry during this period was a dramatic economic collapse. (The GDP fell by more than 40 percent, and employment by more than 80 percent.) This was due not only to the aftereffects of the coup itself and the kleptocratic practices of the junta rulers but also to an infamously "leaky" multilateral trade embargo instigated by the Organization of American States (OAS).

Exiled members of the Aristide administration spent most of the post-coup period in the United States. Negotiations between the coup junta, Aristide, the U.S. government, the World Bank, the International Monetary Fund (IMF), the OAS, the UN, and other "friends of Haiti" waxed and waned sporadically. While the junta leaders were being pressured to step down, Aristide was being pushed to accept an array of neoliberal fiscal policies to be implemented upon his return.[8] On several occasions, it appeared as though the elected government was on the verge of being reinstalled, when suddenly talks would collapse. Finally, on October 15, 1994, the Aristide administration was returned to its tattered nation. "Our *papa* is back!" the people cried, and once again mustered up the courage to hope for better days.

Aristide and his government had not come back alone. Also flying in on the wings of "Operation Restore Democracy," the U.S.-led multinational military intervention that ushered Aristide's government home, were hundreds of foreign diplomats, development professionals, economists, planners, technicians, and others. Intent on taking advantage of this unprecedented opportunity to bring Haiti into the democratic and developed world, they carried with them millions of dollars and briefcases stuffed with ambitious program plans. A new era, they asserted, was about to begin. As Vander Zaag reports: "This massive influx of aid was targeted to all sectors of the economy and society—balance of payments support, structural reform of the economy, reform and training of the police and judiciary, regional development, agriculture, health and social development. . . . Development was definitely big business again in Haiti" (1999, 85).

Several years and numerous programs later, most Haitians have yet to see the "new era" promised them. Many charge that this is largely because recent foreign development and democratization interventions have moved only a questionable degree away from the colonial–neocolonial interventions of earlier eras.

New Legacies

What is the antecedent for community development theory and practice . . . ? In a broad sense it derives from problems of the colonial economy studied. . . . In this tradition, the conventional explanation for "backwardness" and "underdevelopment" is based on notions of dualism whereby an imported social system clashes with an indigenous system. In this view, it is in the interest of colonial powers to "eradicate barbarous customs" and raise the standards of living. In order to promote these goals, a strategy is required that leads people to "want what they need" and then "do what they want." (G. Smucker 1986, 94)

What I saw was her poverty. What she saw was the poverty of the aid we were able to offer—its inability to tackle the root causes of the anger and bring about permanent change. (Ransom 1996, 8)

Sometimes [Konstantin Levin] had a deep admiration for the strength, gentleness, and justice of the people, but very often, when their common undertaking called for either qualities, he was incensed by their carelessness, slovenness, drunkenness and deceit. (Tolstoy 1939, *Anna Karenina*)

The legacies of subjugation, exploitation, and political instability discussed above have left the overwhelming majority of Haitians in a state of grinding poverty. Statistics on Haiti consistently place it well below all other countries in the hemisphere in terms of economic well-being.[9] Estimates of the average per capita income hover around $250,[10] though the majority of the population (most of them peasants cultivating "non-arable" land) are said to earn less than $100 a year, and live well below the World Bank's absolute poverty line.[11] Eighty-six percent of the rural population is unable to obtain even 75 percent of their daily caloric needs. Both in the capital and the countryside, infants and children die often from diseases related to malnutrition or illnesses readily cured by adequate resources and care. The crude death rate is approximately 25 per 1,000. Infant mortality is said to fall between 94 and 110 per 1,000 live births. Life expectancy figures range from forty-three to fifty-five years. Estimates of illiteracy range from 60 to almost 90 percent. There is barely one physician for every ten thousand people, and substantially fewer than that in rural areas, since most doctors are concentrated in Port-au-Prince, provincial capitals, and other large towns. Only 13 percent of the population has access to potable drinking water, 6 percent to electricity, and 5 percent to a telephone.

Such facts and figures made Haiti a premiere destination for development and relief aid long before "Operation Restore Democracy" landed in Port-au-Prince. Since the 1940s when, as Trouillot puts it, "a parade of acronyms" descended upon the struggling nation (1990, 140), poor Haitians have been the targets of incalculable sums of aid money and innumerable projects aimed at helping them. In fact, foreign aid has often comprised the bulk of the country's national budget (nearly 80% in 1997). According to a report published in the Haitian Creole weekly newspaper *Libète*, there were more than seven hundred NGOs (nongovernmental organizations) working in Haiti in 1996 (Meme 1996).[12]

Fueled by North-Western coffers, political agendas, and expertise, NGOs, IGOs (intergovernmental organizations), international lending institutions, and religious missions have amassed a great deal of power in Haiti during recent years. In many ways, in fact, they seem to constitute a sort of shadow government. Particularly in the countryside and urban *bidonvils* (shantytowns), for instance, they have supplied many of the services that governments are generally expected to provide: roads, potable water, medical clinics, schools. They also have played influential roles in local governance and in determining domestic and foreign policies.

How far have these efforts gone in helping the Haitian population? Jean-Claude Bajeux notes that "as the twenty-first century approaches, Haitian society is sliding backward in every way" (1994, 37). Like many Haitians, Bajeux credits international aid to Haiti with playing more than a small part in this regression:

> Together with the failure of our institutions through repeated incursions of the military into politics, and through the misrule of the two Duvaliers, which merely reinforced longstanding structures of privilege, we must also cite the failure of international aid that served in the end only to enrich a small minority of Haitians. . . . [Aid to Haiti] deserves a place in future economic textbooks as a stunning example of international aid that, instead of helping a country to progress, merely hastened its impoverishment and increased the gap between rich and poor (1994, 37).

Other scholars have echoed Bajeux's analysis of the impact of international aid on Haiti and have added detailed studies of both particular projects and major trends. These analysts have explained how aid has not only failed consistently to benefit poor Haitians but, in many cases, has also actively undermined their own attempts to improve their situation. An example is the $7.7 million Export and Investment Promotion Program, designed and financed by USAID in the 1980s. This program, directed at increasing Haiti's exports and tying its economy to the U.S. market, succeeded at making Haiti "ninth in the world in the assembly of U.S. goods for consumption" (McGowan 1997, 6) and generated unprecedented profits for U.S. businesses and Haitian middlemen. But its impact on most Haitians was overwhelmingly negative. "Real wages fell nine percent between 1980 and 1985," McGowan reports, and "Haiti's per capita agricultural production also declined" (1997, 6). DeWind and Kinley reveal that because of these and other windfalls, export-led development strategies have pushed thousands of rural Haitians to leave their land and migrate, either to the shantytowns (bidonvil-s) of Port-au-Prince or to Miami (1986, 142). Farmer (1992) suggests that such foreign assistance policies have had a number of other, less direct but equally tragic consequences, and highlights in particular the ways they have exacerbated Haiti's AIDS crisis.

A particularly revealing narrative on international development aid to Haiti is found in studies by Diederich (1985), Abbott (1988), and Farmer (1992, 1994b). These analysts chronicle how a U.S.-led, multimillion-dollar pig eradication project devastated the rural economy, led to significant increases in hunger, threatened religious practices, undermined certain social relations, and was altogether "the worst calamity every to befall the peasant" (an American veterinarian, quoted in Diederich 1985, 225).

The story of the "swine aid" project, the effects of which continue to be felt in Haiti today, begins in the late 1970s. In 1978, African swine fever was detected in the Dominican Republic. Because the spread of the deadly disease into U.S. markets would have meant huge losses to the multibillion dollar U.S. pork industry, the U.S. government immediately began an investigation into the pig population of Haiti. Diederich (1985) reports that infected Haitian pigs were first detected in 1979 in the Artibonite Valley. Whereas generally, "when African Swine Fever strikes, 99 percent of the pigs that catch the virus die" (225), in Haiti, this was not the case. Evidently, the number of pigs that died there was quite small, and within a couple of years, the deaths had nearly stopped altogether. (Some have speculated that Haitian pigs were actually resistant to the malady).

In the meantime, however, U.S. officials had backed a multinational campaign to eradicate the Dominican Republic's 1.4 million pig population and had begun planning a similar project for Haiti. Funded with $23 million from the U.S. government and staffed by technicians and field experts from Mexico, Canada, and the Dominican Republic, the Haitian operation (called PEPPADEP, Programme pour l'Eradication de la Peste Porcine Africaine et pour le Développement de l'Elvage Porcin) began in 1982. By June 1983, PEPPADEP agents had destroyed nearly every pig in Haiti (estimated at 1.3 million).

To understand the devastating effects this project had on Haiti and, in particular, on the well-being of the peasantry; one must first know a bit about the Haitian pig and the purposes it had served. Called *kochon kreyòl* (Creole pig), or alternatively, *kochon djòl long* (long-snout pig), or *kochon planch* (plank pig), Haitian pigs were notoriously ugly—and hearty—creatures. These black, scrawny, long-nosed animals were thought to be a crossbreed between the Spanish hog brought to Hispañola by some of the first colonists and a wild boar native to the island. "Over a period of 500 years," Diederich explains, "the black pig had become a lean and degenerate scavenger. It was perfectly adapted to some of the most miserable raising conditions in the world, and could go two or three days without food" (1985, 225).

Thus streamlined for survival, this pig required little care. Peasants generally kept their pigs close to their homes, where they could forage around in household scraps for food. In the process, they served as garbage disposals, helped to fertilize the soil of surrounding fields, and attacked insects destructive to crops. In the cities, they satisfied themselves by rummaging around on garbage heaps. Peasants report that besides supplying them with meat, kochon kreyòl-s also served as their primary source of lard and cooking oil. Their skin provided leather. Most important, Creole pigs had been for most rural Haitians the equivalent of a savings account. Again, Diederich explains: "With no banking system available to him, the peasant relied on hog production as a bank account to meet his most pressing obligations: baptism, health care, schooling, funerals, religious ceremonies, and protection against urban-based loan sharks who would grab his land at the first opportunity" (1985, 225).

The pig eradication project of the early 1980s was, in a sense, the Haitian peasant's Great Stock Market Crash. Abbott reports (1988, 274–75) that within months of the operation, school attendance dropped (as parents had nothing to sell to pay for fees, uniforms, and supplies), while malnutrition began to climb. Even religious life was disrupted and spiritual well-being threatened, since certain ceremonies for the lwa-s cannot be properly carried out without the sacrifice of a black pig.

The small remuneration paid to owners for the loss of their animals did little to cushion the effects of this nearly overnight loss of their primary source of economic security. Nor did the restocking initiative written into the PEPPADEP program make up for much of the damage. Indeed, it proved a near-complete failure, and added its own share of insults—and ironies—to this tale of "aid."

The pigs sent to replace the black pigs of the Haitian mountains were purchased from industrial farms in the plains of the midwestern United States. PEPPADEP gave them away free of charge or for modest prices, but only with certain conditions. To receive one of these *kochon blan*-s (foreign [white] pigs), one had to construct a tin-roofed, concrete-floored shelter in which to house it. More than a few peasants noted in telling me about this stipulation that it meant providing these creatures with a better home than they could provide their own children. "My own family doesn't live under a tin roof!" Moreover, as Farmer notes, "Although the new pigs . . . were very large, they were manifestly more fragile than their predecessors. They fell ill and required veterinary intervention; they turned their noses up at the garbage that had been the mainstay of the native pigs' diet. The *kochon blan* fared well only on expensive wheat-based, vitamin-enriched feed" (1992, 40).

Farmer estimates that the cost of providing a pig with this feed for a year ranged between $120 and $250—figures exceeding the annual income of most rural Haitians. Not surprisingly, these finicky, fragile animals died quickly on Haitian terrain. I have visited numerous communities where the repopulation program was implemented and have yet to find one where it actually worked. Most of these locations have no pigs at all to show for it but, rather, a handful of abandoned shelters and a collection of bitter memories. Because administrators often sought to implement the program by working through local community groups, its failures also left behind new rivalries between neighbors in many communities. (Farmer [1992] found this to be the case in the Do Kay community as well.)

Rarely have rural Haitians told me about this series of events, often referred to as "the pig massacre," without capitalizing on its symbolic ironies. All too tempting are the parallels between themselves and the skinny, black, "degenerated" (to use Diederich's term), but hearty, beasts doomed to martyrdom—ostensibly in the name of progress but actually in the interest of another breed: a fat, white, manicured, foreign breed from the north. Many people have pointed out that the destruction of their pigs has led to increased dependency on American imports ("it allowed them to come in and take our market"), and have speculated that this was one of the ultimate objectives of the program. "Now they come back and make money selling us their hotdogs!"[13] Also coloring accounts of the "swine aid" fiasco are widely circulating reports of kochon blan-s devouring Haitian infants and toddlers, and committing other monstrous crimes against local people.

Such experiences with aid undermining the interests of the aided are now familiar to Haitians.[14] This has led many Haitians, particularly those involved in the popular movement, to see foreign-sponsored development and democratization initiatives as inherently exploitative strategies—as being aimed primarily at breeding dependency and undermining grass-roots efforts directed at real change. It is not uncommon to hear that these aims constitute a coherent and coordinated agenda, which is often referred to as the "American Plan." The leader of a peasant women's organization summed up her analysis of foreign aid this way: "Everywhere you look, you see projects piling up . . . in every little corner of the country, projects. But they're not really benefiting the country . . . it's not development you see here, but *en*velopment!"

In spite of such critiques, the dollars, professionals, and program plans have continued to fly in. As suggested earlier, foreign aid to Haiti picked up dramatically following the 1994 restoration of the Aristide administration. By January 1995, nineteen multinational institutions and fourteen govern-ments had pledged $2.1 billion for a five-year recovery program. Of the $2.1 billion sum, $1.2 billion was to be dispersed in the form of loans (mostly from the Inter-American Development Bank [IDB], the World Bank, and the International Monetary Fund [IMF]), and the rest as grants. More than U.S. $88 million was designated to be spent on humanitarian as-sistance, with $60.5 million of it coming from the United States (WOH-PAPDA, 1996). But Haitian government officials have been hesitant to ac-cept some of the stipulations placed on much of that aid. Because of this, together with the continuing instability in the Haitian government and dis-putes among U.S. politicians about the democratic integrity of the Aristide and Préval administrations, some of the funds were never released. (R. White reports that by October 1997, around $1 billion had been spent [R. White 1997, 6; WOH-PAPDA, 1996].)

Just as the economic and political agendas of the Haitian state and elite have been fueled by their chronic "othering" of the Haitian masses, so too has aid to Haiti been buttressed by "aiders'" constructions of the "aided." I have found in my work among numerous international agencies a fairly consistent descriptive image of the Haitian poor. This image consists of four intertwined and multifaceted characteristics: a preference for depend-ency on more powerful others (a dependency mentality, or, as it is some-times called, a slave mentality); a fatalism leading to apathy and resigna-tion; an inability to think analytically or constructively about their situation; and a chronic resistance to working cooperatively and effectively in the in-terest of the collective good.

These characteristics are often articulated in surprisingly candid terms. The following excerpts are from notes I took during conversations with for-eigners working in the Grand'Anse department in 1995 and 1996.

A Canadian CIVPOL officer[15] offered me his perceptions of the Haitian peo-ple during an interview [in March 1995]: "They have a very different way of

thinking, and a very different way of doing things. The grace of God, everything depends on the grace of God . . . Nobody treats anything with respect,
except property. For property they have respect. . . . This is a very violent society, they don't have any other concept of how to deal with conflict. They
don't know how to work things out, to negotiate. . . . They have no real concept of justice. . . . They don't value human life down here like we do. They
don't have a concept of other people having human rights. They are very
naive, and very superstitious. . . . They don't have the same ability as we do,
the same opportunities to read, to consult outside sources, other perspectives. . . . They still have a slave mentality. . . . [To get them to do anything]
you have to take them by the hand and lead them every step of the way."

I spoke with a woman who had moved to the Grand'Anse from Quebec to
"teach the population how to improve their lot," and to encourage them to
work together in developing their communities. She was exasperated with
Haitians. . . . Most of them, she said, are content to just sit around and say
" 'Ah! Why should I go? It'll get done for me!' " As long as people "have
enough to put in their stomachs," she continued, "two or three lovers, and
clothes on their backs, they couldn't care less about anything else." There are
times, she sighed, when she is convinced that "it's us, the *blan*-s, who want the
country to change, but for them, they don't give a damn."

Although generally circulated in informal, exclusively *blan* (expatriate),
off-the-record conversations, at times such perceptions find their way into
the written policies of aid agencies. A case in point is provided by the orientation materials of the OTI/IOM communal governance and community development program. One of the most well-funded and influential
programs functioning in the country during the first several years after
Aristide's return, the OTI/IOM program worked in more than 2,300 communities throughout the country.) Along with messages to foreign program staff about the importance of working in "collaboration" and "partnership" with the local people, its orientation materials included these
lessons and tips:

> A slave mentality remains prevails in Haiti—grass root [sic] mentality: you
> are the boss, I have to do what you say but you have to help me and take care
> of my family. . . . In Haiti, the masses *accept their fate, work hard to survive*, so
> hard that they have neither the time nor the energy to fight to improve their
> lot (they are locked in this survival mode). Their life is ruled by simple faith
> (italics in the original).[16]

The author goes on to describe Haitians' "individualistic" nature and the
problems posed by their inability to understand democratic ideals. It is
later suggested, however, that techniques such as elementary graphics de-

picting "happy faces working together" might be enough to win over these simple-minded folk to the organization's democratization agenda.

What explains the prevalence of such characterizations among international aid professionals? My own observations reveal that those perpetuating these reductionistic and prejudice-laden stereotypes are for the most part well intentioned, smart, conscientious people. They are people who are concerned with doing work that is productive, personally enriching, and genuinely helpful to the populations where they live. They are people who tend to see themselves as both politically and socially progressive, and culturally open-minded—people who would never think of voicing what Dalton calls "hard racisms" (1995, 93). So what is happening here? A closer look reveals that aiders' characterizations of their clients are less paradoxical than nearly inevitable.

Arturo Escobar, Gustavo Esteva, and numerous others have shown us that at the very foundation of the theory and practice of the development industry (and, I would add, the democratization campaigns now central to it) is the modernist premise that the causes of Third World poverty reside not in the forces that enrich and empower a few of the world's people and immiserate the rest but lie instead in the deficiencies and delinquencies of poor people and the communities in which they live. To be about the business of international development and democratization is to be about "placing the majority of the world's cultures into a single category the sole characteristic of which is the absence of certain characteristics of the industrialized countries" (Lummis 1996, 63). It is, to use Fabian's terms (1983), to be engaged in a systemic denial of coevalness. The very occupations of aid agents depend on it.

Still, during the past few decades, a number of national and foreign-based agencies have made serious efforts to move away from traditional models of aid and to correct the legacies described by Bajeaux. Attempting to be more responsive to the concerns, values, resources, and agendas of local people, they have tried to resist imposing their own preconceptions and agendas on local communities, shifting instead toward assisting locally emergent efforts to bring about social change. They have hoped that these changes will afford them more success at facilitating transformations that are both sustainable and truly helpful to the poor. Unfortunately, most of the organizations carrying out such efforts are small, both in terms of their budgets and their staffs. Thus, while some have been remarkably successful, those successes have generally been confined to very limited spheres and geographical areas.

Larger aid institutions working in Haiti have also aspired to new models. For the most part, those models have come from progressive trends in the larger aid industry. During the mid-1970s, such trends included an emphasis on "human-centered development." As the 1974 Declaration of Cocoyoc put it, the purpose of development "should not be to develop things, but to develop man" (quoted in Sachs 1993, 14). Accompanying this drive to "humanize" development was a concern for responding to the "basic needs" of the poor. Gradually, there emerged a "recognition of the need to mobilise people who had been bypassed by or written out of the development process and to encourage their participation in project planning and implementation") (Gardner and Lewis 1996, 104). In fact, *participation* was to become one of the major catch-terms of development in the 1990s. Despite its roots in "radical ideas challenging development orthodoxy," participatory development is today "found in the development plans and policy statements of the most mainstream institutions" (Gardner and Lewis 1996, 110; also see Verhelst 1990, 17–23).

Consistent with these global trends, the program files of major aid institutions in Haiti wax eloquent about allowing the poor a more central role in the development process—extolling "local ownership" of programs, "participatory democracy," "empowering women," "respecting the local culture," "building partnerships with the poor," and "strengthening civil society." Such rhetorical changes, however, seem to have had little effect on how the bulk of foreign assistance actually gets distributed. The $2.1 billion pledged by the international community in 1994, for instance, was contingent on the Haitian government's willingness to accept an Emergency Economic Recovery Plan (EERP). Signed in Paris in 1993 during a meeting with representatives from the International Monetary Fund, the World Bank, Western governments and other donors, this plan calls for the implementation of a strict structural adjustment program (SAP) involving government downsizing, privatization of state enterprises, trade liberalization, the maintenance of low wages, and financial deregulation—policies now renowned in the Third World for virtually guaranteeing the increased immiseration of the poor (Ransom 1996).

Nor have changes in lingo seemed to change significantly the opportunities for involvement offered to local people—not, that is, according to most of the peasants with whom I have discussed this new round of aid. Alluding to a number of school construction projects then taking place in the region, one woman in Bamòn observed, " 'Participation' just means that we get to carry a lot of heavy rocks on our heads."

The limited success of the participation model in Haiti is, again, consistent with the business of aid as a whole. As Gardner and Lewis, observe, "Ideas which start their life as radical alternatives all too often become a neutralized and non-threatening part of the mainstream" (1996, 104). Likewise, they explain,

The idea of participation is drawn from radical roots, but in practice has now become so ever-present in development jargon as to be often virtually without meaning. Many critics of development therefore view participation as a degraded term, which has served only to "soften" top-downism and has been successfully stripped of its previous radical connotations (Rahnema 1992). It can allow ideas to be imported into communities and then attributed to them: a token agenda of involvement at one level of the project (usually at the implementation rather than the planning stage) can then be used to legitimise decisions which have already been taken by powerful outsiders. (111)

McIlwaine describes a similar phenomenon within the context of donor efforts to "strengthen civil society." In the end, what most actually do, McIlwaine says, is "impose the concept of civil society onto pre-existing organisations, according them a range of functions. It is invariably the formal, top-down civil society organisations or NGOs which represent civil society in the eyes of donors, with the informal, grassroots organisations which emerge from below playing only a minor role" (1998, 657).

Verhelst echoes this perception in his evaluation of many NGOs' efforts at "stressing the need to respect 'the local culture.'" Their efforts are often limited "to the inclusion of a little local colour in the process of development-cum-Westernization, rather like those international hotels whose restaurants serve, all over the world, the same aseptic breakfast but do so in a picturesque setting with the staff dressed in traditional costume" (1990, 18).

One prominent development professional aptly supports Verhelst's point in his study of culture and development: "The culture-based approach is a worthwhile item to include in the development worker's toolkit" (Kleymeyer 1994, 205).

The participatory development projects I observed being implemented in the Grand'Anse in 1995 and 1996 were very much like what Gardner and Lewis, McIlwaine and Verhelst would have predicted. In many cases, "participating" did mean very little more than carrying rocks on one's head, or being present at a community governance meeting in which development agency staff asked local people to define their own needs, and then presented them with a set of prê-à-porter project possibilities (each with its own pre-formulated set of regulations for "local contributions").

A case in point is the communal governance and community development program sponsored by USAID's Office of Transition Initiatives (OTI) and administered in more than twenty-three hundred Haitian communities by OTI and the International Organization for Migration (IOM)[17] in the years following the 1991–94 post-coup era. Through this multimillion-dollar program,[18] expatriate staff members convened and participated actively in "communal governance meetings" between state officials, civil servants, officers from the UN/OAS military force, national and international NGOs, and other "community leaders" at the national, regional, and local levels. OTI/IOM staff members reported that these meetings were aimed primarily at teaching Haitians from different sectors how to determine priorities, make decisions, and work together in ways that would constitute local democratic governance and bring about local development.

The degree to which the decisions coming out of these meetings actually emerged from local concerns and realities, however, is highly questionable. In 1995, I once observed a U.S. military officer, known at the time as "the chief" of the UN/OAS forces in the Northwest department, assure an IOM staff member there that she should let him know if she ever had problems on the job or if she needed anything. Since "I am the king of this city," he told her, "I can get you whatever you want, whenever you want." He continued by instructing her to make sure she got him what *he* wanted at the communal governance meeting to be held the next day. "I expect you to take charge at the meeting tomorrow," he said, adding "if you don't, you know I'm going to have to come down hard and tell them how it's going to be." Is it surprising that the OTI/IOM program, like so many programs before it, left little more than the shells of unfinished projects in the Bamòn zone?

Indeed, my observations and those of numerous others suggest that other than the handful nationals working for international organizations (most of whom already were better off than most citizens), few Haitians have benefited more from this most recent series of program plans than they had from those of the past. In fact, the situation of the "targeted populations" (for the most part, the peasantry and the urban poor) seems to be declining as rapidly as ever. As a jobless Port-au-Prince resident put it in 1999, five years after the launching of Operation Restore Democracy, "Because we had so much hope that salvation would finally come for our problems. But now, things are dark and getting darker. Democracy has not improved our lives. It is just a word to me."[19]

In the meantime, other interested parties prosper. According to one USAID official, seventy-nine cents of every USAID dollar is actually spent in the United States. (Some estimates are higher, ranging up to 90 percent.)[20] In 1996, a staff member of the OTI/IOM governance and development program reported that their non-Haitian field officers were making around $5,000 per month, and some of them much more. Haitian staff, in the meantime, were making at least ten times more than the salaries of local civil servants with similar levels of training and responsibility. Bestowing such salaries on people who already had financial and social capital ex-

ceeding that of most of their neighbors dramatically exaggerated disparities already existing in the communities where the program worked.

None of this has escaped the attention of peasant "beneficiaries" of aid
programs. A neighbor in Tisous critiqued the hypocrisies inherent in the
skewed distribution of aid resources by calling on the proverb, "They put
the pot on the fire in the name of the children, but it comes off in the
name of the adults." I cannot count the number of times rural Haitians
have told me that when aid workers, government officials, and missionaries
ask for money, it's in the name of the poor; but when it is spent, it is the aid
workers, government officials, and missionaries who truly benefit.

> The people who benefit from development are those who sit with their big
> vests, big neckties in the city. He tells you he's going to raise you up. And
> then when he gets some [funds for development], he never sends anything
> for you. You hear them talking about doing deeds for the poor, but when you
> take a good look, you see the poor never get anything there. (a spiritual
> leader and herbal healer in the Bamòn area)
>
> It's the very same person who offers you help who'll take it back out of
> your hands. . . . We are like a calf they put up to its mother's teat to suckle [to
> bring down her milk], but push aside when the milk begins to flow. We are al-
> lowed only to taste the milk; they collect the rest in the bucket to drink them-
> selves. (a woman who had just finished a day of washing clothes and cooking
> for a group of Canadian expatriates)

Not only are many of the employment and spending patterns of aid organizations exaggerating rather than challenging disparities in wealth and
power; they also result in situations in which the urban-based staff sent out
to work in rural Haitian communities have very little in common with the
people who live there. Is it any wonder that these parties often fear, resent,
and frustrate one another? Again, peasants sometimes use proverbs to describe this situation and to suggest its impact on the potential success of development initiatives, for example, *Ti monben pa grandi anba gwo monben* (A
little monben tree cannot grow under the shade of a big monben tree);
Wòch nan dlo pa konn mizè wòch nan solèy (the rock bathing in the water cannot know the troubles of the rock sweating in the sun).

Also targeted by harsh criticism is the involvement of aid agencies in affairs of the state. Members of peasant groups point out, for instance, that
USAID, while offering hundreds of thousands of impoverished Haitians
food aid on a daily basis, has repeatedly fought against efforts by the Haitian government to raise the minimum wage[21] and discouraged price controls on basic foodstuffs.[22] Recently, representatives of the peasant group
movement have joined other sectors within Haiti's larger "popular move-

ment" in protesting the structural adjustment programs being promoted by USAID, the IMF, the World Bank, and other international donors.[23] These protests have arisen in part from an increasing recognition among the organized poor that even the most progressive, sustainable, and appropriate aid projects will fail to do much good in the long run unless aiders' self-interested capitalist pursuits are tempered.

In sum, like many citizens of today's world, Haiti's peasantry has survived the ravages of colonialism only to be faced with the equally pervasive disciplines of an industry meant to modernize and advance them. There is little solace in the fact that these more recent "envelopments" are less bloody than those of the past; they sometimes prove in the long run to be just as destructive and dehumanizing. It is not surprising, then, that many rural Haitians have very conflicted feelings about participating in initiatives purporting to develop and democratize them. Cognizant of their need for many of the resources offered by these sources, great numbers of peasants have chosen to participate in the aiding (or rather, "being aided") process, at times even actively seeking out the introduction of aid projects into their communities. Yet most seem to remain doubtful (and sometimes fearful) of their benefactors' objectives. This is demonstrated well in an occurrence that took place in 1996.

Early in the year, an explosion of public fear and outrage occurred in several towns throughout Haiti, including Jérémie, when some international aid workers reportedly went into local schools to vaccinate children as a part of a nationwide public health initiative. Whether or not any children became ill or died from the shots (or, in fact, whether any shots were actually given) was never confirmed; but soon parents were hearing that their children were being administered "death shots," as a part of a foreign-aid plot to finally kill off the Haitian people. I was in Jérémie the morning that the panic first erupted there, and saw mothers, fathers, and siblings literally running to school buildings to retrieve their children, crying out with fear for their little ones' lives. Can we characterize this—as a fellow Haiti scholar did when we discussed it—as just another manifestation of the Haitian population's runaway paranoia and megalomania? One only needs to recall the "pig massacre" of the 1980s, or be familiar with some of the other aid initiatives now (in)famous in Haiti, to understand that the fears of these parents were grounded in all-too-many historical precedents. They were perhaps more reasonable than most of us who have sought to "aid" Haiti would like to admit.

Still, these parents know full well that most of them will have little choice but to put their children in the hands of foreign aid agents if they want them to be vaccinated and educated. A friend in Tisous summed up the opinion of many when he explained his decision to pursue funding for a local community-development project from a foreign-based institution: "If you are thirsty, and the only water you've got is putrid, you're obliged to hold your nose and drink."[24]

Persistent Dissidence

Through repression and terror the white masters managed to erect a system of social control to contain and regiment the half million black slaves whose labor created their wealth, but they could not annihilate the slave's human spirit. (Fick 1990, 46)

Those who took the trouble to observe [the slaves] away from their masters and in their intercourse with each other did not fail to see that remarkable liveliness of intellect and vivacity of spirit which so distinguish their descendents in the West Indies today. . . . It was this intelligence which refused to be crushed, these latent possibilities, that frightened the colonists, as it frightens the whites in Africa today. (James 1989 [1963], 17)

The native knows all this, and laughs to himself every time he spots an allusion to the animal world in the other's words. For he knows that he is not an animal; and it is precisely at the moment he realizes his humanity that he begins to sharpen the weapons with which he will secure its victory. (Fanon 1963, 43)

Peyizan malere, nou se wozo, nou se wozo, se wozo nou ye. . . .
Yo met boule nou, yo met koupe rasin nou, lé lapli a tonbe nap boujonnen.

Poor peasants, we are *wozo*, we are *wozo*, we are *wozo*. . . .
They can burn us, they can hack away at our roots, but when the rain falls, we'll sprout again.[25]

Haitian historians tell us that on August 14, 1791, more than two hundred people attended a Vodou[26] ceremony outside the northern village of Bwa Kayiman, a community founded by runaway slaves of the French colony of Saint Domingue. Reportedly brought together by the call of the *lanbi*, or conch-shell horn,[27] the crowd gathered around a Vodou priestess and a Jamaican-born rebel and priest named Boukman Dutty. Bellegarde-Smith provides this translation of the prayer Boukman offered there:

Hidden God in a cloud
is there, watching us.
He sees all the whites do;
the Whitegod demands crimes
ours wants good things.
But our God that is so good
orders vengeance, he will

ride us, assist us.
Throw away the thoughts of
the Whitegod who thirsts for tears, listen to
freedom that speaks to our hearts. (1990, 41)

Just a week following the ceremony at Bwa Kayiman, Boukman led an
insurrection that catalyzed the beginning of the only successful slave revolution in modern history. The enslaved of Saint Domingue had been
confronting, challenging, and "refusing to swallow" control over their
bodies, minds, and spirits long before then, however. Carolyn Fick reports that their resistance had taken "many forms, not all of them overt,
and some of them even self-destructive" (1990, 47). Among those forms
were suicide, marronage (desertion), disguise, document fabrication,
worship of African deities, poisoning, cursing, and numerous armed
struggles.

Just as it was not the beginning, neither was the Saint Domingue Revolution the end of rebellion and revolt in rural Haiti. A number of scholars
have characterized the very emergence of the Haitian peasantry as an instance of resistance (see Mintz 1985, 1973, 132; Dupuy 1989, 98), explaining that rural Haitians became peasants in large part by refusing to cooper-
ate with their earliest leaders' plans to return Haiti to its status as a
prosperous plantation economy.

Peasants resisted coercive labor policies not only "with their feet" but also
through armed rebellion. A peasant rebellion that erupted as early as 1807
in the Grand'Anse region forced Pétion to make significant concessions to
the lower classes, primarily in the form of land redistribution and a relax-
ation of controls over labor. In fact, peasant uprisings are scattered
throughout Haitian history. In the early 1840s, a movement of peasants
from the Jérémie area (called *pikèt*-s because of the wooden spikes they
used as weapons) revolted against labor practices in the region. According
to Dupuy, "By 1844, the *armée souffrante* (army of the poor), as they called
themselves, had transformed the uprising into a veritable *jacquerie*, and
spread terror throughout the southwest" (1989, 97). After yielding for a
time in response to concessions from the government, the southern pikèt-s
revolted once more in the late 1860s, and then again in the 1890s (Dupuy
1989, 110).

Perhaps the most famous popular rebellions are those that occurred during the nineteen-year U.S. occupation of the country. Suzy Castor claims
that "popular resistance [to the Occupation] began the day the Marines arrived on the coast of Haiti from the United States" in 1915 (1988, 127). It
continued, she says, until the Marines finally went home in 1934. Many of

those who served in the *kako* guerilla army, the centerpiece of this "nation-wide struggle for national sovereignty" (158), were peasants from the mountains.

While scholars have offered numerous chronicles of eighteenth-century resistance in Saint Domingue, corresponding studies of contemporary peasants' responses to exploitation and subjugation remain to be done. In fact, one of the most persistent stereotypes of rural Haitians in the current development age is that they have mustered little action in confronting the political, economic, and social conditions pressed upon them. During my 1993 term of service with the UN/OAS International Civilian Mission to Haiti (MICIVIH), other human rights observers repeatedly approached me to express their frustration at the lack of change in the political situation, and asked why the population had not put forth any "real resistance" to the military junta then ruling over them.[28] There was, in fact, little large-scale organization among opponents of the coup regime at the time. Nor were there any signs of guerrilla camps or uprisings forming in the mountains. But James Scott (1985, 1990) has urged us to look closely before concluding that nothing significant was going on, before assuming that people had resigned themselves to their situation or accepted the ideological precepts with which they were being ruled. Indeed, just as Schild found that "the passivity of people in the [Chilean] poblaciones in the 1980s . . . should not be equated with tacit support for the regime, nor, for that matter, with tacit identification with the left" (1997, 131), I have found that much more was going on in rural Haiti at the time than what was meeting our Observer-eyes.

The discursive and organizational practices I highlight in this book reflect the Haitian peasantry's long heritage of resisting the ideological, economic, and political systems to which they have been subjected. However, to indiscriminately label all unsanctioned or dissident discourse and behavior as "resistance" would be to silence many aspects of what speaking and acting "against the grain" have meant in this context.

In discussing the history of Afro-Caribbean populations, Mintz argues against characterizing certain actions as either accommodation or resistance. He does this by explaining that they are not necessarily mutually exclusive. "Some of the most effective forms of *resistance*," he points out, "were built on prior *adaptation*" (1974, 75–81). Burton expands this idea in suggesting that "cultural opposition in the Caribbean [is] double-edged to the extent that an (Afro-) Creole culture cannot, by its very creoleness, get entirely outside the dominant system in order to resist it . . . and so tends unconsciously to reproduce its underlying structures" (1997, 8). Orin Starn describes peasant protests in Latin America as also "defy[ing] neat categorizations 'hegemonic' or 'counterhegemonic'" (1992, 95). Rather, he says, they

> tend to combine both a challenge of and an acceptance of authority. On the one hand, most movements coalesce in opposition to the powers that be—most often big landowners and/or the state. On the other, they accept and reproduce many of the prevailing arrangements of representation and command. Thus admiration for high offices can mix with disdain for local bureaucrats. . . . Making sense of rural politics requires a fine-tuned ethnographic sensitivity to the interlocking nuances of resistance and accommodation. (95)

Such studies have led numerous scholars to criticize Scott and others for "the overuse of 'resistance'."[29] The term, critics argue, has been applied so liberally that virtually any behavior performed by persons who have suffered oppression may be labeled *resistance.* Not only does this render resistance "a seductive but ultimately infertile concept" (Holland and Eisenhart 1990, 57), it also puts us on a slippery slope toward facile romantizations of oppressed peoples as groups of inherently politicized activists, and tempts us to ignore the fact that they also accommodate, submit, and sometimes exploit one another.

Perhaps one of the most potentially disabling handicaps of theories of resistance is that what their objects of study are doing and saying must be conceptualized first and foremost as re-actions to negative forces. In pointing out that "many of the classic struggles at the entry to the industrial revolution turned as much on customs as upon wages or conditions of work," E. P. Thompson (1991, 4–5) stresses that people were both acting out *against* the threats leveled by capitalist development, and acting out *of* their "customary definitions and expectations" (1978, 152). Mintz and Price (1992 [1976]) make similar points in their study of the development of African-American cultures. In his study of the "new social movement" of blacks in Britain, Gilroy emphasizes that "racial subordination is not the sole factor shaping the choices and actions of Britain's black settlers and their British-born children," (1991, 153) and encourages us to see their actions also as "expressive" ones emanating as much from a rich legacy of varied cultural forms as from adverse social conditions (see also Kearney 1996; Giri 1992).

Likewise, I aim to demonstrate that Haitian peasants, in organizing together and constructing analyses of their situation, are not simply responding to or reacting against the forces pressing down upon them. They also are pro-actively thinking, working, mobilizing, and speaking *from* a multifaceted and shifting base of social, cultural, and material resources, and *to-*

ward the realization of a number of positive visions about what a society should be.

There is a final approach to the study of traditionally marginalized peoples I must address here. Scholars have asserted at times that the oppressed actually have *superior* insight into the causes and mechanisms of social problems. Donna Haraway, for instance, suggests there is "good reason to believe vision is better from below the brilliant space platforms of the powerful" (Haraway 1988, 583; see also Brown 1991, 98). In other words, The disenfranchised are not limited by the "necessary illusions" (to use Chomsky's phrase) that so constrain the thought possibilities of those of us who have benefited more handsomely from the systems of distribution that have governed the modern and postmodern world. "The poor, in their popular wisdom," Boff and Boff note, "in fact 'know' much more about poverty than does any economist. Or rather, they know in another way, and in much greater depth" (1987, 30).

June Nash develops a similar position in her study of a Bolivian mining community. (1992). The miners working there, she says, "seemed more prepared to deal with the multivocalic complexity of human consciousness than did social scientists in academic settings" (292).

By insisting that we take seriously the perspectives of those whose voices have been systematically silenced and discounted, such arguments have undoubtedly enriched the attempts of social scientists to understand our postcolonial world and the peoples, problems, movements and societies that compose it. Yet, as David Harvey and Gyatri Spirak have emphasized, these arguments also threaten to move us from well-founded efforts to make audible the long-silenced voices of the marginalized, to exercises in ennobilization—exercises which in the end reveal more about our own thinking than that of those we study. (See Harvey 1996 and Spivak 1988; see also J.M. Smith 1998). We thereby end up reverting to, rather than escaping, the reductionism and denial of coevalness inherent in the "otherings" we set out to contest.

I do not claim, therefore, that Haitian peasants have some sort of *über*-insight into their situation, that they are any less vulnerable to being duped than the rest of us, that they are products of a "rebellious traditional culture" (Thompson 1991, 9), or that they are innately politicized. I propose instead that Haitian peasants have long been thinking critically about their world and their place in it; and have drawn on rich cultural and social stores in expressing and acting on these thoughts in a variety of creative, artistic, and complex ways. Their thoughts and axioms merit attention not only because of their particularities, and the ways those particularities call into question certain North-Western ways of seeing and doing things, but also because of their capacities to illuminate the common concerns and connections and, hence, the potentialities for solidarity between North-Westerners and those we have found it so difficult not to "other." I begin my efforts to illustrate this by inviting the reader to join me in listening to Haitian peasants as they sing.

3

Melodic Machetes

I am of the opinion that the urban elite never achieved anything like hegemony in rural Haiti. While Haitian peasants have strategically adapted to the monopoly of the elite on affairs of the state, there is no solid research to show that they accepted an ideology that justified domination (on the basis of elite superiority) or the "naturalization" of their subordination. To the contrary, there is ample testimony in informal discourse (especially proverbs, peasant songs, and folktales) that reveals a sophisticated class analysis and an ironic and playful commentary on the rationales and mechanisms of their subordination. (Averill 1997, 7)

Jouk nan kè Lafrik bato yo vin chaje.	To the very heart of Africa the boats came to fill up.
Sou do Karayib esklav yo debake	On the back of the Caribbean, the slaves disembarked
Yo pa gen anyen pou yo te pote	They couldn't carry anything with them
Sèlman ti mizik yo pou yo te chante	Only songs for them to sing
Woy, yo se raraman, woy, yo se raraman	*Woy,* they're *rara* men, *woy,* they're *rara* men
Byen alèkile stati yo vin chanje	Since then, their status has changed
Sepandan yo pa janm sispann chante	However, they've never stopped singing
Depi ou tande, lannwit la rive	Listen, when the night falls
Kote gen tanbou se la yo rasanble	Wherever there's a drum, that's where they'll gather
Woy, yo se raraman, woy, yo se raraman	*Woy,* they're *rara* men, *woy,* they're *rara* men.[1]

The Caribbean is renowned for its festive, playful, and provocative music. Throughout the region, music is a central feature of everyday life. In urban areas, the latest tunes are continually blasted from the scurrying minivans. In rural settings, women, men, and children sing to the rhythms of their work and play. The roles of music and verbal arts in these contexts are not limited to entertainment and distraction. Song is also used daily as a means through which to test, exploit, and at times, challenge, the parameters of what is discursively and behaviorally possible. The stages on which these songs are performed are as varied as the messages they deliver.

Rural Footpaths: Stage One

Kami walks down the path below my hut outside Kalfounò with a load of red beans on her head and a sack of mangoes cradled in her arms. Already perspiring under the early morning sun, it is obvious from the gait of her walk that she is not only hurried; she is perturbed. She is on her way to Pinyon today. She had hoped to take several measures of corn, a chicken, and some yams along with her beans and mangoes to sell in the market that will be bustling there tomorrow morning. She also had hoped that she would not be carrying any of it herself. But she had been counting on Eli's mule, and when her father-in-law informed her at the last minute that his mule would be needed at home, she was forced to leave most of her produce behind.

Now, as she staggers under the weight of her diminished load and the prospect of the eight-hour trek ahead of her, she begins to hum a tune. She soon adds lyrics to her impromptu music, and by the time she passes by my garden and heads down the ravine to cross the stream below Eli's yard, I can make out several lines clearly: "Oh mama, oh mama, I work so hard in the man's garden. Oh mama, oh mama, and what do I have to carry away from his land? . . . You think you know your friends, your family . . . then you're left to walk alone. . . . *Woy*, what's happening to our country? Jealousy and stinginess are eating our hearts." By the time Kami is heading up the other side of the ravine, Eli is out in his yard, motioning enthusiastically with his hands and yelling something about his mule and the ingratitude and audacity of women. But Kami, assured that her message has been received, tops the hill without turning back, and soon her load disappears into the landscape.

Sociopolitical Poetics: *Chante Pwen-s*

> The ability to use song as a weapon of social control is a valued skill in Haiti, as it is [in] several other Afro-American settings. Where social norms emphasize the avoidance of direct confrontation, singing, typically under the transparent veil of nondirected, objectified discourse, serves as a vehicle for venting hostilities and exercising power. (Richman 1987, 1)

Consistently constructed as a people lacking the political will and intellectual capacity to contribute constructively to discussions about their society and the direction it should take, the Haitian peasantry has found its voices chronically excluded from its nation's halls of power (see chapter 2). When rural Haitians have attempted to challenge these stereotypes and exclusions through outright dissent or defiance, they have faced brutal retaliation. As the proverb affirms, in Haiti "a cockroach is never in the right while standing before a chicken."

This has not meant that people have been stopped from articulating dissidence. Instead of either buckling under and complying with their systematic exclusion, or "accept[ing] the ideology that [has] justified domination . . . or the 'naturalization' of their subordination" (Averill 1997, 7), many Haitian peasants have responded by creating a number of less-direct though still pointed strategies through which to gain some control over the social order, and some voice in the public sphere.

These strategies draw on a rich store of dynamic cultural resources and involve crafted modes of expression that are at once effective and subtle. Among them is the practice known as *voye pwen*, or "sending points." In the social arena, to voye pwen is to send critical messages through indirect comments or actions. One may overhear such pwen-s on the path to the market (as in Kami's case), on the sidewalks of provincial towns, on the radio, in the midst of ceremonies for the lwa-s,[2] in prayers at church, and on *tap-tap*-s (public transportation vehicles) in Port-au-Prince. Directed at everything from the injustices of domestic life to the social ills of the nation, pwen-s are sent from neighbor to neighbor, from "little man" to "big man," from wife to husband, from employee to employer, from peasant to politician. While this artistic-discursive model boasts relatives in societies scattered throughout the formerly colonized world, in Haiti its development has been particularly elaborate and widespread.

Careful attention to social interaction in Haiti reveals that pwen-s show up virtually everywhere. One of the most common ways Haitians package and deliver pwen-s is through the medium of song.[3] This is no accident. In her work on the resistance strategies of Bedouin women, Lila Abu-Lughod points out that while her informants were generally forbidden to criticize social norms, "certain forms of resistance [e.g., poetry] by the less powerful in Bedouin society could be admired, even by those whose interests the system supported" (1990, 47). Likewise, although poor Haitians "speaking back" to those more powerful than they has been culturally and politically forbidden, the folk music of rural Haiti is an expressive genre that has long been lauded as a national treasure by those at all levels of Haitian society. The Haitian elite has consistently expressed nostalgic pride in the music of the peasantry and at times, has been quite savvy in converting it from cultural capital into economic and political capital. Small bands of musicians dressed in what passes for peasant attire perform regularly at the bars, poolsides, and restaurants of the country's finest hotels. Images of such performances fill the brochures and other media aimed at attracting foreigners. Once they arrive, it is folk musicians who first greet these visitors at the Port-au-Prince airport, plucking out "Haïti Chéri" on rustic guitars, drums, and cha-chas.

There could hardly be a more perfect medium for the development and delivery of pwen-s. Because weaving contestation and nuance into poetic drama is an art that is particularly popular in the countryside, it is not surprising that we find some of the most masterful chante pwen composers and performers among the peasantry. By singing pwen-s, rural Haitians are able to both exploit their society's discursive and behavioral mores and, at times, to push against the limits of those mores.

In general terms, a *chante pwen*,[4] or "pointing song," uses symbolism to chastise, mock, or comment critically on the deeds or character of a person or group of people. Ordinarily, the symbols employed must be transparent enough to ensure that the message gets across but ambiguous enough to protect the singer from becoming a target for retaliation. The art of composing and performing pointing songs, then, depends on making the words and, at times, the rhythms say more than that which meets the ear.

The roots of chante pwen-s in rural Haitian culture are deep and meandering. Bilby hints that chante pwen-s have ancestors in pre-colonial Africa when he writes that several genres of contemporary Caribbean music may be traced to the West African tradition of "songs of derision" (1985, 21; also see Averill 1997). As the lyrics of "Raraman" (excerpted at the beginning of the chapter) remind us, much of the first Haitian music was authored by enslaved Africans in a social context where nearly all singing and dancing constituted defiance. The result was a host of New World "songs of derision," and more.

Humor and playfulness permeate chante pwen-s, a fact recalling Burton's observation that "in the Caribbean all play is oppositional and all oppositionality . . . contains a 'play' element—which most definitely does *not* mean that it is not intensely serious at the same time" (1997, 9, italics in the original). Some pointing songs and the sociopolitical analyses found in them are much more indirect, more imbued with subtlety, and more colored with imagery than others. Generally, these are the ones considered most worthy of praise by Haitians themselves. In fact, the ornate elaboration of these "masks" with highly nuanced images meant to simultaneously reveal and hide is not simply a political strategy. It is seen, rather, as an artistic craft worthy of praise in itself. This, to regard pointing songs simply as protest songs or resistance songs is to risk overlooking some of their key dimensions. They are also important forums for aesthetic innovation and creative performance and, as such, rich repositories for a wide variety of expressions.

Many chante pwen-s, like Kami's, are spontaneously created. Some are performed only once, heard only by a handful of people, and then fade with the passing of the occasion for which they were composed. Others have been passed from person to person, neighborhood to neighborhood, region to region, generation to generation. Some have traveled the length and breadth of the country, and many have been sung for many decades. As they are circulated and passed down, they are edited and elaborated to respond to the unique circumstances in which they are performed. One such song first appeared in the late 1800s. Called "Panama M Tonbe" (My Hat Fell Off), it tells of a journey President Hyppolite (1889–96) made to Jacmel. The story goes that Hyppolite had set out for Jacmel in order to crush an antigovernment movement led by a popular military general and Vodou priest. As Courlander reports, "Hyppolite was said to have sworn to reduce Jacmel to ashes and to wipe out the entire population except one male and one female to repopulate the land" (1973 [1960], 151).

The trip proved less than successful for Hyppolite. Not only was his campaign thwarted, but he also suffered the terrible embarrassment of dropping his hat along the way. Symbolizing his loss of control and stately prestige, this faux pas provided the people with a perfect opportunity for mockery. "Panama M Tonbe" is one of several songs to come out of this story. Its simple little refrain—the words and peppy rhythm of which seem innocent enough on the surface—is used still today along the footpaths, in the marketplaces, and in the fields of rural Haiti to jeer mercilessly at fallen politicians, to make fun of sitting ones, and to warn them of impending doom.

Panama m tonbe,	My hat fell off,
Panama m tonbe,	My hat fell off,
Panama m tonbe, sa ki dèyè,	My hat fell down, whoever is behind,
Ranmanse l pou mwen!	Pick it up for me!

Courlander tells us that "no political aspirant ever went unsung by his peasant army, or unridiculed by his opponent's followers" (1973 [1960], 148). With each new government, coup d'état, and election campaign, new chante pwen-s and new verses for older ones have appeared. When Jean-Claude Duvalier and his family took flight in the wake of a popular uprising on February 7, 1986, songs honoring the event with celebration, bitter criticism of the Duvalier regime, and warnings to its supporters who were left behind were circulating throughout the country almost immediately. Amy Wilentz provides the lyrics of one such song, played by a Port-au-Prince radio station on the day of that famous exit (Wilentz 1989, 57):

Poor Duvalier, he's gone, he's gone.
He's cold in the snow
And Michèle is going to leave him.

I'm just a poor Tonton [Duvalierist henchman]
In a hospital bed.
I've lost my machete
And I'm no longer a man. . . .

Sometimes chante pwen-s are aimed at little more than having fun. A chante pwen sung in Tisous tells about a girl called Melina.

Melina o	Melina, oh
Ou pa wont o?	Are you not ashamed, ohhh?
Melina	Melina
Ou pase larivye ou pa bese!	You cross the river without bending down!

Local residents said this song was an old one and probably originated somewhere else. The meaning of the song was clear to all, however; not knowing who Melina was did not prevent everyone from thoroughly enjoying a chance to chastise her for not bathing herself "down there" often enough.

While I was unable to learn from my neighbors the full histories of many of the chante pwen-s they performed, I observed first-hand the composition of others. Such was the case with a song that emerged during my final few months in Tisous. Having lived there more than a year by that time, I had developed a close relationship with a four-year-old boy named Milo. He was with me on many of the late afternoons when the family from whom I rented my house would bring over my hot meal for the day. On those occasions, Milo and I would eat together the heaping bowl of yams, white sweet potatoes, or ground corn porridge. Generally, it was accompanied by a cup of "sauce" made with oil, garlic, tomatoes, onions, and hot peppers, and occasionally greens, dried fish, beans, or goat meat. Every week or two, I would get rice and beans instead of the usual pile of tubers. This was a real treat, as rice is a relatively expensive carbohydrate and beans are often scarce.

Milo happened to be there on one of those afternoons—only that day, there was no sauce. I told him so as I served up his bowl and sat it down across from mine. "Mmm, this looks good, huh?" I said. "Where's the sauce?" he demanded, lip turned decidedly downward. Surprised by this little boy who generally ate gleefully nearly anything I offered him, I asked, "What do you mean, Milo? I told you—there's no sauce today." "The sauce!" he exclaimed again, "Where's the sauce?" Now getting irritated, I said, "*Milo*, look, if you don't want it, don't eat it, but I don't have any sauce! And what's with your attitude today?" Looking up at me with all the wounded indignation he could muster, he said, "The other day, Benwa was here, and you gave *him* the sauce. And now you won't give it to me!" Suddenly I realized that my jealous companion was talking about the Tabasco sauce I kept on my shelf. Cautioning him against the idea, I handed it over. He poured it liberally over his food, happy to be vindicated—if only for that brief moment before he actually bit into his fiery feast.

I had nearly forgotten about this incident a few days later when I went with Milo to visit his aunt next door. "So what's this I hear," she teased me as we sat in her yard eating coconuts, "about you depriving poor little Milo of the sauce you serve to Benwa?" Milo, nestled in my lap, began to squirm and protest. "You mean to tell me . . . ?" I started to say. Yes, she confirmed, Milo had been going around the neighborhood telling all his little friends about the gross injustice I had done him. On hearing that, I readily consented, despite his pleas, to tell her the whole story. As she laughed uncontrollably and chided him, I realized that he would never live this one down. I was right. Soon other neighbors, already shaking with anticipatory laughter, were coming by to persuade me to tell them all about it. Before long, I began to hear the work parties in the fields striking their machetes to the peppery beat of this tune:

Li bay Benwa sòs	She gave Benwa sauce
Li pa ba m sòs o	She wouldn't give me sauce, ohhh
Li bay Benwa sòs	She gave Benwa sauce
Li pa ba m sòs o	She wouldn't give me sauce, ohhh
Ala yon ti nèg ki visye!	What a little glutton!

Little Milo is only one potential target for this chorus; it will undoubtedly be used in the future to chastise or warn others tempted by the sins of greed and gluttony.

The variety of messages that may be sent through chante pwen-s is further evident in the fact that sending points "is a practice that spans sacred and secular contexts" (Averill 1997, 15). At the Vodou altar, chante pwen-s are very common, as the lwa-s are called on to right wrongs and settle differences among their servants. In fact, the lwa-s themselves are known to sing points of chastisement, warning, and prescriptive advice. Certain songs may actually carry supernatural charms—or alternatively, curses—to their targets.[5]

Whether meant to entertain, to vent frustrations, to manipulate, to resist pacification, to criticize, or to threaten those in power, these decorative masks have been important tools in the hands of a people who have had little voice in their society's sanctioned realms of political discourse—people who have been hunted down, beaten, imprisoned, chased out of the country, tortured, and sometimes killed for speaking their minds on such issues as the fact that their kids are hungry, or that their neighborhoods lack schools, roads, electricity, and health clinics. Recognizing their multiplex value, Haitians have sent points with chante pwen-s as close to home as next door, and as far away as Port-au-Prince and the White House.

Agricultural Work Parties: Stage Two

> At the *combite* [agricultural work party] a man not only learns all the gossip of the day, but enjoys learning and singing the songs which caustically comment on the shortcomings of neighbors, or evaluate the hospitality of those who have called [that is, hosted] the *combites*, or detail scandal, phrased with sufficient directness to allow the reference of the song to remain clear, but warily, so as not to give the individual pilloried ground for direct recrimination. (Herskovitz 1971 [1937], 74)

Given that many of the most accomplished composers of chante pwen-s are peasants, it is not surprising that the agricultural work party (*konbit* or *kòve*) is one of the genre's most prolific stages. One role of music in this context is simply to entertain and energize ("heat up") the workers. Like "Melina," many of the chante pwen-s that arise here are primarily playful, full of jokes and tongue-in-cheek gossip. More than a few pick fun at the supposed sexual prowess and embarrassing romantic entanglements of others. A good example is this one, recorded in Jacques Romain's novel *Masters of the Dew* (1978 [1944], 27):

> Stroke it in!
> Who's that, I yell,
> Inside that house?
> Some man yells back,
> Just me and a cute
> Little cousin of mine—
> And we don't need you!

Other chante pwen-s heard in the fields contain more serious social commentary. These are often directed at the person whose field is being worked. While the agricultural work performed by the rural poor is widely recognized as a center pillar of Haiti's economy, peasant labor is very poorly compensated.[6] In fact, *grandon*-s (owners of large plots of land) are notorious for exploiting the labor of their poorer neighbors without offering adequate reciprocation. Very often, there is little the latter can do to communicate their expectations or challenge their treatment without risking retaliation from the landowner. There is, however, the weapon of song.

If the owner of a field is stingy with his konbit or kòve guests, as the work-day progresses she or he is likely to hear the beat of the drums begin to drag and the animated voices of the workers turn from amusement to drama-tized groans about the hunger pangs in their bellies. Herskovits (1971 [1937], 74–75) offers the lyrics of a song typical of those that rise from fields when workers begin to realize that their long hours under the hot sun may bring them too-meager portions of food and drink at the end of the day.

Down!
I say, messieurs,
I went to that *combite*
I did not eat.
I went, but I found no drink
To drink.
Enough! Up!
I say, messieurs,
I went to that *combite*
I found no food to eat.

Here, as for most chante pwen-s, the workers would be singing not only for the ears of the targeted person (in this case, the landowner). Also meant to hear would be the person's neighbors, family members, and any-one else who happened to be passing by.

James Scott (1985) suggests in *Weapons of the Weak* that wealthier villagers in Sedaka "really cared" if poorer villagers criticized their piety—so much so that such criticisms were a mechanism with which poorer villagers could effect the wealthy's behavior. Just as the reputation of the rich of Sedaka depended on demonstrating the spirit of *tolong* (roughly, "benevolence"), so too in rural Haiti is the honor of local "big guys" contingent (if not, per-haps, to the same degree) on demonstrations of generosity in their rela-tions with their poorer neighbors. Landowners hosting groups of workers in their fields—particularly when those groups are accompanied by ensem-bles of drums, bamboo horns, or flutes—are ever aware that failing to pass around enough sugar-cane rum, to fill workers' bowls with enough corn porridge, or to pay them sufficiently means taking the risk of exposing their (the landowners') reputations to an onslaught of merciless blows from melodic machetes.

Workers may also use song to reinforce the behavior of good landown-ers. Most konbit and kòve participants are just as happy to sing the praises of a host who has been especially beneficent as they would have been to throw scorn and mockery in the direction of one who had been especially stingy. In either case, pointing songs constitute a means through which poorer peasants can exploit sociocultural norms in controlling, at least to some extent, the behavior of wealthier peasants (or, as Haitians themselves might say, a means through which the cockroach can make the chicken dance).

Other popular objects of konbit and kòve pointing songs are nationally known "big guys," that is, those who rule Haiti's notoriously repressive state apparatus. In a song heard coming often from the fields of Tisous even several years after the end of the 1991–1994 post-coup era, locals still complained about the coup's impact on locals' lives.

Ooo	Ohhh . . .
Koudeta kraze peyi m, o	A coup d'état has crushed my country
O oye o o, O oye o o, O oye o o	*O oye o o, O oye o o, O oye o o*
Koudeta kraze peyi m, o	A coup d'état has crushed my country
Ma rele aye, ma rele aye, ma rele aye	I'm crying out *aye*, I'm crying out *aye* . . .
Koudeta kraze peyi m, o	A coup d'état has crushed my country, oh.

In the following konbit/kòve song, peasant laborers highlight the absurdity of the state's dependency on them on the one hand, and its systematic disrespect for their needs on the other:

Wo! The President sends for me!
I haven't drunk, I haven't eaten!
I haven't drunk, I haven't eaten!
Oh, I haven't drunk, I haven't eaten!
The President sends for me, *wo!*
I haven't drunk, I haven't eaten![7]

Other chante pwen-s call out specific leaders for their behavior:

There was a president,
He was Tirésius Augustin Simon Sam.
If they were all like him,
Haiti would be finished![8]

That Tirésius Sam is long dead does not make this song dated. Like the chorus poking fun at Hyppolite's faux pas, the song may still be employed to critique current rulers.

Scott (1985) acknowledges that the resistance strategies of Sedaka peasants have been limited in their ability to challenge substantially the balance of power there. The same might be said for the history of chante pwen-s in rural Haiti. In fact, chante pwen-s have sometimes worked to uphold the status quo. Averill writes that state leaders have managed on numerous occasions to direct the uses of this genre and other musical forms at "intimidat[ing] opponents, tak[ing] people's minds off problems, demonstrat[ing] electoral or grass-roots strength, and solidify[ing] support" (Averill 1997, 13). He explains further:

> Haiti has a fascinating history of praise and honorific music, much of which has been devoted to the various authoritarian figures who have ruled Haiti since independence. . . . When a group gathers to sing and play an *ochan* for a patron or a political figure, it is the power of the group they are trading for patronage and protection—the very audible power of numbers of people at least momentarily allied with the patron. (12–13)

François Duvalier was particularly intentional about mobilizing this cultural resource. During his reign, he sponsored numerous parades and demonstrations in the capital and throughout the countryside, particularly during holiday celebrations and during the weeks leading up to the "elections" he occasionally staged to fabricate popular support for his regime. For these events, the government would offer people food, liquor, or money in exchange for celebrative manifestations of their devotion to their "Papa." Peasants in Bamòn still recall the chants and songs with which they used to proclaim "Long live Duvalier!" and "throw points" at his detractors.

Mardi Gras and Rara Festivities: Stage Three

Other settings in which Haitian peasants compose and perform chante pwen-s include the festival seasons of Mardi Gras, lasting from early January through Shrove Tuesday, and *Rara*, which peaks between Holy Wednesday and Easter Sunday. "Every weekend in the Mardi Gras season," writes Courlander, "the country roads and villages are alive with special music, dancing bands, and traditional kinds of masquerading" (1973 [1960], 105). The cities pulsate with revelry at these times as well. Observe Gillis and Averill (1991), "In the week before Easter, roads all over Haiti swell with bands of revelers, dancers, singers, percussionists, and players of bamboo and tin trumpets . . . led by presidents, colonels, queens and other members of the complex *rara* band hierarchies."

Mardi Gras and Rara performances are famous for songs Courlander describes as "boldly ribald or licentious," "openly sexual," and colored by "an overall tone of secular abandon" (1973 [1960], 106, 109). They are also well known for their highly politicized chante pwen-s. It is in such celebrations that politicians and other powerholders may find their faults and shortcomings most unabashedly, vulgarly, and mercilessly trumpeted through the country's mountain pathways and city streets. One might not think that the singing which goes on during these raucous occasions would matter much to government officials. In fact, the opposite is true. An effective testimony to the power of pointing songs is the fact that Haitian bands known for their politicized lyrics have sometimes been banned from Carnival activities.

A popular "roots" band called Boukman Eksperyans was threatened with this prospect in 1990. In the months before Carnival, President Prosper Avril's military regime was in the midst of a ruthless crackdown on opposition movements. Troubled by the popularity of Boukman's first big hit, "Pran Chenn, Wet Chenn" (Get Angry, Throw Off Your Chains), the government threatened to forbid Boukman from performing in Carnival that year.

As Gage Averill (1997) explains, however, the group outwitted the government by composing as their Carnival song a piece it could hardly refuse. Called "Kè M Pa Sote" (I Am Not Afraid), the song manages to launch a colorful array of insults at the government while failing to mention by name either the government itself or any particular military or government officials. Instead, it uses terms like *those guys, assassins, frauds.* Averill notes that by failing to identify explicitly the targets of the song's points, Boukman "set a crafty trap for the government" (181) and locked it in a Catch-22. If it allowed the band to perform the song, it would be providing a stage for what the population would readily latch onto as an antigovernment demonstration. However, censuring the song would have meant that the government was essentially acknowledging itself as the intended subject of the song's harsh critiques—something it simply could not bring itself to do in the end. "I Am Not Afraid" was an immediate hit.

This song electrified the population, which danced to its beat and chanted its lyrics all over Port-au-Prince as well as in the countryside. Averill goes so far as to suggest that "I Am Not Afraid" may have had a direct impact on President Avril's forced resignation, which occurred just a few weeks after Carnival (1997, 182).

Gwoupman Peyizan Meetings: Stage Four

Civic organizations focused on planning and instigating projects of economic, political, and social change have increased exponentially in number and kind in Haiti during the past few decades, particularly since the ouster of the Duvalier regime in 1986. This movement, commonly called "the popular movement," includes tens of thousands of small neighborhood-based associations referred to as *gwoupman peyizan*-s, or "peasant groupings."[9]

Many gwoupman peyizan-s (GPs) have been closely associated with foreign aid organizations, which commonly provide them with material and financial support, education, and training. Out of these "partnerships" has emerged a fascinating song genre that reflects both the concerns of the contemporary peasantry and the concerns of the international aid complex. Some of the *chan gwoupman*-s are directed at promoting social axioms such as cooperation and volunteerism. Other songs are aimed at motivating people to adopt certain development technologies or practices. Among the most popular GP songs in Kalfounò, for instance, were "The Special Water [Oral Rehydration Formula] Song," and "The Green Manure [Natural Fertilizer] Song." But many of the most popular and most enthusiastically performed pieces are those which send points. The pwen-s of these chan gwoupman-s levy critiques at state officials, church hierarchies, local "big guys," and on many occasions, the GPs' sponsoring organizations themselves. The songs also comment on the structural roots of injustice in Haiti and call for local citizens to instigate fundamental changes in the way their communities and their society function. In many of these songs, the imagery—like that of many Mardi Gras and Rara celebrations, seems nearly to have discarded masks altogether. As a result, the songs have what Scott calls "a double aspect":

> There is the release of resisting domination and, at the same time, the release of finally expressing the response one had previously choked back. Thus, the release of tension generated by constant vigilance and self-censorship must itself be a source of great satisfaction. . . . It is only when this hidden transcript is openly declared that subordinates can fully recognize the extent to which their claims, their dreams, their anger is shared by other subordinates. (1990, 213, 223)

Again, as in the case of the chan madigra-s and the chan rara-s, the threat these openly defiant pieces pose to power relations is not lost on local and national authorities. This was clear during the 1991–94 post-coup era, when the lyrics of chan gwoupman-s were often referenced in giving justification for attacks on the GPs and their members. Even so, a host of new chan gwoupman-s emerged during this time. Many of these were still being sung in Bamòn during my tenure there in 1995–96. Filled with images of chaos, violence, predation, and stubborn resistance, the following song refers to the coup that toppled the Aristide regime in 1991 and brought the junta to power. With the image of a shepherd attacked in his field, it begins by emphasizing the loss and pain exacted on the people (in this case, the scattered sheep) by the coup. It then turns to images from two popular pastimes, the lottery and the cock fight. Whereas the numbers played in the lottery, 29 and 30, most likely refer to the dates of the September coup, the image of the rooster—Aristide's political symbol—is called up to assert that although their president (and the population itself) may be "bleeding," it will not give up the fight. It continues by portraying the junta rulers as predatory animals who "drink the blood of the people," and then directly points at "the shameless bourgeois" and the *tonton makout*s (those who have followed in the footsteps of Duvalier's repressive paramilitary corps). Finally, it swears that "the powers of Ginen" (divine ancestral powers) will overcome these forces of evil.

Kè	Chorus:
Lè yo frape bèje mouton yo te gaye o, ayida wedo	When they struck down the shepherd, the sheep scattered, oh, *ayida wedo*
Adye o san yo	*Adye o san yo*
Lè yo frape bèje mouton yo te gaye o, ayida wedo	When they struck down the shepherd, the sheep scattered, oh, *ayida wedo*
Adye o san yo	*Adye o san yo*
Se te ak cha blendè	With armored tanks
Se te ak mitrayèt	With machine guns
Se te ak gwò wouzi	With Uzi's
Vye frè yo tap kraze ti pèp la.	Their betraying brothers were crushing the people.
Al jwe 29 ak 30 apre ma di rèv mwen fè o	Go play (in the lottery) numbers 29 and 30, then I'll tell you the dream I had
Adye o san yo	*Adye o san yo*
Kòk la al nan gagè yo bay san l pa pèdi o	The fighting rooster went to the rink and shed blood but didn't die
Patizan kriye vi o fòk pari a refèt o.	It's supporters cried "Live!" and "The match must be repeated!"
Chen anraje yo, malfini zele o, reken gran dlo yo	The rabid dogs, the vultures, the sharks
Fò n sispann bwè san pèp la	You must stop drinking the blood of the people
Boujwa san wont ak lidè san manman sòti pou kraze ti peyi a	The shameless bourgeois and the sadist rulers are trying to shatter the country
Tonton makout ak lidè san manman sòti pou kraze ti peyi a	The *tonton makout*s and incorrigible leaders are trying to destroy the country
Yo pa vle demokrasi pran pye lakay nou e e e.	They want to prevent democracy from taking root here, *e e e*
Fwa sa a koudeta sa a pap pase	This time the coup d'état won't succeed
Yo fè siklonn 30 Sektanm pou fwennen lit pèp la	They crafted September 30 to stop the people

Pouvwa ginen bloke yo nan zak	But the powers of Ginen have blocked
bizango sa a e e e	their sorcery, *e e e*
Pouvwa ginen bloke yo nan zak	But the powers of Ginen have blocked
bizango sa a e e e	their sorcery, *e e e*
Fòk tire pye sa a fini anndan lakay nou	This shooting at our feet must be
	stopped inside this house
Fòk chwal sa a fini anndan lakay nou	This horse has got to die here
Zòt fè manti pou ranvèse pouvwa popilè pèp	They use their lies to undermine
ayisyen an	popular power
Pou boujwa machann peyi ka fè milyon yo e e e	So the bourgeois selling off the country
	can make millions, *e e e.*

The period following the post-coup terror has inspired different kinds of chan gwoupman lyrics. The song below appeared in 1995. At the time, the country was crowded with international peacekeeping troops, which had increased the magnitude and scope of their operations after ushering Aristide back into the country in October 1994. As millions of dollars worth of aid slated for promoting democracy and development also poured in, community governance, material aid, and participatory development projects were spreading like wildfire throughout the countryside. By recalling the dehumanizing effects of projects done in the past in the name of humanitarian aid, this song voices the people's misgivings about the motivations and possible outcomes of this latest wave of assistance. I first heard it during a meeting of a "strong women's group" in Bamòn in the spring of 1996. They spontaneously struck up its chorus in responding to my questions about how they would define the terms *democracy* and *development*—and thereby gave me an answer that was as "pointed" as it was indirect.

Meriken kenbe n nan kou o	The Americans have us by the throat,
	Ohhh
Tonton Sam bay nou kle kou o	Uncle Sam is strangling us, Ohhh
Paske nou se piti, yo pran n pou pitimi	Because we're small, they take us for
	nothin'
Nou sèmante 7 fwa nou pap viv kou zonbi	But we solemnly swear we won't live
	like zombies!
Yo touye kochon djol long n yo	They killed our Creole pigs
Yo ba n kochon grimèl o	And gave us their old white pigs
Yo fòse n vann tout ti poul nou	They force us to get rid of our little
	chickens
Yo ba n pye poul pou vann	And then hand us chicken feet to sell
Sak fè sa?	Who's doing this to us?
Tonton Sam o!	Uncle Sam, Ohhh!

A Refugee Camp: Stage Five

Some of the most memorable glimpses I have had into the political uses of song in Haitian society were, ironically, at the U.S. Naval Base in Guantá-namo Bay, Cuba. There, between November 1991 and the summer of 1993, thousands of Haitians who had tried to flee their country in the af-termath of the 1991 coup were interned in a makeshift refugee camp run by a joint task force of the U.S. Armed Services. Living under conditions of confinement they considered cruel and dehumanizing, the refugees used music to keep intact their dignity, rework their identities, and protest their treatment.

Daily, new rhymes and rhythms appeared through which the refugees would voye pwen-s at their U.S. military captors. It was a particularly entic-ing practice in this context, where the subjects being critiqued stared through razor-wire fences right into the faces of those "indirectly" defacing them. Though not comprehending many words, the soldiers were assuredly "catching the point" of much that was sung. Some of the funniest, angriest, and most creative chante pwen-s became known throughout the camp. These pwen-s were not only composed for the refugees' Guantánamo cap-tors. Then-president George Bush, the United Nations, the U.S. govern-ment, and the agents of the junta regime from which the refugees had fled (e.g., Cedras, Honorat, members of the Haitian parliament, and military and paramilitary troops) also were thoroughly mocked and chastised in the lyrics.

Like "I Am Not Afraid," a number of these chante pwen-s doubled as songs inspiring hope in the face of uncertainty, loss, and fear. One of those that did this best also demonstrates how songs not originally meant to voye pwen may later be utilized to do so. I am referring to a Protestant church hymn called "Men Anlè a Lap Vini" (Look, Up There—He's Coming Back). I first learned about the song from a couple we interviewed at the Guantánamo base in January 1992, soon after the refugee camp was set up. The couple reported that they had been forced to flee after a brutal attack at a church service they were attending. Aware of the Protestant church's traditionally conservative, pro-establishment politics and the fact that it was generally exempt from political offensives, I was surprised. "Why on earth did they attack your church?" I asked. They replied that the assault came just as the congregation was finishing up the final stanza of a popular hymn. Glancing nervously from side to side and singing in whispered voices, they offered me the chorus of "Look, Up There."

> *Men anlè a lap vini!*   Look, up there—he's coming back!
> *Men anlè a lap vini!*   Look, up there—he's coming back!

Men anlè a lap vini!	Look, up there—he's coming back!
Men anlè a lap vini!	He's coming back!

While the explicit intention of this song is celebrating the second coming of Christ, the couple reported that following the 1991 coup, it had become a means for Protestant Haitians to express their discontent and voice their insistence that Aristide would return. Since church services were virtually the only sort of community gathering allowed at the time (the junta had declared public gatherings of more than two people illegal), many parishioners took full advantage of this situation. But the veil of protection provided by the church proved fragile. All this rapturous singing infuriated local authorities, who lashed out in a way typical of the post-coup era, and rushed on congregates with guns, machetes, and clubs.

I was to hear this song many more times during my first visit to the camp at Guantánamo. As conditions worsened and despair over the prospects of being repatriated heightened, it became more and more popular among the refugees. It was a tool, one man told me, to "call for the Grace of God," to "show them we won't give up hope," and to "ask for the return of our *papa* [President Aristide]."

Sung with equal fervor was a song I heard in Guantánamo nearly a year later, when I returned to the camp with a team of lawyers seeking the release of the refugees still being held there. At the time, the only interns were Haitians who initially had been granted entry into the United States on political grounds but then had tested positive for the HIV virus. (Some of their spouses and children were with them as well.) Many months had passed since all the others had been transferred to Miami or returned to Haiti, and this remaining group was becoming increasingly desperate to be freed from their razor wire-enclosed compound.

One day I was asked to interpret for a group of journalists touring the camp. At the time of the journalists' visit, several of the adults had been on a hunger strike for more than two weeks and were camping out in the middle of a barren field in order to protest camp conditions. As soon as the journalists appeared with cameras and notebooks in hand, a group of children gathered themselves together in the middle of the field where their parents were striking and began to dance, clap, and sing the points they wanted to send the American people through these visitors:

INS, ou twonpe mwen!	INS, you fooled me!
CRS, ou twonpe mwen!	CRS,[10] you fooled me!
Ou sòti pou kalifye mwen	You came and qualified me once.
Ou tounen pou dekalifye mwen ankò!	Then you came back again to disqualify me!

Mwen pa militè, mwen pa rete nan baz!	I'm not military; I'm not meant to live in a base!
Mwen pa militè, mwen pa rete nan baz!	I'm not military; I'm not meant to live in a base!
Guantánamo—no good! Miami—yes good!	Guantánamo—no good! Miami—yes good!
Guantánamo—no good! Miami—yes good!	Guantánamo—no good! Miami—yes good!

Recording Studios: Stage Six

Most commercially recorded Haitian music is produced by middle- and upper-class musicians residing in Port-au-Prince and in diaspora communities in the United States, Canada, and Europe. Yet, as Bilby has rightly pointed out for Caribbean music in general, we should not "make too sharp a distinction between popular and folk music" (1985, 25) in looking at music in Haiti. In fact, today one of the most popular genres of recorded Haitian music is known as *mizik rasin,* or "roots music." Its name reveals the fact that its artists draw heavily on songs originally composed and performed by the peasantry. Not coincidentally, much mizik rasin is known also for being highly politicized. A good illustration of this is Boukman Eksperyans' soundtrack, *Kalfou Danjere* (Dangerous Crossroads), which appeared in 1992—right in the midst of the bloody and tumultuous post-coup period.

Not as fortunate as "I Am Not Afraid," two of *Kalfou Danjere*'s recordings—the title track and *"Nowèl Enosan"* (Innocent Christmas)—were eventually banned by the government. The pressure did not end there. The band reports on the booklet accompanying the compact disc that military and paramilitary personnel regularly showed up at Boukman concerts during the post-coup era and attempted to intimidate the band into not playing either these two songs or "I Am Not Afraid." Included with the following excerpt from the title track is a translation taken directly from the compact disc's liner notes:

O wo o, kalfou nèg Kongo	*O wo wo,* crossroads of the Kongo people
Si ou touye, ou chaje ak pwoblem	If you kill, you'll be in deep trouble
Nan kalfou, kalfou nè Kongo	At the crossroads, the crossroads of the Kongo people
Si ou vole, ou chahe ak pwoblem	If you steal, you'll be in deep trouble
Nan kalfou, kalfou nè Kongo.	At the crossroads, the crossroads of the Kongo people.
O wo o, kalfou nèg Kongo	*O wo wo,* crossroads of the Kongo people

Magouyè, ou chaje ak pwoblem	Deceivers, you'll be in deep trouble
Nan kalfou nèg Kongo	At the crossroads, the crossroads of the Kongo people.
Si ou manti, ou chaje ak pwoblem	Liars, you'll be in deep trouble
Nan kalfou, kalfou nè Kongo.	At the crossroads, the crossroads of the Kongo people.
O wo o, kalfou nèg Kongo	*O wo wo,* crossroads of the Kongo people
Touye nou pap touye	We're not doing any killing
Jwe nou pap jwe la	We're not going to play that game
Touye nou pap touye e	We're not doing any killing
Ginen pa Bizango	Ginen is not Bizango
Si ou se yon fran Ginen ou pap touye	If you're a sincere Ginen, you won't kill
Ginen pa Bizango	Ginen is not Bizango
Si ou se yon fran Ginen ou pap volè	If you're a sincere Ginen, you won't steal
Ginen pa Bizango	Ginen is not Bizango
Si ou se yon fran Ginen ou pap manti	If you're a sincere Ginen, you won't lie
Ginen pa Bizango	Ginen is not Bizango
Chorus:	Chorus:
Wo wo woy!	*Wo wo woy!*
Si ou pa Ginen rale ko ou	If you're not Ginen, get out of here
Si ou se magouyè rale ko ou	If you are a cheater, get out of here
Si ou se asasen rale ko ou	If you are an assassin, get out of here
Si ou se volè rale ko ou	If you are a thief, get out of here
O wo o, Kalfou nèg Kongo	*O wo o,* crossroads of the Kongo people
O wo o, kalfou nèg Kongo	*O wo o,* crossroads of the Kongo people
Si ou volè, ou chaje ak pwoblem	If you're a thief, you're in deep trouble
Nan kalfou, kalfou nè Kongo.	At the crossroads, the crossroads of the Kongo people.
Magouye ou chaje ak pwoblem	Cheaters, you're in deep trouble
Magouye ou chaje ak pwoblem	Cheaters, you're in deep trouble
Asasen ou chaje ak pwoblem	Assassins, you're in deep trouble
Nan kalfou	In the crossroads
Kalfou nèg Kongo. . . .	Crossroads of the Kongo people.

Here, Boukman asserts that the righteous forces of Ginen (the spiritual homeland of the Haitian people and dwelling place of their deities) are greater than the malicious power of the "Bizango" secret societies, that is, the power to curse, kill, steal from, cheat, and lie to the people. As places that serve as gateways for the entry of the lwa-s into the earthly realm, cross-roads in Haiti are locations of special significance, considered at once holy and dangerous ground. Enemies who dare to pass through the crossroads of a spiritually savvy people risk falling victim to curses they have set there.

Konbit: Burning Rhythms of Haiti (1989) is a compilation that features a va-riety of popular musicians from Port-au-Prince and the diaspora who "excorporate" (to use Averill's term) traditional peasant folk tunes and musical styles in making critical and suggestive assertions about Haitian society. One song featured on *Konbit* is Manno Charlemagne's "Ayiti Pa Fore" (Haiti Is Not a Jungle). Manno has been one of the most well known and well loved of contemporary Haitian musical artists. For many years, he has used the imagery and melodies of peasant songs to celebrate the country's culture, land, and people, as well as to address the economic disparities and political oppressions that define its social structures. Due to the politically engaged nature of his music, Manno has been forced into hiding or exile numerous times during his career. This courage to speak out (and the eloquence with which he has done it) has contributed greatly to his popularity and was undoubtedly central to his election as Port-au-Prince's mayor following President Aristide's return to power in 1994.

"Haiti Is Not a Jungle," a song originally composed in 1974 (see Averill 1997, 164), had reappeared on the scene during the period of political instability and continued repression following Jean-Claude Duvalier's ouster in 1986 and before the country's first successful democratic elections in 1990. This time, Manno used signification techniques from the chante pwen-s of the peasantry to poke fun at the interim regimes and to call for a more complete "uprooting" of corrupt and oppressive forces within the state.

As the piece begins, he sings softly to an acoustic guitar solo about the pains suffered by poor Haitians because of their social circumstances.

Sak fè ou kwè m Ti Jozèf	Why do you call me "Little Joe"?
Jodi yap anmède mwen	Everyone is putting me down
Non m sèvi yon tablati	My name is a doormat
Pòdo m se yon maleng	The skin on my back is torn open
Ke wap pase men sou li.	My wounds are exposed.
Sak fè m pa reyisi tankou konpè Mimi?	Why didn't I succeed like the fat cats?
M pat gen bon pwofesè pou ki te	I didn't have good teachers, who could have
montre m koulè	shown me my colors (taught me something)
Ki pou te ka fè m wè klè.	Who could have helped me to see clearly (learn to read, become educated).
Se yon verite ak endepandans nou antere	It's true, our freedoms have been killed and buried. . . .

Having elicited empathy for a people denied basic rights and respect, Manno then asserts that those who rule them are to blame. Those rulers, he proposes, are like savage beasts bent on devouring the entire population and turning their country into a cruel social jungle. To get this point across, he asks,

Si Ayiti pa fore, sak fè ou jwenn tout bèt ladan l?	If Haiti isn't a jungle, why then all these beasts?
Ou jwenn lyon, ou jwenn tig, ou jwenn rat,	You find lions and tigers, You find rats and cats
Ou jwenn chat ou jwenn menm leyopa . . .	And you even find leopards . . .
Ki leyopa, souple? Yon bann fò malmaske	Which leopards, if you please? A bunch of masked bad guys
Si gen nempòt ti bri, ti bri tankou latòti	If there's any tiny sound, even the noise of a tortoise
Leyopa pran kouri, wi!	These leopards run away, oh yeah!

This is not a randomly chosen collection of carnivorous animals. "Leopards," for instance, refers to an elite, Port-au-Prince-based military unit renowned for its abuses of power. The people of Haiti readily recognized this pwen and delighted in deciphering the others—the cat, the rat, and so forth. Further in the song, Manno picks up the beat and turns to asserting defiantly that even the fiercest attacks of these beasts cannot destroy the courage of the Haitian people. He calls on them, in turn, to rally that courage in defying their leaders' aggressions.

Lè ou fè sa ma pè ou	When you appear you expect me to run,
Paske ou se makout, ou konprann ou ka kraponnen mwen.	Back off, [tonton] makout! You think you can fool me.
Ou rale ouzi ou la, mwen rilaks sou ou!	You pull out your Uzi, I'll just relax!
Ou rale baton gayak la, mwen pi koul sou ou! . . .	You raise your bully club; I stay cool! . . .

By singing Manno's "Haiti Is Not a Jungle," and Boukman's "I Am Not Afraid" and "Kalfou Danjere," Haitians in the alleyways of Port-au-Prince and on the footpaths of the countryside have repeatedly demonstrated the spirit of defiance that Manno was calling on and have gathered the courage to act on it.

Haitians also have performed this and many other political chante pwens in Boston, Montreal, New York, Paris, Washington, D.C., and Miami. Nina Glick Schiller and Georges Fouron have provided a case study of the importance of songs of social criticism among Haitian immigrant communities in their essay "Everywhere We Go, We Are in Danger" (Glick Schiller and Fouron 1990). Here, they describe the prominent role music has played in Haitian immigrants' efforts to adapt to and resist the challenges they face as they live between the worlds of New York City and Haiti. Just as the songs of the peasantry have traveled from the Haitian countryside to the sidewalks of Boston, so too have rural Haitians eagerly adopted and adapted the ideas and information, as well as the rhythms, melodies, and lyrics they have learned on their radios and during their travels. I was surprised when I learned that a certain chante pwen I first heard in the home of an elderly Vodou practitioner in one of the most out-of-the-way hamlets of Bamòn, for example, turned out to have been composed by "roots" musicians in Montreal. In their composition, as well as in their performance and dissemination, chante pwen-s are thoroughly transnationalized endeavors.

In fact, music from the diaspora has often played an important part in political discourses and struggles going on back in Haiti. As Karen Richman (1992) points out, the Lavalas movement that swept through Haiti in 1990 and placed Father Jean-Bertrand Aristide into the presidential office had as its anthem a song composed by the long-exiled Jean-Claude Martineau, known as Koralen. Set to the tune of a traditional Vodou hymn, this moving song, "Ayiti Demen" (Tomorrow's Haiti), has as its chorus *"Lè la libere Ayiti va bèl, o; wa tande, wa tande koze, o . . ."* (When Haiti is liberated, oh how beautiful it will be; you'll hear about it, it'll be something, ohhh . . .). During the 1991–94 post-coup era, "Ayiti Demen" continued to be called forth by Haitians both within and outside the country to express resistance, and to insist that their dream of a better future would not be destroyed.[11]

Reflections on the *Chante Pwen-s*

Recognized by Scott in Malaysia and by the Comaroffs in South Africa, the "space between the tacit and the articulate, the direct and the indirect" (Comaroff and Comaroff 1991, 31) also has constituted an important terrain for discursive struggle in the Caribbean. In Haiti, the chante pwen-s of the peasantry have been a central feature of that terrain.

Noting Jean Comaroff's discussion of the ambiguous nature of the political actions and the consciousness of subordinate groups, Dirks asserts, "But the message *is* ambiguous, and anthropologists are still struggling to open up theoretical and empirical spaces for culturally-constituted counter-hegemonies" (1992, 17, italics in the original). This discussion of chante pwen-s is meant to be such a space. In struggles between hegemonic and counterhegemonic forces in rural Haiti, chante pwen-s are far from being mere decorations (as artistic endeavors are often portrayed in the literature). Often, they constitute the very terrain of struggle, a place where political action is not only inspired but also formulated, debated, and at times enacted. As we have seen, some of that action challenges and some of it supports ruling hegemonies.

Though the composition and performance of chante pwen-s involve masking, these songs should not be characterized as "*hidden* transcripts of the poor" (Scott 1985, 1990). Their messages, while strategically costumed with imagery and nuance, are very much public. Indeed, the songs are so powerful because they *are* so readily understood by the landowner, the father-in-law, and the president; that is, they provide people who generally find themselves silenced in relation to the powers that be with a way to broadcast their sentiments.

But the value of chante pwen-s does not end there. In their analysis of the songs Nepali women compose and perform at the annual Tij festival, Holland and Skinner emphasize that their songs serve as "a site of cultural production and the formation of subjectivities" (1995, 281). Coplan asserts that the *sefela* poetry he found among Basotho wage laborers in South Africa, "demonstrates how people struggling to deal with exploitative and disintegrative social conditions may create for themselves a sense of personal autonomy from within which they may truly act" (1987, 431). The sefela, he says, also allowed the Basotho "a medium of collective self-expression and emotional reflection on the quality of their lives, their hopes and their inalienable human dignity." These features are certainly apparent in chante pwen-s. As they compose, perform, and disseminate chante pwen-s, Haitian peasants actively challenge their reputation as unenlightened and hapless victims of chronic oppression and actively reformulate both individual and collective identities.

Valued both for their highly nuanced aesthetics and for their flexible utility, then, chante pwen-s have been important tools in the struggles of Haiti's poor to construct more dignified and fruitful lives and a more decent society in which to live. Recognizing this, peasants have crafted and sharpened them no less carefully than the blades of their machetes. The extent to which their chante pwen-s also have been employed by other sectors of Haitian society and in a variety of other transnational realms reveals that while the songs are largely grounded in the particular experiences and perspectives of rural Haitians, they speak to concerns, struggles, and desires shared by people everywhere—and provide one of the few ways in which the Haitian peasant can demand of others:

Tande m tande, konnen m konnen,	Listen to me, understand me
Tande m tande, bon pawòl la ap pale . . .	Listen to me, the truth is talking . . .
Tande m tande, bon pawòl la pale	Listen to me, the truth speaks

Bon koze ap pale, bon pawòl ap pale

The truth is talking, the truth is talking,

Kretyen vivan si nou la

All peoples of the world, if you're there

Vin tande . . .

Come and listen. . . . [12]

4

Hoes Striking in Unison:
Cooperative Labor and Community Spirit

As far as the Haitian government goes, we'll never have a system that's to the advantage of the people. . . . they see the state you're in, [and say] you're not fit to develop. . . . So we have to get together, one helping the other, doing what we can, sharing what we have. (member of a Bamòn *kominotè* group)

As for ourselves, if we don't put our heads together, we'll be letting the *fwomi* [tiny black ants] show us up. When a *fwomi* finds a dead cricket, if it's out by itself, it will take a little nibble, then try to move it. When it sees it can't, you see it doesn't give up, it goes away and gathers up all the other little *fwomi*-s in its band. Before two minutes have passed, you'll see them all coming back to the cricket together, picking it up, and carrying it off to their hole. They feast carefree." (Benwa, as he talked to a women's group in Tisous about the importance of working together)

Dèyè mòn gen mòn (Beyond the mountains, still more mountains). A metaphor for life in rural Haiti, this well-known phrase may be applied to the country's geography as well. Crowded with dramatic mountainscapes, it has appeared to many to be altogether impossible to maneuver. As Heinl and Heinl relate in their famous history of the country, "The story goes that in 1801, when Napoleon was planning his attempt to reconquer Haiti, he asked about the terrain. An intelligence officer crumpled a sheet of foolscap and let it fall. 'That Sire,' he said, 'is the terrain'" (1978, 3). Little of Haiti's 27,000 square kilometers of land area comprises arable plains. Approximately 63 percent of its surface slopes more than 20 percent, and more than 40 percent is above 400 meters in elevation (USAID 1985).

But Napoleon's army would likely find those mountains less formidable now, as the thick subtropical forests that once covered them are largely gone. Left in their place are comparatively naked inclines hosting eroded plots of food crops, pepperings of fruit trees, and scattered collections of homes and villages. The deforestation of Haiti's land began with the aggressive efforts of sixteenth-, seventeenth-, and eighteenth-century colonists to extract from it as much wealth as possible, first by mines and, later, mono-crop agriculture. Environmental degradation continued after independence with a wide variety of agricultural and industrial pursuits. It is now carried on as "desperate ecocide" by the Haitian people in their never-ending search for fuel, building materials, and the increasing amounts of cash needed to provide their families with food, medical care, and education.[1] These legacies have left the country more than 98 percent deforested (Hunter 1996–97, 609). "The mountains have grown old," people sometimes say. "You can see their bones poking through their skin."

Most of the small portion of Haiti's land that is arable is controlled by a handful of wealthy landowners, such as the rice growers of the Artibonite Valley. Peasants, meanwhile, cultivate the hillsides, cliffs, and ravines to which their ancestors once fled for protection from slavery and conscripted labor. With the increased rate of environmental degradation of the past several decades, the steady drops in the productivity that have accompanied it, growing population pressure,[2] the shrinkage of the poor's landholdings, increases in wealth stratification, and a variety of other factors—contemporary Haitian peasants now find themselves engaged in an increasingly impossible quest to secure enough land on which to survive.[3] Not surprisingly, they have gotten little constructive assistance from elsewhere. "Never have the Haitian government or the international community made significant, long-term investments in the productive and marketing capacity of small farmers," Lisa McGowan reports, "despite their importance to the local economy and the fact that they make up the majority of the population" (1997, 4).

Among the ways peasants have responded is to crowd the small plots they till with large varieties of species. A field no larger than a fraction of a hectare may host more than a dozen crops. Through purchasing plots, sharecropping, and utilizing an array of other arrangements, most farmers supplement the fields they have inherited near their homes with more distant ones.[4] The majority of people, then, work several fields at once, each of which might be several miles from the others (distances generally traversed on foot). Few of even the harshest bits and pieces of land are left untilled. Seeds are planted in the crevices of jagged rock, in eroded gullies, and on inclines so steep that the first rainfall is sure to sweep the majority of the cultivator's investments into the creek beds below. Thus, while contemporary travelers through Haiti's rugged terrain continue to echo the astonishment of Napoleon's envoy, now it is the sight of cornfields clinging desperately to the sides of sandy cliffs that startle. Medical clinics in Haiti are sometimes visited by individuals who have broken limbs by "falling off" their fields. *"Tè a di, frè m."*

Taking Up the Hoe

> I have a big family. I have big responsibilities. So I go out to my sweet potato patch with my hoe every day. Sometimes when the sun is hot, I get so tired. I'm hungry. I feel like I can't go on. My back hurts. Even the calluses on my hands are sore. So what do I do? I *mare senti* ["tighten my belt," meaning to muster strength and the determination to go on], spit on my hands, rub them together like this . . . , and take up the hoe again. (a farmer and Protestant preacher who lives outside Kalfounò)
> *"Manje a piti, travay la anpil."* (The food is scarce, the work plentiful.)

The set of tools employed by Haitian peasants today is almost identical to (and in some cases more rudimentary than) that adopted and developed by their ancestors on the Saint Domingue plantations and during the first decades of Haitian independence nearly two centuries ago (A. Métraux 1951; Moral 1978). It is a collection, as Murray says, that is "virtually restricted to items manipulated by human beings" (1977, 239). Very few rural Haitians have access to plows or the animals necessary to use them. Even if they did, the harsh slopes of the land they cultivate would generally render them useless.

Most people carry out the majority of their agricultural tasks with little more than a machete or a *koulin* (resembles a machete but has a longer, more narrow blade), and perhaps a long-handled hoe. While many people in the northeastern community of Kalfounò owned a hoe, few people in the Bamòn area did. It was by stooping low over the ground, machete in hand, that they cleared their fields, planted their seeds, and weeded their crops.[5]

Consistent access to fertilizers and pesticides is enjoyed by a miniscule portion of peasants, despite the efforts of many NGOs and foreign companies to promote their use. Access to irrigation is even more rare.[6] While traveling on Haiti's main roads across the country's few flatland areas, one may see waves of water wafting gracefully over large rice fields or flowing down irrigation canals amid rows of sugar cane or banana trees. One can be certain, however, that those fields are owned almost exclusively by Haiti's agricultural elite. The agricultural work of the average peasant cultivator must, in contrast, coincide with the sporadic seasons of rainfall and drought that characterize the subtropical climate.[7]

All of the above factors coalesce to present peasant farmers with the necessity of clearing, planting, weeding, and harvesting very rugged and often geographically dispersed plots of land, with simple tools and under intense time pressures—and very often in a state of chronic malnutrition. Rare is the person who tries to face all these odds alone. "No garden," Murray confirms, "will be worked from beginning to end by a lone cultivator" (1977, 243). But the prioritization of collective labor in rural Haitian agriculture emerges not only from material and economic concerns. It also reflects a larger commitment to sharing labor and resources that goes well beyond pragmatic interests, and comprises one of the very foundations of rural Haitian culture.

Yonn Ede Lòt[8]: Sharing Labor and Resources as a Way of Life

As the sun began its descent toward the hills in the west, I left my porch, where I had been writing up notes from the morning, and walked through my corn patch and across the path into Djouli and Janba's *lakou* (yard or family compound).[9] Most afternoons, I would find Djouli and her children congregated near the outdoor kitchen shelling beans, scraping cassava roots, or huddling over a boiling pot of tubers, anticipating the day's main meal. But today the lakou was quiet and empty, except for the oldest girl, who was singing softly as she swept her broom of bundled branches back and forth across the packed-dirt yard. Looking up from her chore, she told me that her mother was over at Madan Sesa's house.[10] "They're in the coffee," she said, reminding me that for several days I had noticed people in the area collecting the reddening berries from the small wooded groves surrounding their lakou-s.

Arriving at Madan Sesa's lakou moments later, I found the house and yard filled with coffee and people. The Sesa family had been gradually harvesting their trees during most of the week, and coffee at various stages of processing now dominated the main room of the house, the porch, and the ground outside. Djouli was one among several neighbors who had come to lend a hand. The carpenter, Bòs Wojè, was there, too, along with Gi, Lina, Madan Nikola, Janèl (all close neighbors), and children from several households. The crowd invited me to join them and ushered me into the house, clearing away a place to sit. Gi and Sesa were out on the porch, sharing the job of pounding the driest beans in a wooden mortar borrowed from Bèna's lakou just up the nill. The alternating blows of their wooden pestles into the mortar's bowl added with a rhythmic beat still more aroma to the heavy, wet scent of ripe coffee hovering over the lakou. The women—Madan Sesa, Lina, and Djouli—sat on the packed-dirt floor sorting and winnowing once-pounded beans from their chaff and culls. Beans still sticky with life from the trees were spread out on the ground outside the door, where the younger children kept watch and chased away persistent chickens. Those beans nearly dry enough for pounding found a place on straw mats by the porch. Nearby, one of the Sesa's oldest daughters passed through the grove once again and dropped into her skirt pockets the few ripe berries that had managed to escape detection during previous rounds of picking.

I soon slipped onto the floor to sort through beans with the women and listen to them talk about the virtues of having some coffee and fruit trees around the lakou.[11] As important as the way they fill one's morning coffee cup, they explained, is the little bit of cash their yields can put in your pocket every once in a while. They expounded on some of the other treasures found beneath their groves' low canopies: leaves good for boiling in stews; vines, grasses, and flowers for making teas to treat colds, indigestion, fatigue, high blood pressure, and other maladies; and, of course, an array of sweet potatoes, taro, yams, and other tubers.[12]

"If you're a good-hearted person," they continued, "you'll share such riches when you have them. . . . Then, at times when you don't have, you'll always find." Djouli illustrated this for me: "For instance, if there comes a time when I can't afford to drink coffee, I know Sesa will come through for me and give me a little." Sesa nodded as he raised the pestle, adding, "That's just the way it is here, Djeni, *se yonn ede lòt* [it's one helping another]." A little later, I got up to leave. Madan Sesa hurriedly filled a large tin cup with coffee beans and handed it to me, thanking me and saying that since I had helped, I too must share in some of the harvest.

Such scenes were everyday occurrences during my stay in Bamòn, where people constantly called upon and came to the aid of one another. When I questioned neighbors about the constant give and take between them, I was told, "But Djeni, we are all one and the same we."[13]

Sayings and proverbs about interdependence, cooperation, and sharing abound in the language of rural Haitians, and are repeated like collective mantras in their daily conversations. Here is a small sampling:

Men anpil chay pa lou
When the hands are many the burden is light.

Yon sèl dwèt pa manje kalalou
One finger on its own can't eat stew.
(Trying to carry out a difficult task alone is hopeless.)

Pipi gaye pa fè kim.
Urine must fall in the same place in order to make bubbles.
(We have to congregate if we want to create "collective effervescence.")

Kay la pa janm glise san gani.
A house cannot be wattled without the smallest sticks of wood.
(All those who participate in an effort, regardless of how or how much, are
   equally essential to getting it done.)

Bay piti pa chich.
To give just a little is not stingy.

Men ale men vini fè zanmi dire.
Hands bringing in, hands reaching out—this is the basis for lasting
   friendship.

Manje kwit pa gen mèt.
Cooked food belongs to no one.
(It is meant to be divided up indefinitely until all are fed at least a taste.)

Moun ki pa manje poukont li pa janm grangou.
People who don't eat alone are never hungry.
(It is by living in communion with others that one ensures one's needs are
   met.)

Lè nen pran kou, je koule dlo.
When the nose takes a hit, the eyes shed tears.
(If two people are friends, kin, or neighbors, an injury to one automatically
   pains/grieves the other or, alternatively, means that the other is soon to
   suffer.)

Yon sèl nou fèb, ansanm nou fò, ansanm ansanm nou se lavalas!
Alone we are weak, together we are strong, together-together we are an
   avalanche!
(Jean-Bertrand Aristide's 1990 presidential campaign slogan, this rallying cry
   quickly became as popular among Haiti's poor as even the most common
   proverbs, and remains a popular and evocative saying today.)

Although certain chores are commonly performed alone, such as fetch-
ing firewood around the lakou area or leading an animal to graze, collaboration is viewed as highly desirable for most activities and very often essential. Even when faced with tasks for which physical assistance is not actually
necessary, people express a strong preference for laboring in the company
of others. Women and teenage girls rarely make their frequent treks to and
from the region's marketplaces without the company of a few friends, explaining that "company makes the long route short." Once there, it is
among friends that they prefer to locate themselves within the markets. As
they sell, they assist one another in guarding their wares, making change,
and calculating and negotiating prices. Women and teenage girls who live
close together also tend to coordinate their laundry tasks, setting a certain

time and location each week to come together. Most Saturdays, large numbers of such groupings crowd the edges of many of Haiti's rivers, creeks, bays, and wells. Even more colorful than the drying clothes spread over the banks like clustered assortments of "crazy quilts" are the chatting, laughing, rhythmic scrubbing, and singing to be heard as the women work.

Yonn ede lòt, cooperation and reciprocal sharing, is learned early. I cannot count the number of occasions when I have given a small piece of bread or fruit, sometimes hardly more than a mouthful or two, to a toddler or young child who had eaten little that day (and in many cases was suffering from chronic malnutrition), only to watch her/him immediately begin dividing it up among all the other children in the vicinity. If no one was present to share it with, the knee-high recipient would usually say a quiet "Thank you," carefully envelop it in a corner of clothing, and take off toward home, where the tiny gift will be distributed among siblings and parents.

Simply to sit down in one's lakou to shell beans or corn is to virtually issue an invitation for company, as more likely than not, by the time the task is done several passersby will have stopped to join in. Having to work alone, people say, is a sad fate to be avoided if at all possible. Whenever I walked Bamòn's footpaths by myself, people I met along the way would stop me to ask where my "company" was, and sigh in sympathy (or puzzlement) when I responded that I was traveling alone that day. Like people who habitually eat alone or choose to live alone, individuals who seem to prefer to work or travel alone are considered strange. At times, they are viewed as suspicious. To emphasize the doubtful character of another, for instance, neighbors would often mention just that "he eats alone." "Mmm hmm." More deep-seated than an ethical principle, yonn ede lòt, like onè-respe, closely resembles what Bourdieu (1990) calls habitus.[14] It is an embodied understanding of how one must dispose oneself vis-à-vis others.

Many of my neighbors and other acquaintances in Bamòn credited their cooperative traditions with the fact that despite the harshness of the land they work, they continue to coax from it much of the foodstuffs on which they and their fellow Haitians subsist. But I also heard them mourning lapses in yonn ede lòt, as they discussed instances of neighbors stealing from neighbors and kin practicing sorcery on kin; of fierce land disputes and instances of exploitative manipulations. Thievery, suspicion, jealousy, and conflict, my tutors readily acknowledged, also characterize life in their communities. Another common Haitian proverb is "*Depi nan ginen, nèg rayi nèg.*" It asserts that the Haitian people "hated" or were pitted against one another even before leaving Africa—in other words, "since time immemorial." Other sayings and proverbs I heard more than a few times include:

Yonn ede lòt. Milo shares the refreshment of a green coconut with his sister.

Tout ayisyen mechan.
All Haitians are mean-spirited/ruthless.

Tout ayisyen volè.
All Haitians are thieves.

Tout ayisyen sovaj.
All Haitians are savage.

Zanmi pre se zanmi kòd anba bra.
Friends close by are friends with ropes tucked under their arms.
(Even your best friends can't be trusted; while presenting an image of
   sincerity, they may actually be plotting to "hang" you.)

Pa konfiye vant ou bay nenpòteki.
Don't hand your stomach over to just anyone.
(Don't eat out of just anyone's cooking pot; a curse may lurk beneath ges-
   tures of hospitality.)

One manifestation of the divisiveness that can plague rural Haitians' relations with one another is the phenomenon of *baka*. Several people I knew
in Bamòn had experienced baka attacks, and everyone was familiar with a
variety of baka stories. Baka-s are creatures employed by especially greedy

and envious individuals to secretively enrich themselves at the expense of their neighbors. Baka-s are sometimes invisible but often circulate in the form of cats, mongooses, *mabouya*-s (large lizards), and most often, black dogs. Baka owners (some of whom are not individuals but the infamous "secret societies") send their demonic pets out at night to literally "suck" the wealth from their neighbors. As one of my neighbors put it, "If the baka's owner sees that someone has some money, or a large animal, or a pretty [productive] field, he will send [the baka] out to steal her money, suck the blood out of her animals, or pull the produce out of her garden." Baka-s also are sent to siphon out barrels of whiskey, stored produce, or the merchandise of small shops.

Because a baka can devastate a family's (or even an entire neighborhood's) well-being, there is great interest in catching and destroying them. But this is no simple task. If you do manage to catch a baka, "The owner will offer you a lot of money to give it back to him," because "if you kill it, its owner will surely die." He will probably not die immediately, however, so it is essential that you dispose of the baka corpse completely. You must, my neighbors told me, "throw it in a latrine." "You must not even bury it, . . . because if the owner of the baka finds it and digs it up, you'll not survive." The reason that the death of a baka means near-certain death for its owner is that "their souls are tied together." This comes from the way in which baka-s are acquired.

In order to acquire a baka, I was instructed, you must visit a *bòkò* who "practices with two hands"—a Vodou priest willing to practice sorcery. During this visit, the bòkò invokes a *lespri baka* (baka spirit) and transfers it into a material object. The object will most likely be a mundane household item, such as a tool, a bottle, a bowl, a rock, or an egg. The bòkò instructs you to tuck this object under your arm and carry it back home with you. Eventually, a baka will "hatch" from this object. From that time forward, you and the baka are joined at the soul. I was told that even if their baka is never killed, baka owners will suffer before they die, evidently because their souls have been irreversibly tainted with evil. "People who purchase baka-s never fail to die a miserable death."

Although the baka-s carry out their work under the protection of disguise or invisibility and are very difficult to catch, it is not impossible to detect a baka or even to identify its owner. If you see that your corn begins to grow, I was told, and then starts to wither, while at the same time a neighbor's corn grows taller than ever, or if your cow begins to "dry up" (lose weight) even as a neighbor's gets abnormally fat, the chances are good that that neighbor has a baka.

Not surprisingly, reports of baka attacks tend to multiply during seasons of the year when food, money, and other resources are most scarce.[15] Baka

reports, and the tensions and conflicts between peasants that they have precipitated, could be understood as instances of the poor using one another
as scapegoats in their efforts to cope with the hardships they face—many of
which actually emerge from much more distanced and complex relationships than those between neighbors. But scapegoating is only part of the
equation here. I was told on several occasions that it is generally not the
poorest of peasants who become the owners of baka-s, but rather people
who are wealthier than average in the first place. Part of the reason is that
in order to purchase one from a bòkò, "You must be able to pay a lot of
money." Accounts of baka-s, therefore, may also be seen as implicit or even
subconscious critiques of the exploitative stratification inherent in the economic structure of Haitian society.

Observers of life in rural Haiti have tended to highlight either the sorts
of suspicion and animosity reflected in the tales of baka-s, or demonstrations and expressions of yonn ede lòt, in characterizing rural Haitian society and culture. Some visitors who have been especially impressed,
touched or inspired by the latter have lauded yonn ede lòt as an idyllic or
utopian social ethic. A number of prominent anthropologists and other
scholars have sought to account for more negative aspects of life there. In
doing so, they have suggested that the popular rhetoric of yonn ede lòt
and plentiful demonstrations of sharing and cooperation cover up a more
fundamental reality—a reality that has at its base a self-interested, conflic-
tive, and ruthlessly competitive system of pragmatic calculations and manipulations.

Such a perspective is found in the work of Glenn Smucker (1983), who
paints the entire social context in which yonn ede lòt discourses and practices emerge as a scene of masked animosity and mutual exploitation.
There is little evidence, he says, of any true "sense of community solidarity"
in rural Haiti (358, 459–60). Citing anecdotes of peasants stealing from,
sabotaging, casting spells on, competing with, fearing, and bad-talking one
another, Smucker concludes that rural Haitian culture is an environment
in which "egalitarian ethics collide with envy and enmity" (359). People
neither trust one another nor care genuinely about the other, despite the
many expressions of mutual interest and connection that flood their everyday language. In fact, they incessantly engage in beating one another down.
"There is a negativity in social relations: People are changeable, potentially
unreliable, a trait tempered only by special ties and obligations" (449).
They are, in the end, "crabs in a basket" (359).

In this picture, to see Haitian peasants working side by side is not to see
people assisting one another but, rather, to witness a struggle in which individuals maneuver to pull down and climb over others. The "egalitarian
impulse" here, Smucker says, is a deceptive one, in which "poverty is best

shared, and the high and mighty are brought low. This is not the equality of universal democracy with equal rights for all regardless of the person. Rather, this is an ethic of intense personalism, mutuality, crab antics, social pressures on one's peers and subtle forms of sabotage in relation to the pervading authorities and status superiors" (1983, 450).

Although Haitian peasants may continually talk about egalitarianism and interdependence, we are told that in actuality, self-interested give-and-take aimed at leveling, not solidarity rooted in democratic values, are the guiding principles. Smucker cites the failure of certain externally initiated community development programs as evidence of this culturally rooted lack of solidarity. He concludes that "there is no simple economic solution to the crisis of the Haitian peasantry outside of fundamental political and cultural change" (1983, 461). Erasmus also elaborates on the social "backwardness" of rural community life.[16]

Foreign observers are not the only ones to offer such critiques of rural Haitian collectivity and cooperation. On more than a few occasions during my fieldwork, when I mentioned to town-and city-dwellers that Benwa and I were visiting *kòve*-s (communal work parties) in the countryside, my comments were met with looks of surprise and warnings to beware. Some of those work parties, I was told, would undoubtedly be conducted by *sosyete djab*-s, demonic societies that hold midnight meetings in the crossroads at the folds of Haiti's mountains and plot to *manje moun*. (Literally meaning "eat people," this term refers to killing through sorcery.)[17] I was instructed that the "farther up" you go (the farther into the countryside and away from urban areas), the more prevalent these societies are. "Up there, some of them don't even try to hide. . . . They gather *gwo lajounen* [in broad daylight]." One young man from Nazon explained.

> almost all the djab-s are poor country people—it's because of the miserable conditions they live in, "beating water to make butter" [trying to eke out a living under impossible circumstances]. . . . They don't see anything else they can do to get out [of the situation they're in]. Almost all the poorest ones out there are djab-s. . . . In fact, whenever you see a kòve group, you can be sure there are djab-s in it.

What are we to make of the stark contradictions in perceptions of rural Haitian community life? If we take seriously a range of peasants' own reflections and look closely at their everyday practices, we find that both visions—that of romanticized communalism and that of predatory economic rationalization—come up short in helping us understand the ways Haitian peasants work together and share resources. This is perhaps most evident in the context of farming, which is a prime setting for collective labor, and the context in which some of the most long-standing forms of community organization in Haiti have emerged.

Collective Agricultural Labor

As noted, Haitian farmers rarely try to work their fields alone. There are a number of sources to which they commonly turn for assistance. The first of these is family. While documented accounts of labor organization in the countryside during the first several decades of the nineteenth century are scarce, several scholars have suggested that during this time, the extended family, based in the lakou, provided virtually all the labor a farmer could need (Bastien 1985 [1951]; Lundahl 1983; Moral 1978). Lundahl (1983) explains that in the "traditional *lakou* system,"[18] a large extended family, headed by the oldest male (the *mét lakou*), was grouped spatially in a cluster of houses. This "clustered pattern of settlement," he explains, organized the extended family into a "tight-knit unit toward the world." Not only did it allow them to defend themselves against intruders, it also provided a certain type of social order. Moreover, the lakou "constituted a type of cooperative structure based on the extended family" (212–15). Lakou residents developed reciprocal patterns of food sharing, were responsible for helping one another in times of sickness and death, and worked the household's land together.

Bastien (1985 [1951]), Lundahl (1983), Moral (1978), G. Smucker (1983), and others who have written on the subject explain that since those first few decades of the peasantry, the extended-family lakou has given way to nuclear-family households. "A *lakou* today could mean a few huts grouped around a yard of stamped earth in the middle of agricultural plots . . . [with] none of the social structure" of the original lakou, Lundahl says. "With the gradual demise of the *lakou*," he continues, "the peasant has been forced into a situation where all risks have to be borne on an individual or nuclear family basis" (1983, 219, 223; also see Moral 1978, 169–72).

Although there are undeniably far fewer large lakou compounds than there used to be, and rural families are generally more dispersed geographically, my observations suggest that this has hardly meant the "demise" of extended family social structures and patterns of exchange, or the loss of the contemporary lakou's significance in those structures and patterns. I have found, rather, that contemporary lakou-s remain important and multifaceted centers for family and community life. As the headquarters of the extended-family economic activities, they are commercial centers; as dwellings for the lwa-s and the ancestors (who partake in rituals held for them there), they are religious and ancestral centers; and finally, as locations for daily interaction between neighbors and for organizational meetings, they are important community centers.

Few households in the many neighborhoods I have visited in rural Haiti comprise nuclear families exclusively, and many host a variety of extended-family members, non-kin and fictive kin. Moreover, even extended-family members who do not live within a lakou commonly live very close together. Rather than being clustered on the same packed-dirt foundation a few feet from one another, their houses might be across the path or up the hill, usually within a short walk (if not glancing or shouting distance) from each other. Thus, when looking beyond their "own" lakou to the greater community in order to recruit labor assistance, peasants very often still go to brothers, sisters, cousins, nieces, uncles, and fictive kin.[19]

One of the most straightforward ways to recruit labor outside of the immediate family is to hire someone who is less well off financially, to work for wages. As G. Smucker notes for his own field site of L'Artichaut (in northern Haiti), in Bamòn paid labor arrangements "reflect the complexities of a hybrid economic context" (1983, 319).[20] Wage laborers may be hired for the day (jounen), in which case they are expected to work from early morning until mid-day or early afternoon; by the half-day (demijounen); or to work two full shifts in a day (kase double, or "breaking double"). The latter entails working all morning and returning after a mid-day break to work until late afternoon. During my time in Bamòn, the standard wage for a day of work was five goud-s ($0.33),[21] though people were sometimes paid as much as eight goud-s ($0.53) or as little as three goud-s ($.20). Another option is contracting work, or bay djòb. Here one pays others a lump sum (of cash or a combination of cash and produce) to complete a specific task, such as cultivating a crop of beans or taking care of certain livestock. Peasant workers themselves generally prefer taking a djòb over working for a daily wage. In the latter arrangement, as in sharecropping,[22] they are able to work at their own pace and in their own way, and do not have to labor alone, as is sometimes the case for daily wage laborers.[23]

Although monetary wages are very low, the extremely cash-poor state of the peasantry means that only a small percentage of relatively wealthy peasants can fulfill a substantial amount of their labor needs by paying individual wages. Moreover, like a number of other scholars, I have found that in the eyes of rural Haitians, soliciting paid work, especially from one's neighbors, is "regarded as a most miserable way of earning money" (R. Métraux 1952, 7).[24] This does not mean that payment for work is uncommon in the countryside. In fact, much of the labor performed in Bamòn (and many other areas) involves combinations of paid labor and various forms of exchanged labor. Thus, as Escobar found for the production of meaning in Latin America, the production of food in rural Haiti has taken on "a certain hybrid character, partly linked to the market and the transnational cultural system but also partly arising out of embodied communal systems and the local enactments of speaking subjects" (1992, 75).

"The Strike of a Solitary Hoe Makes No Music"[25]

Regardless of whether the labor is paid, exchanged, or both, or whether it is for oneself or for another, the most popular context in which to work is in groups. One of the most predominate collective labor arrangements in the countryside is simple labor rotation. Called *echanj an wonn* (literally, "circular exchange"), it is generally carried out between small groups of neighbors and kin who agree to work in one another's fields for a few hours several days a week. This reciprocal sharing of labor is often carried out through a group structure.

In Bamòn, such groups are called *eskwad,* or sometimes *sori* or *wonn.* The smallest and least complex of all the organizations engaged in cooperative labor, the eskwad is also the most widespread. No matter where one travels in rural Haiti, one is likely to find eskwad-s of some sort, known by such other names as *asosye, chenn,* or *mera.* In most cases, they are either seasonal or semi-permanent labor rotation arrangements between small groups of neighbors and extended family members. A typical eskwad may have anywhere from four to eight members, though some claim ten or more.

Most Bamòn eskwad-s are composed entirely of men or teenage boys. Unlike *atribisyon-s, sosyete-s* and *kominotè-s* (see chapters 5, 6, and 7, respectively), eskwad-s have no officers or other official stratifications among members. They have no group flag and usually no group name. They do not keep a group treasury, and money is generally not involved in their labor exchanges. Neither are their work sessions accompanied by any food, drink, music, or ceremony.

In the Bamòn region, the eskwad-s generally begin working at "six o'clock" (just after sunrise) and before any of the other groups in the region have gathered. After anywhere from two to four hours of labor, their members will either return to their homes for a bite to eat and a short rest, or go directly to another collective work party or to carry out individual chores. During the times of the year when the fields must be cleared and planted, most of the eskwad-s work together at least five, and sometimes six, days a week. A Tisous neighbor summed up the eskwad-s this way: "This morning [the group] works for me, tomorrow for Titonton, the next day for Jan. . . . We don't get anything for our labor, but if I work for you today, tomorrow you owe me mine."

Generally, Benwa explained, "When everyone is satisfied that their fields are in good shape, they will take a break until time for weeding." Some es-kwad-s work year round, however. It is usually the larger ones, with nine or ten members, which "never ever stop," since it takes them longer to get around to every member's fields. Eskwad-s may also decide, having met the needs of all their own members, to work for other people in the neighbor-hood. They receive variable types and amounts of compensation for such labor. As my neighbor in Tisous described it, "After all of our fields are planted, if there is a neighbor who [needs some help], we will work for her/him. [She or he will] give us a *tichoutchou* [a little something]."

Alongside simple labor rotation, at the heart of collective agricultural work in the Haitian countryside are a variety of more complex arrange-ments, generally referred to as *konbit* and *kòve*. These two basic forms of labor organization have served as building blocks for many other types of community organization in rural Haiti. Thus, in order to understand the organizational landscape there, it is essential to have an understanding of what these arrangements are and what they mean to local residents.

Although the terms *kòve* and *konbit* are widely known throughout rural Haiti and among scholars of the peasantry, there is much confusion in the literature about what each of them means, what their origins are, and whether they are good or bad.[26] This is not surprising, given that Haitian peasants' definitions differ significantly, depending on where, when, among whom, and in what context the issue is discussed. An insight that readily emerges from a careful study of these arrangements is that they are dynamic and generative; they are continually being (re)produced and (re)created by those who engage in them. The following descriptions of konbit and kòve are based primarily on my observations of the events, ac-tivities, and social relationships indicated by these terms in the areas where I have studied, and the explanations residents in those areas offered me.

The *Konbit* and the *Kòve*

It is undoubtedly the sound of this combite drum, heard in the mountains or through the brush by travelers, that has so often been mistaken for the "mys-terious booming" of the vodun drum. (Herskovitz 1971 [1937], 72)

And I can see the day arrive when both sides will come face to face:
"Well, brothers," some will say, "are we brothers?"
"Yes, we're brothers," the others will reply.
"Without a grudge?"
"Without a grudge?"

"Really?"

"On with the coumbite?"

"On with the coumbite?"

(Spoken by Manuel, a villager in Jacques Romain's classic novel, *Masters of the Dew*, who envisions bringing together his community in a water project [1978 (1944), 92].)

In many regions of the country and in many expatriate circles, the term *konbit* can evoke a sort of nostalgic romance, calling up images of old-timey "hand-in-hand" cooperation and "heads-together" community spirit. This understanding was common, though not unchallenged, in Kalfounò during my time there (1988–91).

In such contexts, *konbit* commonly refers to virtually any sort of collective effort. In Kalfounò, for instance, there were house-raising and-roofing konbit-s, bean-shelling konbit-s, cassava bread-making konbit-s, and corn-shucking konbit-s. Sometimes people talk about a collection of school children engaged in helping one another with lessons as a "studying konbit." While some konbit-s are quite elaborate and involve careful planning and a substantial time commitment on the part of participants (as is the case for house-raising and -roofing konbit-s), others occur simply by happenstance when a few folks gather to lend someone a hand in completing a simple task, such as shelling enough beans for a family's evening meal.

Konbit generally holds a more specific meaning as well: that of a particular sort of agricultural work party. This event comes about when someone needing assistance to clear, plant, weed, or harvest a field invites people from the local community to come on a particular day to help.[27] There are various customary ways to issue invitations for a konbit, depending on the preferences and needs of the host.[28] For some konbit-s, only certain individuals or groups are invited. Usually, however, invitations are sent out informally to extended family members, friends, and other acquaintances, who then pass the word around the neighborhood. Even though attending means sacrificing an entire day of labor (the work generally lasts from early or mid-morning until late in the afternoon), a person known to be a generous host may find that several dozen people show up for the event.

The person appointed by the host to be the *chèf konbit* (the konbit "chief," or director) orchestrates the work. He is assisted in his task by a group of musicians hired by the host to "encourage" and "heat up" the work. Thus, to the rhythms of the handcrafted drums (accompanied in many cases by bamboo horns, and sometimes conch-shell horns or flutes), and to the call-and-response songs of the *sanba*[29] (song leader), the participants stroke their hoes, machetes, or spades into the ground and make their way through the field.

Kalfounò *konbit.*

To an observer unacquainted with konbit-s, this work party may appear quite disorganized and inefficient. Workers often break line to animate their conversations, argue with the musicians over how a cadence should go, take rests under nearby shade trees, or good-naturedly accost the chèf konbit for his stinginess with the rum.[30] Occasionally, the whole group will pause to rest, snack, pass the bottle around, or enjoy a particularly compelling story or joke. Yet all the while work progresses at an amazingly rapid pace through the field.[31]

In the meantime, a group of women, teenage girls, and children assembled under a tree at a corner of the field have the enormous task of preparing the food. They cook in large aluminum pots balanced over several fires. The konbit host is expected to offer the group *kafe* (literally, "coffee," which generally means a light breakfast consisting of a cup of sweet coffee and some form of *viv*, a starchy vegetable or piece of bread); possibly a small snack, such as boiled sweet potatoes, in the early afternoon; and then a hearty meal when the work is finished in the late afternoon. It used to be customary to slaughter a goat, a cow, or sometimes several animals for large konbit-s.[32] Although konbit meals are no longer "feasts," if done right, they provide workers with more food—and certainly more protein—than many of them are be able to give their entire families in a day. (It is not uncommon to see workers saving portions of their meals for dividing between family members later.)

While many outside observers of the konbit have understood this offering of food and drink to be payment or compensation for the work, konbit participants unfailingly insist that it is no such thing. Rather, they say that it is an extension of hospitality and a gesture of thanks for their "gift" of labor. This misinterpretation has had dire consequences at times, particularly when it has prompted development-minded observers to think of the konbit as a sort of indigenous "food for work" program, and thus a local rationalization for implementing such programs, many of which have disrupted or undermined local cooperative structures and patterns of reciprocation.

The work is hard, but the atmosphere is a festive one, accompanied as it is by drumming and singing, animated conversations, laughter, performance, disputes, and play. At the end of the day, if the host has been generous with food and drink, the workers will say a compliment by transforming the gathering into a full-blown *banbòch*, an impromptu dance party that may well last through the night.

Recall that the lowliest position one can be in as a worker is to be a day-laborer paid by a neighbor. The konbit sets up a relationship in which labor is not so blatantly bought and sold. Despite the sizable sums they have already spent, customarily hosts are still obliged to those who have worked for them. They may reciprocate in the form of their own labor when the guests host konbit-s themselves. A host who is of greater socioeconomic standing might be called upon for other sorts of favors, such as giving loans or renting out plots of land at reasonable rates.

Like the term *konbit, kòve* may indicate a number of different collective labor arrangements. In the Grand'Anse, it has taken on the general connotation that konbit has in many other areas of the country and can indicate most any kind of collective effort. Thus, my neighbors had coffee-processing kòve-s, house-roofing kòve-s, and bean-shelling kòve-s. Sometimes, they would call a parade of children on their way to the spring a "water-fetching kòve." But again, *kòve* is associated with a more particular sort of arrangement.

Its more specific characterization is as a type of agricultural work party that involves both labor exchange and monetary payment. As they are being carried out, Grand'Anse kòve-s resemble the konbit-s of the Northeast and the Central Plateau in many ways but are also quite different.

Many, though not all, kòve-s are conducted to the music of drums, horns, and call-and-response songs like those of the konbit. Even the formations in which the workers arrange themselves to carry out their tasks mirror konbit work patterns. Yet kòve-s are often shorter than konbit-s, lasting only throughout a morning or an afternoon (generally, between three and five hours). Typically, food is not served at a kòve,[33] though the owner of the field is expected to provide rum for the workers on top of the cash paid to the group. Many kòve-s are much smaller than the traditional konbit-s, though the work force may range from as few as six or eight to more than a hundred.

Interestingly, kòve-s were understood in Kalfounò as inherently exploitative. There, the meaning of kòve resembled that of the French term *corvée*, which connotes forced labor and drudgery. I was told by residents there that *kòve* elicited powerfully negative collective memories of chaingangs—namely, those instituted as part of the conscripted-labor projects conducted by U.S. troops during the 1915–34 occupation in order to build roads, military headquarters, and other public structures.[34] In Bamòn, though, the kòve was generally celebrated as the primary organizational mechanism through which rural dwellers are able to get their fields planted. In that region, konbit (also called "invitational kòve-s") were perceived to be more susceptible to exploitation. Benwa explained why:

> They don't do [*konbit*] here anymore, because they say they're not going to let the *grandon* [large landowner] keep making more off of them. . . . They say the grandon, whenever he has built up some money, invites them and gives them a little work and a taste of rum. But the grandon is not going to go help the poor guy when he needs it in his own field. . . . So they [the "poor guys"] prefer to work with their eskwad-s, and to work kòve-s—in other words, where the poor can work to help the poor instead. . . . When you're in a kòve or eskwad, it's yonn ede lòt [one helping another]. And everyone must work. If you don't do your share, you'll not benefit.

Regardless of disagreements about their relative merit, both the konbit and the kòve clearly have been foundational building blocks for much contemporary community-based organization in rural Haiti. This has meant different things in different regions and time periods. During my time in Kalfounò, members of the development-oriented *gwoupman peyizan*-s with which I worked often called upon the spirit of the konbit to recruit participation in events as varied as vaccination campaigns and spring-capping (for potable water) projects. Much more visible was the centrality of the kòve to civil society in the Grand'Anse. There, most field kòve-s are not, like most

Bamòn *kòve* (conducted by a local *kominotè*).

konbit-s in the Northeast and the Central Plateau, carried out by an assembly of invited "guests" who disperse after the work was done. Generally, rather, the workers are members of a semi-permanent or permanent organization. A diverse array of community groups have taken up the kòve and have done so for a diverse array of reasons. In the process, they have elaborated on and developed it in many different ways.

In Bamòn, such groups include the atribisyon and the sosyete. According to their members, both groups, along with the eskwad, have histories as long as the konbit and the kòve themselves—or, as they often put it, as "old as the Old Testament!" But they are hardly things of the past.

Rural Community Groups

They are about *yonn ede lòt*. When someone has a problem, they start up the music. (a kominotè member)

They are our roots. *Kominotè, rara, sosyete, bokal* . . . they've been around since the Old Testament. (a sosyete member)

On first arriving in the Grand'Anse to carry out ethnographic research, I was glad to have under my belt several years' experience working with and studying peasant organizations. I had visited well over a hundred peasant group meetings in the Central Plateau and Northeast departments and in other areas of the country, and had participated in numerous seminars, general assemblies, and training sessions, some of which I had planned and directed. I hardly expected to experience, as Geertz had, the "unnerving business" of not being able to "find my feet" (1973, 13). Yet I had barely settled into Tisous before I found myself decidedly unbalanced. What I discovered in this Grand'Anse community were a number and a variety of groups that much surpassed anything I had anticipated. What is more, most of those I encountered barely resembled what I had understood peasant groups to be! In the fields carrying out kòve-s, many of them looked to me much like the konbit work parties I had known in the Northeast. But they also had officers, regular meeting times, and group flags. I hardly knew what to make of the fact that group names I had never even heard (i.e., of atribisyon-s) were suddenly household terms in conversations with my Tisous neighbors; that groups I had assumed to be virtually extinct for generations (sosyete-s) were everywhere. Astonished and fascinated, I was especially enticed by the ways members of these organizations evaluated them: "They get our fields planted." "They are the *nannan* [heart/meat] of our culture." "They are our roots." "They sustain us."

Little wonder I was not prepared for this scene, for I had learned to think about grass-roots organization in Haiti in a way similar to most other observers, that is, with classifications that left little conceptual space for the types of groups I encountered in Bamòn. In fact, discourse about contemporary grass-roots organization in rural Haiti during the past few years has focused almost solely on peasant groups like the ones I knew in Kalfounò (see chapter 8): organizations that have emerged primarily during the past twenty to thirty years and are closely associated with externally sponsored aid initiatives.

That older, more locally emergent forms of peasant organization such as those I found in Bamòn have been largely overlooked in discussions of grass-roots organization is one of the many ironies found in the literature on rural Haiti. When they have gained attention, groups such as the atribitsyon and the sosyete have generally been portrayed as old-timey folk customs that are largely irrelevant to progressive social-change agendas. Indeed, author after author tells us that "traditional" forums for collective agricultural labor are increasingly dysfunctional and obsolete in a world moving rapidly toward more efficient socioeconomic systems based primarily on individual work and direct monetary compensation. So argued Herskovitz in the 1930s; Alfred Métraux and Erasmus in the 1950s; Moral in the

1960s; Laguerre in the 1970s; Lundahl and Conway in the 1980s, and A. White and Elie in the 1990s (see J. M. Smith 1998).[35]

Lundahl claims the whole nexus of cooperative structures has virtually collapsed. While "co-operative structures have in the past played an important role in the economy," he says, today only "the remnants of these structures can still be found in contemporary Haitian society." He refers to the lakou, the konbit, the eskwad, and the sosyete alike in the past tense (1983, 211, 221–24; Conway 1989, 252). If they have managed to hang on at all, it is as partially disintegrated social artifacts of more authentic historical predecessors. Not willing to let them finally die out, their participants engage in a sort of disingenuous theatrics in which they use a veil of down-home co-operation from the good ol' days to mask their real nature as modern bands of self-interested individual wage laborers whose primary achievement is further enriching the local elite. The *Paysans, Systèmes, et Crises* researchers say of labor-exchange groups:

> The traditional structures and ideological principles of mutual assistance remain, covering up a reality that corresponds more and more to disguised wage labor . . . [thus permitting] the creation and maintenance of networks of dependence, and therefore the rerouting of the work force toward the profit of those who control the most precious production resource: the real estate. (S.A.C.A.D.-F.A.M.V. 1993, 246–47)

Such portrayals contrast starkly with what I was seeing and hearing in Bamòn. The incongruencies between what I had read about peasants in preparing for the field and what I was observing in Bamòn are not uncommon to ethnographers. Consider Alvarez's comments about her work with social movements in Brazil:

> Yet, somehow, I always readily found these putatively disappeared, dead, or dying movements; attended their (still) numerous meetings, events, and rallies; and had animated conversations/interviews with long-time activists who told me of new developments in the movements, new strategies, new challenges confronted, new groups that had emerged, and new issues that had surfaced since my last visit. . . . In light of these observations, I (slowly) arrived at the conclusion that either I or my so-called key informants were deluding ourselves about the vitality of these purportedly dead social movements, or there was a conceptual problem with the conceptual lenses through which some social scientists were viewing movement dynamics in postauthoritarian Brazil. (1997, 88)

Like Alvarez's, my research revealed that the situation was much more complex than what either my initial conclusions or my previous reading indicated. It is indisputable that in many areas of rural Haiti, konbit-s and sosyete-s are more rare than they used to be, and that paid labor has become much more popular in recent years. However, as is demonstrated in my discussions of the atribisyon and the sosyete, what is happening is not nearly so simple or clear-cut as the replacement of cooperative enterprises with systems centered on individual profit. As Susan Eckstein points out in her examination of Latin American social movements, "although many have concluded that agrarian capitalism necessarily undermines village-level solidarity, participation in markets sometimes brings residents resources that can help them strengthen already existing ties and institutions." (1989,).

On receiving the Nobel Prize for Peace, Gabriel García Márquez issued a caution to well-meaning Europeans engaged in analyzing his homeland:

> It is understandable that the rational talents on this side of the world, exalted in the contemplation of their own cultures, should have found themselves without a valid means to interpret us. It is only natural that they insist on measuring us with the yardstick that they use for themselves, forgetting that the ravages of life are not the same for all . . . [But] the interpretation of our reality through patterns not of our own serves only to make us ever more unknown, ever less free, ever more solitary. (1995, 135)

Both Márquez's caution and the *onè-respe* principle I learned from my neighbors compels us to hesitate before accepting the analyses of Haitian peasant organizations that dominate the existing literature.[36] It compels us to switch yardsticks and to search for answers in the organizations themselves. In so doing, it becomes clear that evaluations based on the modernist models of efficiency and progress that populate late twentieth-century studies of rural Haitian society simply cannot account for the ways these organizations "do group."

While my neighbors explained their mutual interdependence by describing themselves as "one and the same we," they hardly considered their community to be a level playing field. Likewise, when talking about themselves as "fingers on the same hand," Haitian peasants mean both that they are joined together and that they are not all the same measure. It is not surprising, then, that as they work collectively for both personal gain and common survival, the members of Haitian peasant organizations paint neither a rose-colored image of happy-camper communalism, nor a picture of passive-aggressive civil war between self-interested individuals. They reveal, rather, a rich system of practices and discourses that can be called upon for varying purposes. I do not take issue with earlier studies, therefore, by asserting that the Haitian peasant groups are, in fact, democratic and efficient as opposed to patriarchal and unproductive, or that their members are barefoot social progressives instead of floundering proto-capitalists. Because of the many, and sometimes extraordinary, things that rural Haitians have to say about them; because they have developed over particular historical periods whose beginnings we cannot know with certainty (eighteenth-century Saint Domingue? fifteenth-century Quisqueya? Fourteenth-century West Africa?); and because they continue to be (re)produced and (re)created as their members respond in different ways to changing material, social, and political conditions—because of all this, there is no final "evaluation" to be made of civil society organizations in rural Haiti. Instead, we need to learn from them.

In this book, I suggest that not only do Haitian peasant groups, particularly those known as "Old Testament" groups, stand as some of the most long-sustained forms of community mobilization practiced by Haitian peasants; they also constitute rich case studies in how collective practices aimed in part at economic ends may involve engagement in other realms, including political, social, artistic, performative, historical, and spiritual ones. As such, they offer challenges to the ways rural community development initiatives tend to be planned and carried out and, more generally, provide insights into how academics and practitioners alike might revise the ways we understand and work with those identified as poor and disempowered.

5

The *Atribisyon*

Atribisyon se nannan kilti bò isit la. Se li ki kenbe kilti a bò isit la.

The *atribisyon* is the core of agriculture around here.
It is what supports our way of life.
(Atribisyon officer)

Atribisyon se rasin nou.

The *atribisyon*, it is our roots.
(Atribisyon member.)

Nou pa wè èd sòti lòt kote; fòk se nou menm ki itil tèt nou.
se gran moun yo ki ba m reskonsablite a.

We don't get any help from elsewhere; it is we who must help each other. . . .
It is the old folks and ancestors who have given me this responsibility.
(Atribisyon officer)

The *atribisyon*-s are small neighborhood-based organizations whose members regularly carry out kòve-s together. They are found in many areas of the Grand'Anse and, according to residents, have populated every hamlet in the Bamòn zone during the past several generations. They usually comprise seven to twelve people, most of them adult men or teenage boys living within easy walking distances from one another.

Atribisyon members take turns working one another's fields. They also work for nonmembers and occasionally perform nonagricultural tasks. The income they earn from their kòve-s is not distributed among the membership but belongs to the group as a whole. Neither is it collected at the time services are rendered but at the end of the year, when it is spent all at once. Herein lies one of the most unusual and distinctive features of atribisyon-s. They take their entire yearly earnings and use them to purchase the makings of a single holiday feast. Called a *rachòt*, this feast is celebrated on the first day of January, Haitian Independence Day.

In an era when peasants' increasingly small plots of land are less likely each season to produce as much as the last harvest's already insufficient yields; when rising inflation continues to exaggerate the cost of even the most basic staples to several times the already forbidding prices of a few years past; and when the prospects for political change that would favor Haiti's poor majority seem to be floundering, I was surprised to discover that the atribisyon-s invest so much time and effort in one annual *fèt*,[1] particularly because individual atribisyon members, like most Haitian peasants, are chronically and sometimes desperately cash poor. Indeed, most atribisyon members have many occasions during the year when a small wage, or a share of their group's earnings, would be just what is needed to relieve the hunger pangs in their children's bellies, get an aching tooth pulled; or purchase badly needed medicines, schoolbooks, and clothes. Yet atribisyon members are resolute in their insistence on "tying up their waists," and forgoing individual and immediate compensation in exchange for an annual community celebration of culinary extravagance. This feast, they explain, boasts a rich store of underlying significance, much of which is rooted in its origins—the celebrations of the former slaves of Saint Domingue following their successful overthrow of colonial rule in 1803.

"One and the Same We": Group Membership and Structure

When I asked neighbors in Tisous how many people in the area were in atribisyon-s, I often received the reply, "All of us!" Indeed, though few of the women I knew participated directly in an atribisyon, all of the men and most of the teenage boys in my immediate neighborhood belonged to at least one; many of them belonged to several. Most households, then, boasted multiple atribisyon memberships and sent people to *kòve atribisyon*-s (atribisyon work sessions) several times a week.

Generally, there is little socioeconomic stratification among atribisyon members. Most of the adults are *tipeyizan*-s, or "small peasants." They have small landholdings of less than a hectare, a limited number of small livestock, and a modest two-or three-room house. These houses generally have a packed-dirt floor and thatched roof, along with an outdoor kitchen and possibly a simple latrine. Members may have been close neighbors all their lives. Many groups consist mainly of one or two extended families, partly because aging or chronically ill group members often "pass down" their memberships, and sometimes their leadership positions, to others in their families. According to members, this system helps ensure the groups' sustainability and vibrancy.

Most atribisyon-s have four or five officers, or *chèf*-s: a *chaje kòve*, a *laplas*, a secretary, a treasurer, and often a *konsèy*, or "adviser." The chaje kòve, or kòve chief, is sometimes referred to as the "president" and has the most responsibility. He oversees the group's work calendar and functions as its spokesperson, negotiating dates and fees with the people who hire the group to do kòve-s. He also has the delicate task of making sure the rum they drink during their kòve-s is justly divided between the workers. Finally, he is in charge of calling the group together on workdays by sounding the group's conch-shell horn, which he keeps under his care. The laplas is considered the chief assistant to the chaje kòve, and carries out many of the latter's responsibilities. Sometimes called the *derijè* (director) or *gouvènè* (governor), he also oversees—and if necessary, directs—the work of the group during kòve-s. The secretary maintains the group roster and keeps track of the attendance of members at kòve-s throughout the year. The treasurer notes how much money is owed the group for each kòve.

Although the officers are officially in charge of guiding and overseeing an atribisyon's work, there is generally little distinction between them and other members in terms of responsibilities and status. Decision making tends to be done through informal, consensus-directed discussions out in the field. Likewise, atribisyon officers do not tend to be offered the special privileges commonly enjoyed by the officers of other groups (e.g., exemptions from work and free kòve). The image of group members as "fingers on the same hand" seems to be especially appropriate for the atribisyon-s: some members may be a bit more prominent than others, but for the most part, each is seen as equally valuable and given equal importance. The roles and status of women in atribisyon-s underlines this fact.

Although men and teenage boys comprise the bulk of atribisyon membership in Bamòn, when women do participate, they often serve as treasurers. In fact, many atribisyon-s actively recruit women for this post. Especially sought after are older women who have proven themselves to be astute *timachann*-s (small commerçantes) and trustworthy managers of family or community funds. Female atribisyon members may also take on the responsibility of providing workers with water and sometimes nourishment during their work sessions. In addition, they play important roles in planning and carrying out the end-of-year rachòt. Thus, while their numbers are generally small and their roles specialized, women who do belong to atribisyon-s are seen as full-fledged members and have equal claim on the earnings collected at the end of the year.

An Anatomy of *Atribisyon* Labor

As early as the second or third week of January, the conch shell horns begin to sound each morning, sprinkling the jagged mountainsides, sporadic plains, and twisting ravines of the area with small groups of men clustered close together. Leaning forward and bent over their machetes, they slash at fodder, uproot grasses, and talk about the first planting season of the year.

Each atribisyon has one or two weekdays set aside for their kòve-s, which tend to last between three and five hours. Just what a kòve atribisyon entails varies according to the season of the year. The groups are busiest during the year's driest seasons, which tend to fall between January and early April, and again between July and September or into October. During those periods the ground must be cleared for planting—the most labor-intensive and time-consuming of all agricultural tasks. Later, atribisyon members also gather to plant, weed, and harvest.

During much of the year, atribisyon-s function much like simple labor-rotation groups, as the group moves back and forth between the fields of their members. But once all their members' fields have been worked, atribisyon-s are available for hire by others. The costs of hiring these groups are significantly lower than those involved in hiring most other labor teams. In general, when a person hires an atribisyon to work a field, the amount of money she must pay is calculated according to the number of workers. The standard wage for a kòve atribisyon in the Grand'Anse during my time there was five goud-s ($0.33) per person, though groups were sometimes paid only four goud-s ($0.25) for each worker. Depending on the size of the group, the generosity or financial means of the owner, and the relationship between the two parties, the atribisyon might also be offered a small measure of rum as "encouragement."

Atribisyon-s are not only available to work the region's fields. During times of the year when there is less agricultural work to be done (between weeding and harvesting, for instance), they are often hired to roof or rethatch houses. An atribisyon might also be employed to transport an especially large or heavy load, such as planks, tin, or large poles for construction; to make lye for painting a house or public building; or to carry out any of a number of other projects involving extended hours of heavy labor. For these sorts of tasks, an atribisyon most often negotiates with the owner one lump sum rather than a collective daily wage.

Compared to the larger, more structurally complex sosyete-s, atribisyon-s are not a very boisterous or flamboyant bunch. They have no flashy material artifacts—no colorful group flags or banners to wave as they go to and from their work. Neither do they generally employ musical instruments to

"heat up" their labor. Though they often sing, chat, and joke with one another as they toil over the ground and carry their loads, there is little pomp
and circumstance in their kòve-s and little partying afterward. Even when
their workload is minimal, they expend no time or money hosting ceremonies or entertainment events but simply take up other tasks. Their noses
thus fixed firmly to the grindstone, they attack the area's stubborn soils plot
by small plot, cover its houses, carry its loads, and anticipate the year's end.

Once October finally rolls around, atribisyon officers, and often entire
groups, begin to make their rounds through the area in order to remind
clients of their debts. They solicit payment throughout the month of November and into December. An atribisyon might have worked for as many
as thirty or forty different people during the year, and for some of them
several times. Members of a local atribisyon of twelve people told me that
their group might earn somewhere between 1,500 and 3,500 goud-s
($100–$235) in a year.

When the atribisyon has collected its fees for the year, the group selects
an animal, either in the immediate area or in one of the region's weekly
markets. If the year has been a good one, they will buy a cow. If not, or if the
price of meat is especially high at the time, they will settle for a couple of
goats. If the year has been a particularly bad one, they will have to divide up
only one goat. On December 31, they kill their chosen animal and separate
it equally among the members of the group. Suddenly all the exhausting
hours of bending underneath the hot sun, all the joint pains, the calluses,
and the deprivations of the as year are blessed and forgotten as the communal feasting ensues.

"It is very difficult for people around here to get their fields cultivated," a
Bamòn resident told Benwa and me. "The earth here is hard, and hard to
work. . . . It is the atribisyon that allows people to get their fields prepared
when they need it. . . . If it wasn't for the atribisyon, peasant agriculture
would collapse." People in Bamòn repeatedly insisted that atribisyon labor
is one of the best sources of labor available in the region. Reasons they gave
for this include (1) the appropriate size of the groups, (2) the system of
payment deferral, (3) cost exemptions for group members, (4) ready avail-
ability, and (5) flexibility.

The small size of an atribisyon ensures that every member gets a "turn" at
receiving the group's services at least every few weeks, in contrast to sosyete
members, who must often wait an entire season or even longer. It also
means that atribisyon labor tends to cost much less than the labor of larger
organizations, which generally charge the same amount per worker per
kòve but have many more members (so many, in fact, that employing them
would be overkill for the needs of most peasants). Because the landholdings of most rural Haitians are small and are often dispersed among several

different plots, a group of seven to twelve workers can usually clear, plant, or weed an entire field in a single morning.

Another, and perhaps the most important, economic incentive for hiring an atribisyon is that one is not required to pay immediately but, rather, in November or December. This policy is greatly appreciated by peasant farmers, since labor needs are highest just at the times of the year when funds are most scarce. In Bamòn, most of the harvests from the past year's corn, beans, and cassava crops are long gone by mid-February, and even sweet potatoes, yams, and other tubers are becoming scarce. Yet it is at this very time, when there is little to eat and even less to sell for cash, that the most intensive clearing and planting work of the year must be done. By the time the atribisyon-s are collecting on their debts in October, November and December, on the other hand, most people have just gathered their fields' second harvests, and therefore have more funds at their disposal at this time than they will at any other time of the year.

The consistent weekly schedules they hold, not to mention the sheer number of groups concentrated within a relatively small geographic area, mean that atribisyon-s constitute a readily available and generally very reliable source of labor. Still another factor increasing their cost efficiency is the atribisyon's flexibility. Because their memberships are small and comprise people living near one another, they can be summoned without extended notice and can rearrange their schedules at the last minute. They are also willing to negotiate prices according to the varying needs and resources of their clientele.

Together, these factors make the atribisyon-s more dependable, efficient, and affordable than any other labor-getting strategy around, especially for those who are atribisyon members themselves. But economic rationale is not the only reason my neighbors in Tisous have so enthusiastically embraced the atribisyon system. Certainly, it does not sufficiently explain why people in desperate need of cash and the goods and services it can provide would decline a relatively steady income flow during the year in favor of a few days of communal feasting. It was by participating in an atribisyon's end-of-year feast that I first began to glimpse some of the other factors at work.

Feasting on History: The *Rachòt*

Moun yo manje anpil vyann. Menmsi yo pa ka manje l vre, jou saaaaa . . . Mmph!

The people eat *a lot* of meat [on Independence Day]. Even if they aren't able to eat meat the rest of the year, that daaaay. . . . *Mmph!*
  (a neighbor in Tisous)

A Bamòn *atribisyon* plants corn in a member's field.

Whack! Whack! Whack! I woke up on a cool December morning to the distant sound of machetes hacking through bone and flesh. Wondering where the sound was coming from, I stepped outside my door, rubbed my sun-startled eyes, and peered out over my corn patch to my neighbors' yard. But the noise seemed to be coming from several directions. Down by the creek? Over the knob? Just up the path? In Tèwouj?

Whack! Tooooooa! Tooooooa! The strikes of machetes were joined by the smooth airy tones of a conch shell. As I stood on my porch trying to locate some of the sounds in the air, Benwa walked up the path and into my yard. He reminded me that it was December 31, the day before Independence Day, and time to make final preparations for celebrating the historic victory of the Saint Domingue Revolution and the official founding of the country of Haiti on January 1, 1804. For many Haitian communities, this meant that it was also time for the slaughtering of animals and the distribution of meat.

Coming down the path in front of my house was a group of children on their way to the spring. Seeming even more animated than usual, they giggled and talked excitedly as they tapped quick cadences on their empty gallon jugs and buckets. Even Mari's children in the house just across the path seemed caught up in the aura of anxious anticipation that filled the neighborhood. Many a morning and afternoon I had listened for hours to the droning cries of the youngest ones, who had not yet learned the futility of weeping for want of food. Sometimes when the evening pot was taken off the fire and its contents separated out, the crying became even louder, as the children realized that once again, there was not enough to satisfy. Despite unending cycles of hard labor and self-deprivation, their parents, like many others in rural Haiti, simply could not seem to entice the earth, the marketplace, or the lwa-s to yield enough to satisfy their aching bellies. But for a few days, things would be different, even for Mari's kids.

Benwa told me how the next day, heaping plates of *griyo* (spicy fried meat), rice, bean sauce, plantains, and bowls of golden pumpkin stew would be passed around the neighborhood, as families invited one another to partake in feasts. For the next week or so, he said, people would travel around the region, wishing one another a year of prosperity. Some would have relatives and friends coming from Jérémie, Port-au-Prince, perhaps even overseas. As of this evening, luscious smells would begin to waft from the thatched roofs of Tisous' kitchens—the undisputed social centers of community life during the next few days. People greeting one another on the path would stop to chat an extra few minutes, "their mouths coated with a delicious film of spicy grease." After twelve long months of carefully rationing each allotment of protein and fat, Mari and the other mothers of Tisous would finally satiate the hunger of their children, their men, and the deities with generous portions of flesh and fat, an indulgence rarely matched in the everyday lives of the rural poor. It was to God and the atribisyon-s, Benwa concluded, that they owed their thanks.

At the time, I was unable understand the connection between all the feasting and the groups I had seen out working in the fields day after day, so I asked Benwa what he meant. Soon he was leading me through a neighbor's field, across a creek, up a nearby mountainside, and into the lakou of Ton Mano. As we approached the grove of banana, coconut, and coffee trees surrounding Ton Mano's home, we heard a chorus of jovial chatter, animated arguments, and laughter. When we arrived, we found the members of Atribisyon Kay Mano gathered with other neighbors and friends around a recently butchered cow. The carcass, already divided into several allotments, had been arranged neatly on a large bed of palm fronds and banana leaves. An older member of the group (who I knew as both a *touchè* healer[2] and a carpenter) sat on the ground near a door of Ton Mano's house with another man. He was "posing" a small gourd on the man's swollen ankle, which he would momentarily slit with a razor blade in order to "draw out the spoiled blood." Ton Mano and several other men passed around a small bottle of rum. The festive tone of the occasion was accentuated by the hum of static-laced Dominican music coming from a radio inside the house.

Between the kitchen and the house sat Ton Mano's oldest son, Souri, who was surgically dividing up a bovine skull with his machete. He interrupted his meticulous chopping to tell me that each atribisyon member must get the same proportion of meat. Even the head, he explained, must be separated out so all can have a bit, "even if they only get to taste the eye."[3] In the kitchen, Madan Mano, the atribisyon's treasurer and Mano's wife, was cooking up the intestines and other delectable parts of the cow's insides into a meaty soup. This would be shared by the group that evening before each person headed home with his or her own succulent Independence Day feast, which would likely be distributed again among several fires and many bowls.

Ton Mano's eyes lit up when I asked him to tell me about what was going on. Giving Benwa and me a chair and promising us a gift of meat, Ton Mano confirmed, "Yes, you need to know about these things!" He began with 1804.

In that year, having finally defeated the armies of Napoleon and rid itself of one of the most vicious slave systems in recorded history, the citizenship of the first black republic in the New World celebrated their independence. Ton Mano explained, "They called together all the *nèg mawon*-s [the people who had deserted the slave plantations to hide in the mountains, where they had organized resistance efforts against the colonists]. They slaughtered cattle and ate *soup joumou* [a rich stew made of meat and vegetables in a base of tropical pumpkin]." While the colonists had ruled the land, they had been denied such delicacies. Slaves were not considered to merit the same food that "humans" ate. But now the formerly enslaved ate and ate and ate, to their hearts' content. "Since that time, it has become impossible for peasants to buy meat all the time. But although, yes, we are poor, we *are humans,* and we should all be able to eat meat, even if it's only once a year! . . . So people in every little corner of the countryside decided to join together and *fè kòve.*" And that is how the atribisyon was born.

Like many other atribisyon members with whom I later spoke, Ton Mano explained to me as he pointed back to 1804 and highlighted his group's roots in that most heroic period of Haiti's two-hundred-year history, that in continuing their kòve work and the rachòt, the atribisyon-s are honoring their formerly enslaved ancestors and keeping alive those ancestors' traditions and aspirations. Members emphasized this dimension of the group by underlining the atribisyon-s continued use of the lanbi. This instrument, they recalled, was blown by the *nèg mawon*-s to call people together in order to plan and carry out attacks against the colonists during the Saint Domingue Revolution.

Ton Mano highlighted with his group's lanbi their respect for and connection to their more immediate ancestors as well. After he had fetched

Atribisyon Kay Mano's well-worn shell, given me a brief lesson in lanbi-blowing, and laughed heartily at my less-than-stellar premiere perform-ance, he explained in a somber tone and with carefully enunciated words, "It was my grandfather who used to sound this lanbi. It is from his hands that my father got it, and he then gave it to me." He continued, "I am now getting old"; he had put sixty-seven years behind him. "A few years ago, I handed over my responsibilities to Souri here. . . . That's the way it works. When someone gets old, he gives his place to a younger person. . . . there is Souri's son there," he added, pointing to a toddler lingering bashfully at the edge of the yard. "One day he will take [Souri's] place."

Reflections on the *Atribisyon*

Despite the enormous and unrelenting odds working against Haitian peas-ant farmers, the small rugged plots of Bamòn continue to get planted year after year, providing the area with a lifeline of sustenance. Many people in the Bamòn area give atribisyon-s much of the credit. But the services of-fered by the atribisyon-s do not end there. As Ton Mano and other atribisyon members explained to me, to participate in these groups is not only to furnish oneself, one's extended family, and one's community with essential labor. The atribisyon-s also provide members with an opportunity to *viv kòm moun*, to "live as humans should," if only for a few days out of the year. The rachòt's power to do this can be better understood if we consider the cravings for meat and fatty food experienced by those who are chroni-cally undernourished.

On a visit to Haiti during the 1991–94 post-coup era, I was speaking with a young farmer about the embargo then levied on the country by the inter-national community. The conversation about the resultant exaggeration of prices in the marketplace and grave scarcity of funds led to a conversation about disparities in wealth. "I've heard," he said, "that there are places where people have *too* much to eat, so much that they throw food away . . . and so much money that they can't spend it all. . . . *Mmph!*" A while later, I asked him what he would do if he had "too much money." He leaned slowly back in his chair and with a dreamy look in his eye, smiled and said, "I'd drink oil and eat greasy food *every* day!"

The rachòt is in a sense, then, a fantasy come true. But again, the reasons for and meanings of the feasting do not end there. Atribisyon members stressed that this communion with their "living brothers and sisters" is also an opportunity to honor their ancestors and uphold those ancestors' dreams. I was told, in fact, that many of the rachòt-s are also *manje lemò-s*, or "feasts for the dead," where those who have come before are ceremoniously invited to partake.

First among the ancestors remembered and honored with the rachòt-s are the former slaves who were the first citizens of the Haitian nation. By remembering and reenacting their celebrations nearly two hundred years before, atribisyon members are asserting a certain type of personal and collective identity, one that stands in stark contrast to the ways they are now viewed by the world. Haitian peasants have repeatedly commented to me on having been treated by the powers that be "as though we are beasts." Readily acknowledging that they are "dirt poor" and have little power, they insist nonetheless that they remain "the children of Toussaint and Dessalines"—the descendants of heroes, and humans with the right to "eat meat." In the process of doing so, atribisyon members offer an implicit critique of the harsh deprivations and uncertainties that characterize present-day life in rural Haiti; moreover, they paint a picture of the way life *should* be, a picture of how humans *should* be able to live.

Until such a society is realized, the atribisyon's rachòt serves as a forum through which members promise to themselves, each other, and their ancestors that just as their enslaved ancestors insisted on their right to "eat soup joumou," they too will face the unrelenting pressures of daily life with an insistence on their humanity and on the inalienable dignity affixed to it.

6

The *Sosyete*

We started [our *sosyete*] in order to help out when a brother has a problem—like when there is a death in his family. If the person is poor, if he has a little plot of land or a little chicken, maybe that's all he has. We decided we wanted to save him from having to sell off that last little plot of land and last little chicken. (Sosyete Prankè Officer)

It is not unusual while out roaming the footpaths of the Grand 'Anse to come across festive parades of machete-wielding peasants. Directed by men and women sporting flags and batons, those who follow kick up the dust with their marching and dancing, and fill the air with their songs. Their singing is led by a band of men tapping on handmade drums and tin canisters and blowing smooth, deep notes from lengths of bamboo and plastic piping. As they address one another with titles like "division general," "flag queen," and "governor," one might well wonder, "Is this a roving fête? A mock paramilitary unit? One of the dreaded Haitian 'secret societies'" This group is none of the above, the inquisitive onlooker is told. It is a *sosyete*, one of the oldest civic organizations in Haiti, and still one of the most popular in this region of the country.

As with the atribisyon and the eskwad, the sosyete is described by Bamòn residents as existing "since the Old Testament." Also like these groups, collective agricultural labor is a central feature of the sosyete's work and identity. But the sosyete-s contribute in distinct ways to the economic, material, social, and spiritual well-being of their members and communities. Like the atribisyon-s, most sosyete-s can be hired to roof or rethatch houses, transport heavy loads, or carry out various other tasks. They also function more generally as mutual aid associations, offering their members assistance and support during times of sickness and death. They often provide members and their larger communities with an informal judicial system as well, thereby allowing locals to regulate interpersonal disputes without having to appeal to the state court system—renowned for humiliating and exploiting poor Haitians. A related service entails posing as advocates for or a "force behind" members who find themselves in conflict with non-group members. In addition, some Bamòn sosyete-s host religious ceremonies, such as funeral rites and feasts for the ancestors, and provide entertainment for their communities by way of dances, holiday festivities, and parades.

Sosyete-s are subdivided into several types. In the Bamòn area during my time there, sosyete-s included *sosyete bokal . . . sosyete nago . . . sosyete baka . . . sosyete kongo . . . sosyete vyelon . . . sosyete madigra, sosyete zouya . . . sosyete boutka,* and *sosyete vaksin.* Additional categories of sosyete-s may be found in other areas of Haiti. Although a variety of distinguishing factors may be identified in the ways these different sosyete-s function, a sosyete's primary defining characteristic is its music—the sorts of musical instruments in its band (*batri*), and the repertoire of *rit*-s (rhythms or cadences)[1] and songs it employs.[2]

Structure and Leadership

Two of the characteristics most obviously distinguishing sosyete-s from the other Old Testament groups are their size and structural complexity. A sosyete in Bamòn may have fifty, eighty, or even well over a hundred members, making it the largest of all the community groups engaged in communal labor.[3] Unlike an atribisyon, a sosyete's membership generally represents several different neighborhoods, so many of its members will be neither kin nor close acquaintances. Rarely will the distance between two members' homes be more than a half-hour's walk, though, and it is unlikely that any two of a sosyete's members were complete strangers before joining the group. A number of sosyete members told us that although the other members had voted on their admittance, their membership was essentially "passed down" to them from parents or siblings who were preparing for death or had become unable to work. They explained that this membership inheritance system, like that of the atribisyon's, has been a key reason their groups have managed to stay together for several decades.

There tends to be more variation in socioeconomic status among sosyete members than is typical of the eskwad-s and the atribisyon-s. Even though very few are wealthy enough to be considered *gwo nèg*-s (big men/big shots), some sosyete members are significantly better off than most of their neighbors. (They might, for instance, own a house with a tin roof, several animals, and an unusually large, contiguous plot of land.) A few others might be altogether landless. Most group members, though, tend to fall between these two extremes: they are tipeyizan but not *pov malere*, people whose families are "struggling" but who generally manage to have at least one substantial meal a day, and to provide their children with at least a few years of formal schooling. As with the atribisyon-s, the majority of Bamòn sosyete members are men. However, most sosyete-s in the area boast at least three to five female members.

The sosyete-s have many leadership positions, each with its responsibilities and aura of honor. Although the rosters of officers vary among groups, the list in Table 6.1 is representative of the sosyete-s Benwa and I visited in Bamòn.

Table 6.1.   Sosyete Officers and Their Roles.[4]

President (*Prezidan*)	The president leads the group in making decisions. This post is the most prestigious and is usually filled by an older man recognized for his popular authority and wisdom. He is responsible for calling the *konsèy*-s (meetings), which occur either on a periodic basis (not usually more than once a month), or whenever the group needs to discuss specific problems or make decisions about issues that have come up. He presides over these meetings and is looked to for guidance in the discussions that arise.
Governor of the People (*Gouvènè de Pèp*)	The governor is, in effect, the president's chief administrator. He often takes a more active role than the president himself in directing and overseeing the activities of the group, such as the work sessions, mutual aid operations, and meetings. A. Métraux (1971) describes him as "a sort of foreman." "He has responsibility over all of us," one sosyete member explained. "If people want to do something, it is he they ask for permission." The prestige associated with his post is second only to that of the presidency.
Army General (*Jal Lame*)	The army general's primary responsibility is to lead the group as it proceeds to and from its kòve-s (work sessions) and other events, and as it carries out the other processions, dances, and ceremonial procedures involved in the group's work. To do this, he walks ahead of the other members of the group and its musical band, carrying in his hand a wooden baton the size of a short walking cane or a billy stick, and moving it up and down, back and forth much like a drum major or drill sergeant. The jal lame may also be seen helping the chaje kòve coordinate workers as they carry out kòve-s.
Division General (*Jeneral Divizyon*)	The division general is essentially the group's *simidor/sanba* (band leader and primary songwriter). He generally plays an instrument, usually a drum, but might simply lead the music with his voice and perhaps the use of a baton much like that of the army general's.
Kòve Chief (*Chaje Kòve*)	The kòve chief's major role seems to be distributing the rum among members during group events. "It's no easy task," Benwa assured me. This officer's efforts to carry out an equitable distribution is often challenged by group members, who plague him with their attempts to get more than what he might deem to be their rightful allotments.
Chief Assistant to the kòve Chief (*Chaje Laplas / Laplas*)	In part a liaison and messenger for the group, the laplas is responsible for informing members about the times and places of their work sessions. He is also responsible for

Table 6.1.   Sosyete Officers and Their Roles. (*cont.*)

	running errands for the group, for instance, when the group needs to purchase something, or needs to communicate with an individual or group in another region. In addition, he makes sure a small fire is built in the field before each kòve, so that members will have a source for lighting their pipes or hand-rolled cigarettes during the workday. He may join the army general in leading the group's processions. In fact, sometimes the responsibilities of the army general are assumed by the laplas, or vice-versa. (A. Métraux [1951] cites several different subtypes of the laplas position in his analysis of Marbial sosyete-s.)
Secretary (*Sekretè*)	The secretary assists the governor and the president in presiding over the group's konsèy-s (business meetings). He also "holds the notebook" containing records of the group's activities and its membership list. He keeps track of members' participation in the kòve-s and reports to the rest of the group when a member has been especially negligent or is having problems. The responsibilities of this post are such that, if available, a person who has attended some years of school is generally chosen.
Treasurer (*Trezòye*)	The role of the treasurer, which involves keeping track of the group's monetary transactions and holding its collective funds, may or may not be filled by the same person serving as secretary. Women are very often chosen to fill this position, generally for the same reasons women are recruited to be treasurers in atribisyon-s.
Exploring General (*Jeneral Dekouvèt*)	Before a kòve, the exploring general inspects the terrain to be worked by the group. It is only after the exploring general reports his findings back to the governor that a kòve can begin. Not only does his job involve searching for rough areas the workers may find especially challenging, as A. Métraux notes, he also "beats the bounds of the field in search of hypothetical enemies" (1951, 1971).
Depot Mistress/Queen (*Metrès; Renn Deapo*)	The position of depot mistress is always staffed by a woman. Her job involves guarding the stash of drinking vessels and other possessions left in her care by the workers at the beginning of a kòve. She may also assist the kòve chief, though not always under his supervision, in distributing rum to the workers.
Councillor Team (*Konsèy*)	A sosyete's councillor team generally consists of a handful of older men or women. Many can no longer work in the fields. They are valued instead for their experience and wisdom. They are to be consulted before any major decisions are made concerning the group and receive gestures of respect sometimes surpassing those enjoyed by the other officers.
Monitor (*Monitè*)	The monitor is a *prèt savann*, or bush priest, who is chosen by the group to conduct the proceedings for the wakes, funerals, burials, and other religiously imbued ceremonies sponsored by the group. Most have received extensive training in the Catholic church as acolytes or assistants to priests during their youth or early adulthood years. The prèt savann-s also draw

Table 6.1.   Sosyete Officers and Their Roles. (*cont.*)

	heavily on Vodou rites and, increasingly, Protestantism, thus offering the group a dynamic montage of ritual.
Silencing General (*Jeneral Silans*)	The silencing general is in charge of quieting members of the group when they become too noisy or rowdy.
Suppliers (*Founisè*-s)	The suppliers provide the group with its musical instruments, the rum needed for group meetings and ceremonies, and other materials necessary to conducting its work, ceremonies, and mutual aid operations. Most groups thus have a *founisè batri* (musical instrument supplier), a *sèkèyliye* (coffin supplier), and a *founisè sik* (sugar supplier). Some also have one or more members designated as *founisè savon ak lwil doliv*-s (soap and vegetable oil suppliers).
Flag Queen (*Renn Drapo*)	The flag queen is assigned the task of carrying the group's flag during processions and ceremonies, and assisting the army general in leading the group. Some groups have two flags and, thus, two flag queens. Many groups do not bring out their flags except on special occasions, and some no longer have flags at all. Thus, according to sosyete participants, flag queens are much more rare than they used to be.
Soldiers (*Solda*-s)	Members not holding an office are called "soldiers."
Workers (*Wòm*-s)	All members (lay members and officers alike) are "workers" when a kòve is taking place.

Other offices we learned about include a number of "ministers" and "queens": finance minister (*ministè finans*), judiciary minister (*ministè kasasyon*), war minister (*ministè lagè*), supervising queen (*renn dirijèz*), combat queen (*renn konba*), basket queen (*renn panye*), and Queen Victoria (*Renn Viktòya*). Older members of Bamòn sosyete-s, in talking about the earlier, grander days, told us of a special sort of queen previously common among sosyete-s in the area—*the* queen. As R.B. Hall (1929) and Wirkus and Dudley (1931) report in their discussions of sosyete-s functioning on the island of La Gonâve in the 1920s, the office of queen has at times been the most powerful and prestigious of sosyete positions. The queens they describe not only ruled over individual sosyete-s but over entire regions of sosyete-s, and thus provided a centralized organizational structure the likes of which seem not to exist today.

Also mentioned by the older members of the groups, but evidently no longer found in the Bamòn area, are *wa*-s, or "kings." These dignitaries would join the queens in overseeing the groups' processions and ceremonies, and in carrying the group flags. They also carried the *jon*-s, swords usually constructed from scraps of tin. Locals reported that many kings were skilled jugglers and were renowned for the creative and difficult feats they performed with their swords. "They could make [the swords] dance," and could even make them disappear and reappear magically. In fact, some of the swords were known to "dance in the air on their own." Consistent with Wirkus and Dudley's account (1931) of La Gonâve sosyete-s, Bamòn residents described the kings as having less status and responsibility than the queens. This distinction was less clear when people spoke of *lanpèrè*-s; these are "emperors," who, like the queen, seem to have played much the same sort of role as contemporary presidents, though with more ceremony. Also mentioned were colonel (*kowonèl*), major (*majò*), prosecuting attorney (*komisè*), supporting president (*prezidan soutiyenn*), confidence president (*prezidan konfiyans*), drill sergeant[5] (*sèjan de zanm*), police general (*jeneral lapolis*), deputy (*depite*), and district officer (*adjwen awòndisman*).

Officers may either "inherit" their positions (like Souri had his father's atribisyon presidency), be appointed by other officers, or be elected by the membership. Within the past couple of decades, many Bamòn sosyete-s have moved from systems of inheritance or appointment to elections. One sosyete that has undergone "democratizing" changes is Sosyete Kòk Kalite (The Winning Rooster Society), a sosyete bokal founded in 1937. When Benwa and I visited this group one afternoon as it worked in a field several kilometers from Tisous, Jeje, its president, explained to me how this had happened. "Before, when an old member was dying," he said, "he would chose his replacement." Now, however, "when one of the leaders of the group needs to be replaced, all of the members of the group vote."

Jeje said they realized they needed to change the old system when they observed how some of the newer organizations in the area were functioning. He specifically cited the influence of two Catholic church-affiliated programs that showed up in the area in the mid-to-late 1980s: a literacy and consciousness-raising campaign called Misyon Alfa, and the TKL (*Ti Kominote Legliz*, or Small Church Community) movement. Both programs, Jeje reported, encouraged participants in the community groups they sponsored to reflect critically on social injustices and to challenge those injustices both at a national and a local level. They also offered training in democratic styles of community organization and leadership. When people who belonged to sosyete-s went to TKL meetings or Misyon Alfa literacy centers, they took back to their sosyete-s these lessons: "They would say no, we shouldn't do it that [old] way anymore." It is likely that democratizing influences also came from members of the Bamòn community who traveled to and from Haiti's urban areas at the time, and witnessed the rise of other popular movement organizations there.

People who are known as particularly good or resourceful leaders may find themselves holding positions in a couple of different sosyete-s, or in both sosyete-s and other groups as well. Souri, the president of the Atribisyon Monklè, served as the president of another atribisyon and held offices in a gwoupman peyizan (see chapter 7), an eskwad, and a sosyete madigra. In addition, he often took the place of his aging father in the workdays and meetings of another sosyete madigra. Some people hold more than one office within a particular sosyete. For example, Tonpyè, the president of Sosyete Prankè (a sosyete bokal), was its coffin supplier, and the group's division general served as the rum supplier.

Before examining case studies of particular sosyete-s, it is worthwhile to reflect briefly on the sosyete leadership structure. What are we to make of the array of dignitaries listed in Table 6.1? Of the many references to military and state government posts? What sort of real authority does the "army general" actually have? The "silence general"? What purposes, in other words, do these posts serve for sosyete members?

The answers to these questions are not immediately clear, and students of the sosyete have offered mixed assessments. Alfred Métraux concluded from his research that they were little more than fun and games: "In the society known as 'Fleur de rose' ten out of fifteen members held some rank and the others complained of their humble status and aspired to the dignity of office. Besides a president and his ministers, each society includes generals and governors. Their duties varied, but, of course it is all make believe" (1960, 39).

In assessing the roles officers play in their groups, he adds that although the "governors" do actually lead the workers, "some resounding titles exist merely to tickle the imagination and the ear of their holders, and their origin often lies simply in a pun." To take the sosyete offices seriously, Métraux insists, would be "to misinterpret the spirit of the societies" (1971, 33).

Likewise, Vallès explains that its militaristic-political façade does not change anything about the nature and functions of the sosyete (1967, 121). In contrast to Métraux's and Vallès' assessments, Laguerre (1975) assures us that sosyete hierarchies are a deadly serious matter. Claiming that they function as avenues for the systematic exploitation of some group members by others, Laguerre sees these hierarchies as the primary reason sosyete-s will never be able to function with any real integrity or productivity (1975, 55).

Laguerre reports that the officers rarely, if ever, contribute anything of real value to the group, aside from satiating the members' thirst for pomp and circumstance. For him, sosyete officers are parasites—local patriarchs who stock up on social prestige and material wealth by taking advantage of the labor of their poorer neighbors. He claims, moreover, that their system of hierarchical rule allows the sosyete-s to "safeguard a military and governmental structure that parallels the structure of the army and the national government" (1975, 56). The harshness of this latter critique is underlined by the fact that Laguerre was writing during the time of the notoriously oppressive Duvalier regime.

Anglade (1977, 71) also takes seriously the military aspect of sosyete officer corps. In contrast to Laguerre's assessment, however, he suggests that they reflect the organizing principles of the celebrated *kako* and *pikèt*, rural guerilla armies with roots in pre-emancipation St. Domingue.

Historical records offer no substantial evidence that sosyete-s have ever performed any real military functions—either to buttress or to challenge state rule. Although Bamòn sosyete members insisted repeatedly that in 1959, "we were recognized by the state," the Haitian government's approach to peasant groups has, for the most part, fluctuated between benign neglect, aggressive hostility, and self-interested manipulation. As Smucker and Noriac put it, throughout Haitian history, there has been an "onerous restriction on independent legal status for peasant organizations" (1996, 21). This approach began even as early as the first decades of Haitian independence. Leyburn notes that Boyer's Rural Code, aimed to "reorder the agricultural life of Haiti," actually forbade "cooperative enterprise" among farmers (1941, 67).

Despite the political changes that have occurred in Haiti during the past fifteen years (including the adoption of a new Constitution, the dismissal of the Code Rurale, and the election of former popular-movement activists to departmental and national offices), Smucker and Noriac tell us that there is still no "law on associations adapted to the needs of grass-roots peasant organizations. . . . As a result most peasant organizations are unable to defend themselves in court, legally borrow money, sign legally for grants, own property, establish a bank account, bring suit in a court of law, defend their rights as an organization, or legally represent individual members or officers" (1996, 21; also see Elie 1992; Vallès 1967).

Yet Bamòn sosyete members are not entirely off-base in claiming that they once "collaborated with the state." What they are referring to are occasional incidences in which Papa Doc Duvalier's government sent them alimentary aid.[6] Numerous Bamòn residents, among them many group members, complained to Benwa and me that the major purpose of this aid was not to alleviate hunger but was intended, rather, to bribe the population into supporting the Duvalier regime. On receiving it, locals reported, groups like the sosyete-s would be obliged to parade into town dancing, drumming, singing, and shouting "Long live Duvalier!" on election day. In fact, sosyete-s, like the *kominotè*-s (chapter 7), were renowned for their willingness to trade festive demonstrations of loyalty for a few bottles of whiskey, a few measures of food, or some pocket change. As for USAID and the other foreign agencies that provided the supplies and funding for these aid distributions, many rural Haitians suspect that they were happy to assist Duvalier in placating the peasantry, and thereby preempting any real efforts of local people to change the conditions in which they lived. As Farmer (1992, 1996) points out, though such accusations are sometimes interpreted as the paranoid imaginings of the poor, there is actually a good deal of evidence in patterns of aid and foreign policy that would back them up.[7]

That sosyete-s have had only marginal, unbalanced, and erratic relation-ships with the state, and have not significantly mimicked its structures, should not lead us to conclude that their hierarchies of officers are super-fluous, or that these officers have been merely figureheads or performers. A. Métraux's assertion that "the dignitaries themselves do not take their lofty status very seriously" (1951, 73) sometimes rang true during our visits to the groups, but sosyete members showed and told Benwa and me on many other occasions that they were taking them quite seriously indeed. "Soldiers" and officers alike frequently attested to the crucial value of cer-tain officers' leadership and contributions. "That's the monitor over there. We offer him a free kòve every once in a while, because without him, we would not be able to provide our members with decent burials." "Tonpyè has been our president for years and years, and he took it [the presidency] from his father. We'd fall apart without him." "A good division general is the key to a good kòve. Some of them don't know what they are doing. But Tison—ahhh, he's good!"

As we will see, ceremonial manifestations of respect for officers comprise a part of each kòve and konsèy (group meeting). Yet members seemed to move quite easily from expressing somber deference for officers, to poking jabs at those same "honoraries." On occasion, it even appeared to me that the officers' pomp-and-circumstance displays were intended as much as mockeries of their own positions (and therefore of the state?) as status-building gestures.

The following case studies suggest that Laguerre's claims that sosyete of-ficers are essentially parasites are also exaggerated, at least in reference to Bamòn sosyete-s. In these sosyete-s, officers did receive certain material re-wards for their leadership, such as a few extra sips of rum here and there, and occasionally an extra kòve. Still, every active member was due a kòve in time. Everyone also was entitled to a dignified burial, to assistance in times of sickness, and to an equal share in the earnings of the group. Plus, as Al-fred Métraux and Vallès have reminded us, all sosyete members, regardless of status, are expected to "stoop in the fields."[8] Group members insisted that while some officers have tried to take advantage of their positions, lazy, exploitative officers have been the exception, not the rule. Moreover—de-spite Laguerre's suggestion that the abuse of power within sosyete-s has be-come worse in recent decades—both a chronological analysis of studies on sosyete-s, as well as comparative descriptions by peasants themselves, sug-gest that the structures of contemporary sosyete-s have become less, not more, hierarchical than those of former groups. For instance, older sources on sosyete-s speak extensively of queens, kings, and emperors, yet such po-sitions are rarely seen today. Roles played by those dignitaries seem to be carried out instead by a greater number of less-prestigious officers closer in status and power with lay group members.[9] And in some sosyete-s, it seems that nearly everyone has a special role to play.

The sosyete-s of Bamòn, then, do not resemble Laguerre's circles of crass exploitation or Alfred Métraux's less-than-serious games of "high-sounding titles" and pomp and circumstance as much as they resemble Rhoda Métraux's hierarchical families of collaborators:

> In their titles, the societies echo the relationship of official to ordinary citizen, parent to child, and vice versa. In their organization, the societies also reflect the social hierarchy, for heading them, one finds the men who are important in other aspects as well. . . . At the same time, all those who are members work together more or less equally and more or less equally benefit by the performance of the group, whether their recompense is work on their fields or payment for work done elsewhere. The main exceptions are the organizer and the effective leader, both of whom get work done for them without their working, in return for their organizing abilities and for the role they play in giving and presiding over dances and feasts. . . . When the members are paid by someone who hires the society, it is on one scale; when they eat, it is approximately the same food. (1952, 17–18)

The sosyete-s' long-term success at structuring and organizing communal labor tasks in an ever more challenging environment cannot be understood without acknowledging the ways they have combined seemingly incongruent characteristics—hierarchy with egalitarian values, long-suffering work with fun-loving play, and performance with worship.

Case Studies of Bamòn *Sosyete-s*

Sosyete Prankè

The members of the sosyete bokal Sosyete Prankè (Take Heart) were among my most careful tutors as I sought to learn about sosyete-s. Benwa and I first met this group during a community meeting we organized soon after I moved to Tisous. We had called the meeting to officially introduce ourselves, confirm the community's willingness to host our work, and ask residents to participate in formulating our plans. People came from Janpyè, Savanèt, Timache, Tisous, Monapik, Tèwouj, Mòn Gagè, and other neighborhoods in the upper Bamòn area. We talked about many things as the crowd of forty or so sat in a jagged circle formation on the narrow wooden benches of the one-room building that served as the area's Catholic chapel, primary school, and community meetinghouse.

To our delight, participants questioned us extensively about what I had come to do. As was often the case, most had assumed that I had come as part of a development assistance program, and found it hard to digest the idea that I had come to "study" the groups I was asking about, not aid, teach, or employ them. Nor had they expected me to be as interested in what I might learn from them about *effective* community organizing, as I would be in gathering information on what they did not have and were not able to do. Once mine and Benwa's objectives were more or less clear, we received a mixture of responses. A few people seemed to hesitate in taking us seriously, and others seemed to distrust my intentions. Most, however, expressed a combination of amusement, friendly curiosity, and a hospitable willingness to help us in our task. Some even said, with tentative enthusiasm, that it was about time a foreigner had come to listen instead of lecture, and to "discover the reality we're living in."[10]

Several invitations to upcoming group meetings and work days were offered, advice was given on how we might go about our research, and information about groups in the area was listed off so rapidly that I simply couldn't get it all down. (Luckily, Benwa's memory was a more effective recording device than my pen.)

Although several sosyete-s were represented at the meeting, Prankè members were especially vocal and provided a substantial portion of the information we received that day. An elderly Prankè officer, for example, gave a vivid description of what I would come to understand as a fundamental objective of the sosyete-s. His sosyete, he explained, formed

> because we saw that the peasants, instead of going forward, we were going backwards. We started it in order to help out when a brother has a problem—like when there is a death in his family. If the person is poor, if he has a little plot of land or a little chicken, maybe that's all he has. We decided we wanted save him from having to sell off that last little plot of land and last little chicken [to pay for the burial].

As he ended his discourse, others began talking about helping out in the fields and coming to one another's aid during times of crisis. Several people emphasized that by participating in these activities, they were not only improving their own and their children's chances of survival, but also demonstrating their loyalty to their ancestors' traditions and aspirations. A number of those ancestors were mentioned by name.

Someone soon noted that many sosyete-s have names that reflect the spirit of these objectives. Common titles include Charite (Charity), Kanpe Fèm (Standing Firm), Men Dan Lan Men (Hand in Hand). But the most admired titles seem to be those boasting of a group's strength, beauty, bravery, or prowess: Flè Pi Bèl de Bamòn (The Most Beautiful Flower of

Bamòn), Zetwal Briyant (Brilliant Star), Solèy Laviktwa (Victory Sun), and Towo Vayan (Valiant Bull).

Like other sosyete-s represented in the meeting that day, Prankè members located their group's birth in the 1950s. (Most agreed that it was 1955.) They counted some young people among their eighty-five members, although the current president and a handful of others still participating in the group had been founders. Other sosyete-s represented at the meeting began in the 1930s and a few as late as the 1970s.

After about three hours of animated conversation, debate, question-and-answer exchanges, and information sharing, the community meeting in Tè-wouj began to wind down. When we had wrapped things up with a Catholic prayer-song, Prankè members said that they should be getting to the kòve they had scheduled for that day. Would Benwa and I like to join them, they asked. Of course! Obviously surprised by our response, they and the others immediately began telling me that the walk would be long and difficult, and that I was welcome to reconsider. Chuckling in amusement at my insistence that I could handle it, several officers and members led us out of the chapel and south toward the mountains of Anwòmòn, a rural section neighboring Bamòn. Aware that it was past noon and that we would likely have nothing to eat until we returned in the early evening, they took us to the nearby field of a member, where we grabbed a few sticks of sugarcane to hold us over. As we walked and crunched on the juicy sticks of cane, they told us about the group's kòve-s.

Like the atribisyon-s, each sosyete has a certain day of the week when its members join together to carry out kòve-s. They usually congregate after everyone has had time to put in a few hours with their eskwad-s or atribisyon-s. It is therefore common for kòve sosyete-s to begin as late as noon or even early afternoon. Their kòve-s tend to last somewhere between three and five hours, depending on the size of the field, the number of workers deployed, and the amount of rum bestowed on them. Again, like the atribisyson-s, sosyete-s provide labor on a rotating basis to group members and also hire themselves out. Other similarities with atribisyon-s include the fact that they are busiest during pre-planting and planting seasons but continue to function during other parts of the year. In those periods, they may be employed to carry out nonagricultural tasks, or they may conduct public works projects, hold business meetings, and organize ceremonies or holiday celebrations, as well. Unlike the atribisyon-s, the money earned by sosyete-s is not designated for an annual feast. Most of it, rather, is set aside as a mutual aid fund.

On this day, Prankè was working in a field more than an hour's walk away. This is not unusual; sosyete members commonly spend two hours or more walking both to and from the fields they work. The handful of officers accompanying Benwa and me got us to the work site before most of the other sosyete members had arrived. It was not long, though, until we heard the others approaching.

Wo o o o
taka taka taka taka [drum beats]
Aye o o o
taka taka ta

Wo o o o
taka taka taka taka
Aye o o o
taka taka ta

A sosyete's processions to and from the field are more than simple work commutes. They are festive highlights of their work days. As usual, the trip had begun on this day when the group's division general stepped out of his lakou and proceeded through the Tèwouj, Tisous, and Mònapik neighborhoods. With the beating of the *siynal* rhythm on the *bokal* drum that hung from his waist, he alerted everyone in the area that it was time for the other members to come join him. Bokal-s, the signature instrument of the sosyete bokal-s, are 5 gallon rectangular tins. Covered with rust and dents from many years of use, these makeshift drums were originally vessels for holding vegetable oil. They were first adopted by sosyete musicians in the 1950s, when they entered Haiti as part of the "disaster relief" shipments sent from the U.S. government to the Duvalier regime. Prankè boasts a musical corps of two bokal-s, five *banbou* horns (four made from lengths of bamboo and one from PVC piping), as well as a *tinbal* (a two-headed drum slung over the shoulder or around the neck), and a *bourèt* (small, hand-held drums resembling tambourines in size and shape but without cymbals).

As the "division general" made his rounds through members' neighborhoods, the other musicians joined him, and soon the music and chants of Prankè's siynal were reverberating throughout the area. One by one, Prankè members heard the summons, grabbed their machetes, and fell in line with the musicians. As the group thus paraded along the narrow footpaths through the countryside, group members greeted neighbors and friends they met along the way. Women, children, and men looked up from the cooking pots, animals, and fields they were tending to watch and listen. Some joined in the march for while.

Eventually, we saw the procession top Goat Mountain and descend in our direction—marching, dancing, and singing their way to the field.

Wo, bokal samdi ap bat, o.	The Saturday *bokal* is sounding, oh.
Wo o o, mennen bokal la, o. . . .	*Wo*, lead the *bokal*, oh. . . .

Wo, bokal samdi ap bat, o.	The Saturday *bokal* is out, oh.
Wo o o, mennen bokal la, o. . . .	*Wo,* lead the *bokal,* oh. . . .

Out in front of this festive procession of workers was the army general, directing the crew with the motions of his baton. The laplas carried the flag today, as the flag queen had accompanied our party to the field.[11] When the strutting, singing, machete-wielding, cursing, laughing workers finally arrived at the field, they spent the next few minutes surveying the area. As the exploring general carried out his inspections of the field's terrain and boundaries, the others joked among themselves and discussed the work to be done. Soon Mèt Neve, the man for whom they would be working, walked down from his house to join them. As indicated by the title *Mèt* (Master)[12] with which the group leaders addressed him, Mèt Neve is considered one of the "notables" of the area. He is a *grandon,* a man whose large landholdings make him one of the most wealthy people in the Bamòn rural section. The group had arrived later than expected (the sun had begun its descent from its midday summit) and was still missing a few expected members. (Around forty-five people showed up that day.) Mèt Neve knew better than to chastise them too harshly, though, and thus risk being the victim of the jokes and songs soon to set the rhythm of the group's work. Instead, he waited with tried patience at the side of the field as they sporadically organized themselves.

Now it was time for the official greeting, or *salitasyon,* between Neve and the group. This short ritual began as the band changed rhythms from the siynal to a *rapèl,* and followed the army general out into the field, where they marched around in roughly circular patterns. The rest of the group fell in behind, while responding in a somewhat distracted unison to the lines sung out by the division general. Once the army general had gestured to the four cardinal points of the field, he ordered the group to halt. As the drummers then switched to an *ochan* cadence, the general wordlessly and with grave seriousness invited Mèt Neve into their circle, saluting him with flowing motions of his baton and the straw hat he took from his head. Finally, he formally announced the group's arrival and readiness to work. Mèt Neve answered him with a salute and a welcome, and ceremoniously presented the workers with the task before them—clearing the field of brush in preparation for planting.

The division general and the band, changing rhythms again, followed the army general as he divided the workers into two lines. It was in this formation, called *de kolonn,* or "two columns," that they would move through the field. Typical of large kòve-s and konbit-s, this pattern sets up a competitive game. The "team" that finishes clearing, planting, or weeding its section first celebrates its victory with songs that boast of its valor and chide the slower group. This sort of good-natured competition, members reported, results in the work getting done faster and more enthusiastically.

Also inspiring their efforts was the music of the band and the call-and-response singing led by the division general.

Kote yo mare ti bèf la?	Where have they tied the calf?
Nan ravin nan, wo	In the ravine, *wo*
Kote yo mare ti kabrit la?	Where have they tied the little goat?
Nan ravin nan, wo	In the ravine, *wo* . . .
Pa rele, pa kriye, wo	Don't yell, don't cry out, *wo*
Fò ou pa kriye si m fè chemn pa mwen	You musn't complain if I make my own path
Map sèvi vre Ginen	I'm serving the true ancestral spirits
Ou menm ou nan de chemen	You, you are walking two paths
Kite m chache lavi mwen	Let make my way in life
Kote Ginen a vle.	Following the ancestral spirits.

As in the konbit, the songs heard at kòve sosyete-s range from Vodou hymns calling on the lwa-s to political commentaries about state officials or verses poking fun at neighbors caught in embarrassing or scandalous acts. Some are old, familiar folk classics known throughout Haiti. Others belong to the region or are hallmarks of the group itself. Still others are composed on the spot. Even the most familiar are continually edited and expanded, so that one rarely hears a song with exactly the same words on two different occasions. Many of these songs are *chante pwen-s* (see chapter 3).

One of Prankè's newest songs was about a young man from the area who had died mysteriously after several days and nights of parading around with his sosyete madigra during the Carnival season.

Tifrè, m pale ou pa mache lannwit	Tifrè, I told you not to go out at night
Lè m pale Tifrè, Tifrè ba m pwoblem	When I warned Tifrè, he gave me a hard time
Sa bay Tifrè pwoblèm	Tifrè had a problem with that
Men kounyeya Tifrè gen pwoblèm!	But now does Tifrè ever have problems!

Thus singing as they went, the two columns swept down and across the field, attacking everything in their paths. They chopped away cornstalks tangled in vines, mercilessly pruned the small trees scattered about, scraped low-growing weeds from the ground, tossed aside the largest rocks, and otherwise hacked at, pulled up, or tore down nearly everything else they came across.

In the meantime, the three women group members present (Prankè has five female members) gathered in a corner of the field. On days when the sosyete plants, harvests, or carries out other tasks, the women work alongside the men. But this day, the task at hand was clearing the land—which most people in the area consider men's work—so the women went about doing other things. One of their responsibilities was "guarding the bottles." Whereas the *mèt kòve* (the person hiring the group to work) is expected to supply the sosyete with rum during the kòve, it is customary for each group member to come with his or her own drinking vessel. The bottle depot frees the workers from having to hold on to them or keep them lodged in their pockets while they work. Prankè's members had left the depot mistress and her assistants with quite a variety of containers: some had brought old medicine bottles, others tin cups, others rusting aluminum cans that once held tomato paste or evaporated milk. Some of the vessels, equipped to lend spice or medicinal properties to the brew, were stuffed with a variety of leaves and bark, or hot peppers. When time came for a drink, a worker was expected to ask the mistress for his bottle and then return it to her or one of her helpers after he imbibed.

Members told me this arrangement ensures that no arguments arise over whether someone has tampered with another worker's bottle (which might be done either to steal a swig of rum or, more seriously, to leave behind a curse against the bottle's owner). Also placed under the women's care were shirts, extra tools, musical instruments, and other things shed from the bodies and clothes of the men over the course of the work session. As they sat by the depot, the women chatted, teased the men who came for an occasional drink, shouted "encouragements" to the workers in the field, took a few swigs from the kòve chief's jugs, and occasionally joined in the singing.

The women also kept watch over the "smoking fire,"[13] and went to and from a nearby stream to fetch drinking water. Later in the day, as the men neared the field's edges, the women would "clean" the fields, by removing the fodder trash generated by the men and gathering it into large piles so it could be burned and then scattered about the field as fertilizer.

Standing at the edge of Neve's field, I noted that some members of the group seemed to be working quite a bit more diligently than others. I found this to be the case at nearly every kòve sosyete I attended. Contrary to what Laguerre would have predicted, the divide did not fall along officer—nonofficer lines. When I asked about it, I was told simply that "different people have different capacities." In fact, the discrepancies did not seem to be especially bothersome to anyone except me. This is not to say that there are no expectations regarding levels of participation in sosyete-s. A person who chronically fails to put forth a sincere effort in the activities of the group is destined to become the object of ruthless song lyrics and mocking labels such as "General Do-nothing," and may be subjected to fines or to any number of other disciplinary measures. Also disdained, however, is the person who is *regadan*, that is, who appears to "calculate" the relative amounts of work done by different people. I have heard over and over such statements as, "Not everyone has the same *kouraj* [strength]," "You never know what problems may be weighing on someone," and "All sticks in the bundle have the same value, but they're not all the same length." People who insist that everyone must do the same amount of work are just as likely to become the brunt of mockery as those who are chronically lazy.

As the kòve progressed, the wear and tear on the muscles and energy of the workers was revived by occasional sips of rum. By the end of the day, many of the members had had more than a few tastes, and they were ready to conclude with a festive flair—even though their limbs were exhausted and their "large intestines [were] eating [their] small intestines" with hunger. The band revived itself and began to play more enthusiastically as some of the workers added dancing to the final moments of their labor. Soon the women were taking part, laughing and singing as they joined in. Eventually, nearly everyone joined in the spontaneous party. This partying not only served as a means for the group to boast the quality of its work and display its "fiery" character. It also constituted an indirect gesture of appreciation to Neve, as it proclaimed to the neighborhood his generosity. Enjoying the fête himself, Neve knew that had he kept too tight a grip on his purse and failed to provide enough rum to meet the group's expectations; the surrounding hills and valleys would have been informed of his stinginess instead.

Unfortunately, Benwa and I had to leave shortly after the dancing began and thus were not able to be with the group as it concluded the kòve and headed home. We were able to observe Prankè ending the day on other occasions, however. One of those was when the group came to my lakou and presented me with a gift kòve. This evolved out of a visit Benwa and I had made to a group meeting the previous week. At the end of that meeting, an officer had announced that they were so pleased by our visit that they would give me a kòve the next week to "clean up" the area around my house "and make everything pretty for Christmas."

The group conducted its work that mid-December day much like it had when working Neve's field. Having fully cleared the small cornfield around my house, kitchen, and outhouse, they radically trimmed the trees planted around its border (my request that some of the foliage be left was met with indulgent laughter, then duly ignored) and even scraped the moss off the rock wall between the corn patch and my front door—all within a couple of hours. Some of the workers then moved to the path outside my gate, filling in the treacherous holes and gullies left by the rainy season. Like Neve, I had been careful to provide the group with a generous—though not dangerously extravagant—supply of rum. It had begun to do its trick soon into the work day and helped to create an increasingly jovial mood. Still, I was somehow persuaded to send someone out to purchase an extra half-gallon when the jugs were emptied earlier than expected.

When the maintenance on the path was nearing completion, the band stepped up the rhythm, increased the volume, and soon nearly everyone, together with more than a dozen neighbors and passersby, had joined in the dancing and singing. Pulled along by the depot mistress, I hoped I could get my *blan* feet moving in a somewhat appropriate fashion. I had little problem; most of us were bunched together so closely around the band that our individual movements coordinated themselves into one shuffling, dancing body. We thus moved with the band from one end of my lakou to the other, and then back again. By this time, others were taking over for the division general in leading the call-and-response tunes, while some of my neighbors who were musicians in other sosyete bokal-s joined or replaced Sosyete Prankè's musicians. Occasionally, the tight nest of shaking, twisting, shuffling bodies would open up, as individual women and men took turns claiming the spotlight and working miracles with the spirited agility of their feet or the blurred motions of their hands on goat hide.

O o o	Ohhh . . .
Koudeta kraze peyi m, o	A coup d'état has crushed my country
O oye o o, O oye o o, O oye o o	*O oye o o, O oye o o, O oye o o*
Koudeta kraze peyi m, o	A coup d'état has crushed my country
Ma rele aye, ma rele aye, ma rele aye	I'm crying out *aye*, I'm crying out *aye* . . .
Koudeta kraze peyi m, o	A coup d'état has crushed my country.[14]

After nearly an hour, the army general led the group back into the lakou, signaling that it was time to call it a day. But before leaving, the group had one more exercise to carry out: the closing *salitasyon*. The army general led the division general and the band as they traced large circles in the freshly cleared garden. Most of the other officers and some of the other members joined them. The dancing and singing took on a more serious air, as the beat of the drums, the singing, and the moving bodies slowed significantly. Arguments over whether the drummers were tapping out the right tune, and what exactly should be done next by whom, eventually precipitated a momentary lull in the music. This gave participants a chance to call for the others still out in the path and to gather into a more uniform circle.

Soon it was time to *antre chèf,* or "enter the chiefs," a ritual that involves not only honoring the leaders of the group but also presenting the day's work to God, to the lwa-s, and to the owner of the field.

The ritual began with the army general moving to the center of the circle and performing a dance in which he slowly and ceremoniously moved his

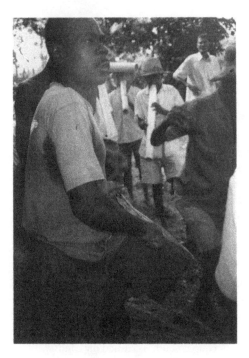

Sosyete Prankè celebrates the end of a hard day's work.

baton back and forth, and up and down across the front of his body. He soon went to the group's president and, with gestures resembling fluid salutes and bows, brought him out into the circle. The president danced along with him, using the straw hat he had taken from his head to match the general's motions in mirror image. Eventually, the army general delivered the president back to the periphery of the circle and chose another officer to take his place. After he had thus taken turns dancing with the sosyete's highest officers, he invited visitors from the neighborhood who were officers in other groups to join him. He then called on Benwa and, finally, myself. All of this was accomplished without a word from the army general, whose silence contributed to the gravely serious air of his orchestrations. Also honored by the gestures of the army general and those who danced with him were the ancestors and the lwa-s, as was evidenced by gestures made to the four "corners" of the circle.

While attending a ceremony conducted by a local Vodou priest later that month, it struck me that the practice of antre chèf I had observed in kòve sosyete-s was very similar to how he "entered" us into his *ounfò* (temple). The music, the silent dancing, the hand and full-body gestures, the circular processions all became suddenly familiar, as I recalled similar rites in other Vodou services I had attended in the past. When I told Benwa about this later, he said "Of course! . . . The *sosyete bokal,* the [*sosyete*] *kongo,* the [*sosyete*] *baka,* the [*sosyete*] *madigra,* they all come directly out of the Vodou heritage." Both Alfred Métraux (1972 [1959]) and Maya Deren (1970 [1937]) briefly point to such links in their discussions of the Vodou societies that congregate around particular priests and priestesses (see J. M. Smith 1998). For the sosyete, worship—like labor, performance, and play—is a necessary part of a good day's work.

When all the dancing, bowing, and saluting was completed, the music stopped. Then, in a expansive display of ceremonial verbosity, the governor gave a speech saying that the group was presenting its work to God and to the owner of the field. Their humble group, he continued, hoped that both would be honored by it and find it pleasing. He reaffirmed the group's pleasure that Benwa and I had shown interest in them and had visited them in the fields and during their meetings. He expressed in flamboyantly poetic terms the group's pride in the job they had done that day, and again stated that he hoped I had found this "little gesture" acceptable. Following his lead, I gathered all the oral courage I could muster and crafted what I hoped was a sufficiently elegant expression of my appreciation for the virtues of their organization, their generosity to me, and the quality of their labor. Evidently satisfied with my response, the band began to play again, and the circle dispersed. Part of the group followed the music back out the gate and began the dancing procession back toward their homes. Others lingered a while in my yard, exchanging with me more gestures of mutual appreciation, and taunting me with comments about my sad marital status and their schemes for how it might be changed.

The sosyete-s hold occasional meetings, or *konsèy*-s (literally, "councils"), at which they discuss group business. Some of the groups meet regularly, usually no more than once a month. Some sit together only every three months or so. The president may call a konsèy whenever something comes up that must be discussed among the entire group. Benwa explained that generally, the konsèy-s "do not have a fixed agenda." They are held, he explained, "so that everyone can say what is in their hearts concerning the sosyete, what pleases them and what doesn't, too. . . . Every type of subject [involving the group] has its place at a konsèy."

Exactly what a konsèy entails seems to vary quite a bit. A couple of those I visited were spontaneous, held in a field after the completion of a kòve and not lasting longer than about an hour. Others are scheduled in advance and last an entire afternoon, or perhaps into the evening. Such was the Prankè konsèy Benwa and I visited in December 1995. That Sunday afternoon, we arrived at the home of the president around three o'clock, just as the meeting was getting started. More than thirty people were gathered in the yard, on the porch, and inside the tiny stone-and-thatch house. The band, which had been touring the area and sending out the sinyal beat, had entered the president's lakou and was playing the *doub ochan* rhythm, indicating that it was time to "enter the chiefs." The army general responded affirmatively and set about ceremoniously directing the entry of the officers into the house. He half-walked, half-danced his way over to each one, greeting them wordlessly with somber nods, bows, turns, and the circumscribed motions of his baton. Reciprocating his gestures, they each rose from their places on the porch and went inside. With the same honor-bestowing gestures he had used to direct the entry of the officers, the general then ushered in Benwa and me. Though the small room was already crowded, Benwa and I were immediately offered two places on one of the scarce cane-bottom chairs, which had been turned on their sides to accommodate four to five people. Once we were seated, members of the group took turns offering us greetings and handshakes, addressing him as "brother" and "neighbor," and me as "sister," "daughter," and *blan* (foreigner).

A few more people had to be ushered in before the meeting could begin. Led in after us was a very old man who had just ambled up the path on a horse. He was given a seat along with two other men at the small wooden table placed in the center of the room. I was told that he was the *prèt savann* (bush [lay] priest) who directs funeral rites and other religious ceremonies for the group. The secretary, a much younger man, was seated at the opposite end. In front of him on the tattered white tablecloth was a notebook containing the group's membership and attendance lists and other written records. Beside the secretary was the group's president. These three officers were the only people in the room to have a chair to themselves. The laplas stood near the table, across from the monitor. Standing next to him, the governor was preparing to conduct the meeting. Most of the other members either stood against the wall or made seats out of other objects, such as the large rocks piled up in the corners of the room. Still others remained out on the porch and in the yard. During the course of the meeting, people would wander in and out of the house, sometimes participating enthusiastically in the discussions led by the officers, and sometimes carrying on lively conversations all their own.

The next three hours were filled with much animated discussion, decorated by elaborate verbal artwork, bursts of laughter, and occasionally, passionate confrontation. The agenda for the day, presented by the governor, was only partially preformulated, and topics were brought up by other officers and lay members throughout the meeting. Heading the list of concerns were complaints about a decline in attendance at the kòve-s and konsèy-s, and what might be done to turn it around. From the animated conversation that afternoon, I gathered that Prankè's officers had gotten a bit too lenient with the group's attendance rules and were now trying to persuade members of the seriousness of their intent to enforce those rules more faithfully.[15] That might mean subjecting members to a range of penalties.

Penalties levied against sosyete slackers include the *baraj*, in which the rest of the group marches together to the delinquent's home and "seiges" it. Bombarding all present with "pointing songs" and aggressive drumming, they put up the sosyete's flag at the door and claim the residence as their own. They then proceed to interrogate the person, asking for explanations of her absences and warning her of the penalties she is to suffer. As A. Métraux notes, "The culprit may get off comparatively lightly if [she or] he is repentant and humble, and treats the society's envoy courteously" (1951, 81). In that case, she might be required to hand over only a little food and rum. But if she is indignant and refuses to repent, the group will likely seize one of her animals, which will then be slaughtered for a feast. A harsh punishment indeed in a context where livestock is second only to land in its monetary value.

Yet the disciplinary measures taken by sosyete-s to keep their members in line are rarely meted out without a large dose of humor. A baraj can be as much a teasing, it seems, as a punishment—again, given that the victim responds in an acceptable manner. If that is the case, members claimed, she will be welcomed immediately back into the good graces of the group and, subsequently, might be respected all the more for it. The idea is to chastise, not to inflict real harm. Only the most relentlessly negligent members will finally be called before the group at a konsèy and dismissed altogether.

Another popular form of punishment among certain sosyete-s is called the *pikèt*, or "pick." Generally administered when someone has repeatedly shown up late to kòve-s, it involves making the person spend some tedious time alone in the middle of the field where the group is working. He has to stand on one foot, while resting the other on the pointed tip of a stick protruding from the ground. Once again, this practice seems to blur the lines between the painfully serious and a giddy good time.

Following the discussion of absenteeism, the governor instructed the group to decide what to do about a member they "had welcomed as a brother into the group" but who was being negligent. This person had been invited to attend this meeting and was asked to state his defense. "I am your child," he began, "and all of you here are mothers and fathers to me. I have come today to ask your forgiveness for my negligence and backsliding, and to beg you to accept me once again into your fold." He explained that he knew they were doubting him, as he had failed since joining the sosyete to show up for the konsèy-s and kòve-s. He admitted that it was all his fault. He hoped they would forgive him, allow him to pay his debts, and let him remain a member. After a long discussion, the group decided that "when a child stumbles into the water, his father must reach down and lift him up," and that they should do likewise and help him out. They settled on requiring him to pay only eight goud-s in fines despite all of the kòve-s he had missed, and to consider him a brand-new member. The man was very pleased, and promised to express his gratitude and renewed commitment by bringing the group some rum.

A little later, the elderly man who was identified as the group's monitor and a member of its councillor team announced that he had something "to lay before the group for judgment." Before he continued, the monitor was given a formal introduction by the governor, who emphasized that they were honored by his presence. The governor praised his service as Prankè's monitor since 1964 and stated that they would be happy to hear his concerns. Using his cane, the monitor hoisted up his weathered body from his chair, slowly removed his hat from the whitened hair underneath, and made a lengthy speech in which he expounded on the virtues of the sosyete. He highlighted his commitment to the group and pointed out that he had helped to found it before many of the current members were even born. He said that even though most of those with whom he had first worked were long dead, he was still committed to serving the group.

Reciting two familiar proverbs—"One finger can't eat stew all by itself," nor can "one finger kill a head lice"—he said he hoped they did not mind that he had to "send someone in [his] place" to the kòve-s, as his old body no longer had the strength for it. He asked if this "child" had pleased them with his labor. The group assured him that he had. He was glad, he said, but added he had learned that on several occasions, the young man had lied to him about going to a work session and had sneaked off somewhere else instead. He said that although he had already chastised him, he had come today to "judge" the young man in front of the sosyete. He simply could not afford to continue paying three- or five-goud compensation fees every time the guy skipped out. Reflecting the general trend of Bamòn sosyete-s toward becoming more "democratic," the group politely refused the old man's suggestion. The consensus they reached was that they would be happy to judge the "accused" but not behind his back. Because he had not shown up to the meeting, several people explained, they could not conduct a true hearing. They would do it, but only in his presence, where his own account could be heard. The monitor accepted the decision, thanked them, and again took his seat.

The meeting hardly followed *Robert's Rules of Order*. Sometimes, two or more participants spoke at once, and people constantly wandered in and out the room. Some of the members participated in nearly all the discussions; others spent almost the whole meeting out in the yard carrying on their own conversations. Most of the decisions were made through the informally assessed consensus of those participating at the time. While the officers leading the meeting clearly possessed a certain degree of authority over the proceedings and ruled on certain issues without contest, their opinions were openly challenged on several occasions—and at times were ignored altogether as those made by other members were affirmed and accepted. When a disagreement would threaten to become too heated, someone would usually jump in with a comment designed to break the tension with laughter. Often, two people who had just been engaged in a verbal sparring match would in the next moment be embracing one another warmly. The addresses "brother," "sister," "grandfather," and "papa" were used constantly, as were common *yonn ede lòt* (one helping another) proverbs (see chapter 4).

About halfway through the meeting, Benwa and I were again recognized and were more formally introduced. In the round of flowery, proverb-laden speeches that followed, the governor and several other group members complimented us on our work and expressed their appreciation for our interest in the group. Finally, they invited me to say a few words. Longing for more shiny oratorical jewels with which to dress my speech, I nonetheless managed to express how honored and grateful I was to be with them, how much I admired their work, and how much I was looking forward to learning more about it. Benwa then took his turn on the floor and lauded the group with more refined phrases. When he was finished, they applauded us and then went back to conducting their business.

Other topics of discussion included the need for a new drummer. (One of the group's two bokal drums did not have a "child.") No decision was made on this issue, except that a search would begin. There was also a brief and somewhat confusing financial and attendance report given by the secretary. And, of course, another rum distribution. Near the end of the meeting, people began to approach the secretary with the dues they owed for absences from kòve-s. Some disagreements ensued, and several times the rest of the membership was called on to judge whether the memory of the secretary or the memory of the indebted member was more accurate.

As the meeting came to a close, one of the members again spoke up and said that he was very pleased with the presence of "the sister" and hoped that if I ever needed any services I would call on them to aid me. He then proposed that the group give me a *kòve gratis*, a free work session, to thank me for coming. Everyone agreed, and they all offered Benwa and me another round of handshakes. The officers suggested that they carry out the kòve the very next Tuesday. I happily accepted the offer, touched by the warm welcome I had received and grateful to feel in the crowd (at least for a moment) as much like a daughter and a sister as a blan.

Sosyete Ann Leve Ansanm

By being loyal and active participants in one or more sosyete-s, members ensure that they and their loved ones will be aided in times of crisis by those with whom they work. Sosyete members invariably highlighted this benefit in describing the advantages of sosyete participation. As Tonpyè, the president of Prankè put it, sosyete-s have thereby prevented many members from losing "that last little plot of land and last little chicken." A case study of the *sosyete baka* Sosyete Ann Leve Ansanm (Let Us Rise Up Together Society) demonstrates how this works.

Benwa and I first visited Ann Leve Ansanm during a kòve they were conducting in the Mòn Gagè abitasyon (Benwa's neighborhood and the home community of many of Leve Ansanm's members). To our questions about the history of the group, members responded that it has undergone some significant changes in the past few decades. One change they highlighted was suspending the practice of holding *manje lemò*-s, feasts for the ancestors. Until several years ago, when enough money accumulated in the treasury (perhaps every three or four years), they would buy a cow, a few gallons of rum, and other delicacies, and hold a huge feast to which they would invite all of the group's deceased presidents and other former members.

But times are different, they said. Their president, Dyedonnen, explained that as economic pressures on group members increased over the years and "life became so terribly hard, we saw that we could not continue eating what we made." So in 1988, they gave up the tradition of ancestor feasts. They had always reserved a portion of their funds for mutual aid projects; now, almost all of it is spent that way. In fact, on the very day of our first visit, Ann Leve Ansanm was working in the field of a member who had been ill for some time.[16]

Not only do groups come to the aid of sick members by helping to maintain their fields; it is also common for sosyete-s to draw from their treasuries in order to help those members attain the care they need (e.g., by paying for medicines or the services of health-care practitioners). They also are ready to carry members and, in many cases, members' relatives, over miles of rough terrain in order to get them to a well-reputed ougan, leaf doctor, clinic, or hospital.[17]

Sosyete-s also provide members assistance during times of death. In rural Haiti, a dignified burial is at once a social and religious necessity and an extremely costly undertaking. Pulling it off has been for countless peasant families the catalyst that sent them tumbling "from poverty into misery." It is not uncommon for precious landholdings and animals to be sold or impossible debts to be assumed in order to bury a family member with dignity. Many members suggested that its role as a funeral society is the most important social service the sosyete provides.

Whenever a member dies, or in some cases, when the spouse, child, or parent of a member dies, the group immediately mobilizes. The coffin supplier (usually a carpenter by trade) begins to build a coffin or fetches one he has already made. The rum supplier fills the allotted number of bottles the group is to contribute. To relieve the family of some of the costs of cooking for the onslaught of mourners they will host during the coming days and possibly weeks, many groups also have a vegetable-oil and soap supplier and a sugar supplier. (As in many sosyete-s, these roles were filled in Ann Leve Ansanm by a woman who regularly bought and sold these products in local markets.) Less typically, the groups have a coffee supplier.

Not only must all the clothes that had belonged to the deceased be washed, but the entire inventory of clothes and linens in the house where the deceased had lived must also be taken to the creek for scrubbing. Thus, Ann Leve Ansanm offered a few bars of laundry soap. Some sosyete-s provide other items—laundry bleach or certain types of foodstuffs, such as rice or beans. In addition to material items, Ann Leve Ansanm officers would take some money from the treasury for the family. If possible, they said, they would offer 75–100 goud-s.

In the hours following the death, female members who are not suppliers go to fetch water, while non-supplier men collect bundles of firewood. Soon they are all descending on the *kay lanmò*, the grieving household. The band leads the way, drumming the appropriate cadences and directing the group in songs suitable for the occasion. By the time most of the sosyete's members arrive with their contributions, the body has been bathed with soap, leaves, and perfumes; it has been dressed in white and laid out on a clean bed in the main room of the house.[18]

The prèt savann who serves as the group's religious monitor greets the family, comforts them, and instructs them on additional things they must do to prepare the body and to provide an appropriate setting for the death rites he will conduct. He then takes his place inside, at a table placed near the body. There he will reside throughout most of the wake, leading mourners through many repetitive hours of singing, praying, chanting, and offering libations. The sounds of their droning voices accentuate the somber atmosphere created by the presence of the reclining corpse, the lamp under the coffin, the candles on the table, and the white sheets hung about the room. Most of what the prèt savann speaks and sings comes from the yellowed and frayed liturgical books he has carried with him. He rarely reads, however, as most of the relevant Latin- and French-language verses contained therein are lodged firmly in his voluminous memory.[19]

Other sosyete members, in the meantime, participate in the wake along with others from the community. As some join family members in reciting the "canticles" led by the prèt savann, others console those overcome with grief. A brother is held as he sits in a daze and chants songs of mourning; a mother is calmed after she finishes a round of heart-searing wails; a sister is restrained from hurting herself as her body flails about in sorrow. While women members help with the endless rounds of cooking, cleaning, and serving, most of the men carry out the less-strenuous task of providing "distraction"—sitting in the yard playing Haitian-style dominoes and cards, joking with one another, and drinking rum. The sosyete's band also strikes up a tune now and then, thereby lightening the mood. Thus the time passes in tears, laughter, prayers, curses, embraces, wails, arguments, chants, whispers, gossip, comings and goings, drinking, and eating. No one is left alone, and no expressions of anguish, regret, or loss are unacceptable. Group members will stay with the family around the clock, at least until the burial.

Finally, the coffin supplier arrives, signaling that the moment has come to take the body to its grave. The monitor guides family members as they place the body in the coffin and undertake the unbearable task of nailing on the lid. Male members of the sosyete then take up their role as pallbearers. The band leads the crowd in a slow, sometimes haphazard, processional to the gravesite, which may be anywhere from a few hundred yards to several miles away. This journey is not always an entirely somber one. Very often, the pallbearers have had more than a little rum during the course of the wake and enthusiastically *jouke* the casket along the way. This involves turning it around, taking it off the path in all directions (sometimes to the infuriated cries of those whose crops get trampled in the process), dipping it and lifting it up, shaking it, and otherwise trying to "confuse" the soul of the deceased so that it will not try to return to its home after the corpse is buried to haunt the family or their neighborhood.

At the gravesite, the prèt savann again leads everyone in a series of prayers, songs, and recitations. Finally, the pallbearers lower the coffin into the grave and family members throw the first few fistfuls of earth on it. After the burial is concluded, attendees return to the grieving house and wash their hands in a basin of water infused with a mixture of medicinal leaves. Many group members will spend the rest of the day, and possibly the coming night, with the family. The following morning, the women will empty the grieving house of all its clothes and linens and head to the river for the "laundry kòve." Members will take turns maintaining a near-constant presence at the house during the coming week or two, as they continue to offer comfort and help with the formidable chores involved in hosting other visitors.

During the first nine days after the burial, a series of rituals called *lime lanp* (lighting the lamp) is performed. For this, the lamp[20] that had been placed beneath the deceased's bed during the wake is burned periodically, "so that the person's soul won't lose its way on its journey." It sits on a white cloth-draped table in the main room of the grieving house. Behind, around, and above the table, white sheets have been hung. Often these are adorned with decorative and symbolic designs cut from leaves and black cloth. Under the table is a set of the person's clothes. On top of the table sits a variety of objects: bottles of libations for the lwa-s, a tin cup of "holy water" blessed by the prèt savann, a copy of the Bible, decorative plants, lwa-possessed stones, a crucifix, tattered reproductions of Catholic icons, and a photograph or other mementos of the deceased.

Sometimes the lamp is lit every three evenings, sometimes every evening. The sosyete's prèt savann performs the lamp-lighting ritual and leads the attendees in songs and prayers from his books. On the ninth day, the entire community joins the family and the sosyete at the grieving house for the *nevenn*, a final rite similar to the Latin Americans *novena*. The entire day is spent singing the "canticles." Participants also consume sweet coffee, whiskey, and snacks; play cards and dominoes; grieve; and socialize. While the nevenn thus resembles the wake in some ways, its liturgies, like its décor, is distinct. This day, the prayers and songs are ones that "recommend" the person's soul to heaven and finally send it on its way. This is done not only in the interest of the deceased. If the soul is not sent properly to "the other side," it may very well meddle in and possibly plague with misfortune the lives of those who remain.[21] My neighbor, Bèna, once explained to me that nevenn participants are essentially telling the soul, "We got along well together. Now we are friends no more. You've died. We have nothing to do with each other anymore. I owe you nothing. Go on your way."

In talking with me about the services their group had provided its members, several of Ann Leve Ansanm's members cited the Haitian proverb *"Ti patat fè chay"*—even little sweet potatoes, when put together, can make a big load. They reported that while the value of the materials provided by their sosyete in cases of death was considerable, the burden put on the group was minimal (particularly in comparison to how the expenses would have affected an individual family). They explained that most of the materials were provided by suppliers, who tended to be a little bit better off than other members and thus could cope with the sudden expenses. Moreover, the suppliers did not have to be compensated immediately or in kind for their contributions but, rather, with "free kòve-s" down the road.

As previously mentioned, receiving an honorable burial is of great concern to rural Haitians. Such a burial requires that others properly carry out an extensive set of rituals, ceremonies, and adornments, the costs of which are well beyond the means of most peasants. Yet if the rites are not done, or if community participation in them is feeble, not only is the reputation of the deceased and her family threatened; the soul is actually in danger of losing its way on its journey to the other world. By being an active member of a sosyete, one preempts this nightmare while, at the same time, protecting one's relatives from the economic ruin that might result from trying to provide everything themselves. What the sosyete-s offer here, then, is a sort of informal life insurance policy—but more than that. By "surrounding" them in times of crisis, they also ensure their members that they will not have to take on the most trying moments of their lives alone.

Many sosyete-s also conduct public works projects. For instance, several years ago, Ann Leve Ansanm joined with a number of Bamòn sosyete-s and other local organizations to provide the manual labor necessary for building the public school and Catholic chapel in Mon Gagè. They also help maintain the area's dirt roads and footpaths. The solitary dirt road that traverses the length of Bamòn is a winding, mountainous one made impassable nearly every rainy season with ruts, gullies, holes, and ravines. Even though none of the residents of the area possesses a vehicle, a dump truck passes through twice a week to transport people and goods to and from Jérémie. Foreign NGOs and missions working in the area also use the road with frequency. Because these parties offer valuable services to locals (e.g., occasionally transporting people to and from the hospital in Jérémie), Ann Leve Ansanm and other groups have periodically volunteered to work together in patching up the road. The vehicles' owners have sometimes compensated them (in cash, rum, or food) for their services, sometimes not.

Sosyete Solèy Leve

Somewhere in the darkness can be heard the discordant notes, always the same, of a flute; they get farther away, cease. Then I think not about death but about the living who are gone, and I hear the sound of their voices, and it is as if I saw the various shades of their lives, the colours they were, yellow, blue, pink or black, faded colours, intermingled and distant, and I try to find the thread of my life, too. (the narrator of Simone Schwarz-Bart's novel *The Bridge of Beyond* [1982, 169])

Not all of the sosyete-s in Bamòn had totally done away with the practice of holding dances and feasts for the ancestors. Among those still hosting such events at the time of my tenure there was a sosyete kongo called

A *sosyete's* lay priest (*prèt savann*) conducts a feast for the ancestors.

Sosyete Solèy Leve (Rising Sun Society). Sosyete kongo-s, residents said, were known "in the good old days" for their close connection with the *ounfò* (Vodou temple) and for the elaborate festivities they orchestrated. Solèy Leve, which was based in the greater Savanèt and Mòn Gagè area, was one of the few sosyete kongo-s left in Bamòn by the time I arrived. Benwa's uncle was the president of the group, and we went to see him one day to find out more about it.

As we visited with him on the porch of his home, drinking from green coconuts and looking out on a bird's-eyes view of Mòn Gagè, Ton Dyemèt told us that his group, too, was nearly a thing of the past. He explained that it had been around for a long, long time. Since the group was older than any of the current members, he said, no one was sure when it had started. Perhaps when their grandparents were young men and women. At one time, it had boasted two hundred members but now had between thirty and fifty.

The pride in Ton Dyemèt's eyes turned quickly to sad regret as he remarked that in the past few years, "people died and there was no one to replace them. . . . The young people are not interested in carrying it on."

And, he said, it had been a very long time since they had hosted one of their famous kongo dances. It was through those, he explained, that they had demonstrated their loyalty to the *lwa kongo*-s, the ancestors and deities of the kongo lineage. Severing past relationships with one's spiritual caregivers and kin is not only alienating in itself. In rural Haiti, it also makes one more vulnerable to worldly misfortune and is sometimes fatal. Has this been the real cause of the droughts that have plagued the area during the past few years? Of the recent deaths in Ton Dyemèt's family? Of the failure of his children to excel in school? Ton Dyemèt wonders.

When Solèy Leve was at its height, Ton Dyemèt explained, it had a queen and a king to lead their processions and dances. These highest dignitaries were accompanied by a large number of flag queens. They even had an emperor with a *jòn*, a magical sword that the emperor could make dance on its own. There were more women members in his sosyete-s than you find in most, Ton Dyemèt said. "It is they who were the most important [participants] in the dances. They dressed in white, and wore white scarves."[22]

Shortly after that first visit with Ton Dyemèt, Benwa and I returned to his house and asked if he thought the group would consider putting on a kongo dance if we took care of all the expenses. He immediately accepted the offer and set the date for the following Saturday. He said they would need a gallon of rum, a *demika* (a small soda bottle) of cane syrup, some *kasav* (a flat bread made from grated manioc root), some *tablèt*-s (coconut and peanut candies made with cane syrup), and some *bonbon lamidon*-s (sweet wafers made of manioc starch, sugar, and spices)—"just a little something so we can show them [the lwa kongo-s] that even though we've been very negligent lately, we haven't forgotten them."

The kongo dance was held on Saturday afternoon, just as Ton Dyemèt had said. Benwa and I joined the group as they proceeded to the lakou of one of the area's most renowned Vodou priestesses. When we all arrived there, the music stopped suddenly, and one of the musicians announced that this was the "capital" of the sosyete kongo (the site of the founder's former home). With that, we entered the lakou and made our way to a large concrete tomb. There a candle was lit, a few pennies tossed to the ground, and several sips of rum poured out as participants called on the lwa kongo-s, asking them to look upon the sosyete with favor and to bless the upcoming dance.

When the music started up again, the group began to dance and sing its way out the gate and up the path. Once we arrived at the lakou where the dance was to be held (also the former home of a deceased group leader), libations were offered (this time at the gateway) to the lwa kongo-s. These libations consisted of rum, dark cane syrup, candles, and several brief oratories. Without the flags, the sword, or the queen and king, this procedure was not the elaborate ceremony it would have been a few decades ago. It was not long until all the offerings had been presented to everyone's satisfaction, and the dancing started.

The crowd had grown to more than thirty people by that time. Around one third of the participants were women, and nearly every age group seemed to be represented. Several people had complained earlier about how late it was getting and how tired and hungry they were. (Most of them had been out in the fields since morning and had consumed little more than a few gulps of rum.) But no one seemed anxious to leave once the drumming began, and for several hours the participants danced and sang kongo songs:

Mariyani o, wale	Mariyani oh, you're leaving
Mariyani o, wale	Mariyani oh, you're leaving
Mariyani o, wale. wa yo	Mariyani oh, you're leaving, *wa yo*
Nan barye wap tann mwen	Wait for me at the gate.
Mariyani o, male	Mariyani oh, I'm leaving
Mariyani o, male	Mariyani oh, I'm leaving, *wa*
Mariyani o, male, wa yo	Mariyani oh, I'm leaving, *wa yo*
Nan barye wap tann mwen.	Wait for me at the gate.
Nan Ginen o	In Ginen,[23] oh
Nan Ginen o	In Ginen, oh
Montre m chemen pou m al nan Ginen.	Show me the path so I can go to Ginen.
Mabouya nan won avèk fanm li	The lizard is in the circle with his woman.
Nou vini gade pou n al pale.	You've come to look so you can go talk.[24]
Tiwawa, leve pou nou pale	Tiwawa, wake up so we can talk
Tiwawa, leve pou nou danse	Tiwawa, wake up so we can dance
Wawa o, leve pou nou koze nan peyi a	Wawa oh, wake up so we can get going.
O Tiwawa	Oh, Tiwawa
Wawa Ginen, m di nou leve,	Wawa Ginen, I'm telling you to wake
mezanmi . . .	up, *mezanmi . . .* [25]
Jou Granwòl o te pale avè m, papa	The day Granwòl [an ancestral lwa] spoke to me, papa
Kilès ki te konnen, o?	Who knew about it, oh?
Granwòl o, m pral nonmen non ou ase	Granwòl, I'm going to name your name often[to serve you well]
Non ou ase	Your name is enough

Jou m angaje ma sove.	The day I commit to serving you, I'll be saved.
Woule! Woule! Woule!	*Woule! Woule! Woule!* [sung to instigate a drum roll]

Once the dancing winded down, we all gathered to arrange a modest offering of food for the lwa kongo-s under a coconut tree. We shared the rest of the food among ourselves, finishing it off with the last few sips of rum as the sun set a golden orange around our rustic communion circle.

Sosyete Endyen Desalin

Another type of sosyete well known for its festive flair is the *sosyete madigra*. Sosyete-s of this kind, unlike the sosyete kongo-s, remain populous in the Bamòn zone. Sosyete madigra-s closely resemble other sosyete-s during most of the year, as they labor in the fields, transport loads, conduct wakes, and cover houses. The resemblance ends at the beginning of the Carnival season, however. During this period, lasting form early January through Shrove Tuesday, they "disguise themselves" with madigra costumes and parade around the area. They entertain residents with their festive music, mock battles, and theatrics, and in the process, solicit tips. Many of them also head off to villages and towns to participate in the Carnival parades held there.

The Bamòn area has several different kinds of sosyete madigra. The *madigra endyen* (Indian *madigra*), I was told, is the "oldest and most popular" type of sosyete madigra there. I asked Benwa to explain where the term *endyen* comes from. He replied:

> Christopher Columbus got lost, and called the people he found here Indians, even though he'd not arrived in India. Those people wore short skirts made of shredded material, the same as what the *madigra* put on. They say that Christopher Columbus "discovered the Americas," but that's not true at all, or there would not be people who were already there. He just got lost.

People often spoke of the "Indians" who lived on Haitian soil before them as distant ancestors of sorts, a kinship that seemed engendered by their being fellow victims of the cruelties and humiliations meted out by European colonists.

In early January, after the holiday season and before the year's worst bout of hard work and hunger has set in, the madigra endyen-s of Bamòn begin making their costumes. Taking some money from the group's treasury, a few of the members travel to Jérémie to buy some modest materials, such as

crêpe paper, red pieces of used clothing, and other inexpensive and colorful items. They also purchase or gather from the households of members
cardboard boxes, paper, pieces of tin for horns, towels, and a host of other
odds and ends. They craft these into "Indian costumes" and other imagina-
tive, often outrageous, disguises. They then take up their musical instruments and begin their processions.

Some sosyete madigra-s parade and dance their afternoons and evenings
away throughout the entire Carnival season. Some groups travel great distances, visiting other neighborhoods and villages for days at a time. Many of
the sosyete madigra-s, however, "step out" only a few days before Mardi Gras
itself and stay fairly close to home.

Such was the Sosyete Endyen Desalin. A madigra endyen named after
Haiti's founding father, Jean-Jacques Dessalines, it was based near Tisous
and was one of the most popular sosyete madigra-s in the area. Not until
just before sunset on Ash Wednesday did I hear them coming from down
the path.

[*Taka taka taka ta*]

Madan Mora, sak fè ou keyi joumou Mora?	Madam Mora, why'd you go and pick Mora's pumpkin?
Madan Mora, sak fè ou keyi joumou Mora?	Madam Mora, why'd you go and pick Mora's pumpkin?
Mora fache jistan l mande divòs, o!	Mora was so mad he wants a divorce!

That year, 1996, only two members of the group were dressed as Indians.
Their costumes, which included large headdresses, were constructed of
clothing, cardboard, and hundreds of strips of red, blue, and white crêpe
paper. Each held a stick sword in his hand. The other star of the show was a
man wearing a red dress, a woman's wig, and a pair of women's glasses.
When the group neared my lakou, they stopped momentarily and then ran
in through the gate, the two Indians taking the lead. As they took over my
yard, the lead Indian led the singing, in the sosyete's typical call-and-
response style:

Se frè nou ye	We are all brothers
M ka di ou bonswa	I can tell you "Good evening"
Se sè nou ye	We are all sisters
M ka di ou bonswa	I can tell you "Good evening"
Se frè ak sè n ye	We are all sisters and brothers
M ka di ou bonswa!	I can tell you "Good evening!"

As the band continued with a number of other songs, the two Indians
danced around in the middle of a circle formed by the growing crowd in

my front yard and corn patch. Few could resist joining in. Old men grabbed drums away from the musicians, women flirted with the Indians, and toddlers giggled and jumped up and down as they ran in circles around the dancers. At one point, "the lady in red" approached me with her plastic offering plate and, after her, the drummers and the Indians. Once they were all satisfied with contributions, I was rewarded with dances in which the Indians used their wooden swords to ceremoniously spar with one another. Other men jumped into the theatrical battle while the spectators cheered, laughed, and clapped. As night descended, the glows and shadows cast by the small lamp I had placed on the front stoop accentuated the drama of the mock battles, and occasional "Indian cries" pierced the air. A festive, colorful, playful time for adults and children alike. After a while, the group sang and ceremoniously signed their good-bye's and thank-you's, and then made their way over to Djouli's house. Benwa reminded me as they left, "When a madigra dances in your field, you will have a good harvest."

It was well after midnight when I heard the sounds of Sosyete Endyen Dessalin finally fade away. They were on their way to end the festival season with a ceremony called "the fire in the crossroads." At the beginning of the Mardi Gras season, they had made a doll, a *serès*. "She is the mother of all [sosyete] madigra," they said. Describing the final ceremony ("passed down to us by the ancestors"), Benwa explained that they put this doll in a room of the house that serves as the headquarters of the group. Then:

> on the final day, Mardi Gras Tuesday, when they go out, they take her with them. While they are in the streets, she might be in someone's shoulder bag. . . . When their parading is done, when it's time for them to return home, they go to a crossroads and build a fire. All the *madigra*-s build the fire, but not all of them have a serès. . . . Then they take a little piece of paper from each costume, and they put all of those, together with the doll, into the fire, and burn it. They yell, "*Anmwe!*" [a cry of distress], the same way as when someone dies. They beat the rhythm *ladrapa*, the same rhythm they play when someone dies. In other words, the madigra has died for the year, and they have buried it.

Though they will continue to function as a sosyete during the remainder of the year, the festivities are no more. In continuing, Benwa explained that the same doll can be called on to help regulate problems within the group:

> It is that same serès [they use] when a member "eats" the mardigra's money all by himself. . . They have a Vodou ceremony in the same way they do as

when they're calling the other lwa-s. They call on the serès, and send her into the head of the person who stole the money. She enters the person's head. All day long, the rhythms of the madigra will be playing in that person's head. The person won't be able to think another thought. [She or he] is sure to go insane. They call that *foli madigra* [madigra madness]. That person might start dressing in madigra costumes and spend the rest of [his or her] life that way. . . . The [sosyete] *rara* do that, too. The crazy guy you see around Bòdlo and Bwamari, it was a rara's money he stole. Now he's always dressed "like a Jew," wearing *rara* clothes. Of course, when the rara have their ceremonies, they do not call the doll serès; they have another name they call her.

Sosyete Endyen Desalin joins Sosyete Solèy Leve in continuing to uphold certain other "festive" traditions now deemed too costly by most of the other sosyete-s in the area. Although they can no longer pull it off as an annual event, every few years, when the group saves up enough money, they hold a *manje lemò* (feast for the dead/ancestors). For this, they buy a cow or a couple of goats, along with rice, beans, plantains, and other foodstuffs, and celebrate wholeheartedly. They accompany their ceremonious presentations of offerings to the ancestors and the lwa-s with much dancing (known as *bal bourèt*), eating, and drinking.

They also "go to the water" to give offerings to the *simbi*-s, the mermaid-like lwa-s who reside in Haiti's rivers, creeks, and basins. They do this, Benwa explained, because "the Indians, the Taino, went down into the water when the Spanish were making them suffer so miserably. . . . People say that it is those people who are the simbi-s."

Reflections on the *Sosyete*

> Survival itself, in certain circumstances, is heroic. To live through mean times without becoming mean-spirited is heroic. (Barbara Kingsolver, quoted in Epstein 1996, 34)

The sosyete-s are by no means flawless civic institutions. Bamòn residents charge that some of them are more helpful to large landowners than to the zone's "small peasants," and thereby exaggerate, not challenge, disparities in wealth. Gender-based discriminations are evident in a number of sosyete traditions. Many are plagued with corruption, mismanagement, and other problems. They often fail to be as productive or efficient as they might. But to assume that these hierarchically organized, not especially efficient, occasionally less than serious, sometimes floundering organizations have little to teach us would be a grave error. Like the area's atribisyon-s, the sosyete-s of Bamòn are praised by many there for their ability to effectively mobilize agricultural labor. Looking at sosyete-s as labor-producing mechanisms, however, is to see only one of their many dimensions.

In fact, sosyete members in Bamòn tended to highlight other aspects of their groups in explaining their reasons for belonging to them. Among the most predominant of these are the mutual aid services provided by sosyete-s in times of sickness and death. Assistance with wakes and death rites seemed to be the most valued services of all. The economic benefits these practices offer individual group members can hardly be overstated, and they have saved many a peasant from economic ruin. But again, personal economic interest is hardly the full story.

As in the rachòt of the atribisyon, people are able to assert and maintain their dignity and humanity through these arrangements, and to gain a certain amount of control over generally unwieldy circumstances. In the sosyete-s, rural Haitians—generally disparaged or dismissed in the larger society—are offered opportunities to perform as effective leaders, as creative artists, as talented musicians, as productive workers, as responsible citizens. They are provided ways to bypass the state courts in regulating local disputes. They are assured of receiving companionship and solidarity in some of the most difficult moments of life, and are equipped with the resources to offer the same to others. They are able to pay homage to the deities and the ancestors in ways they could not afford on their own, and to continue certain traditions that were entrusted to them by their ancestors but have been threatened by the pressures of contemporary life. Finally, they are able to occasionally interrupt what sometimes seems like an ever more back-breaking struggle to get by, and to inject into their lives some flamboyance, extravagance, and celebration.

7

The *Gwoupman Peyizan*

We have tied our umbilical cords together so that we can move our country forward . . . , so that
we can live as humans were meant to live . . . so that we can have decent homes, health clinics,
schools, roads, good hospitals, [so that] we can realize our rights as people, so that we can live
as *humans*. (a leader of peasant women's organizations in the Grand'Anse)

During the past several decades, there has been a marked transformation
in the nature of civic organization in rural Haiti. At the center of this transformation is the emergence and growth of the *gwoupman peyizan* (GP)
movement. *Gwoupman peyizan* (literally, "peasant grouping") is a label used
for a wide variety of local organizations, most of which aim to bring about
social, economic, or political change. They have come of age largely within
the context of externally initiated development and democratization initiatives, and reflect the agendas of such initiatives to a much greater degree
than do the atribisyon-s and the sosyete-s. Thus, while these organizations
share certain characteristics and concerns with more long-standing, more
organically emergent organizations such as the sosyete and the atribisyon,
they exhibit important distinctions.

Sustainable agriculture, preventative health education, adult literacy,
civic education, income generation, human rights, democratization, and
women's issues are among the areas on which the GPs have focused their
energies. Instead of the elaborate array of officers found in the sosyete-s or
the modest and informal leadership arrangements typical of atribisyon-s,
the structures of GPs—like their objectives—tend to resemble more closely
those common to the "new social movements" of contemporary Latin
America. As with the "Old Testament" groups, membership composition is
commonly grounded in kinship ties and residential proximity, though
here, women and young adults are more prominent and often take on
more active leadership roles.

Among the most important characteristics of the GPs is the context they have provided for the rural poor to expose and analyze the structural causes of their impoverishment and disempowerment (see R. Maguire 1990, 31). As a result, these groups have not only had a profound impact on community life in rural Haiti but also have been influential at the national level. They were central to the widespread consciousness-raising and persistent mobilization that led to the 1986 overthrow of the Duvalier regime, in the democratization campaigns that followed the Duvaliers' departure, in the push for a new constitution, in the election of President Aristide in 1990, and in the crusade to bring about his return following the 1991 coup d'état. Yet in analyses of the popular movement in Haiti, GPs have received relatively little attention. As is true for much of the literature on social movements in Latin America, studies of social movements in Haiti tend to focus on organizations that are very large, that are aimed at gaining political power, or that are based in urban areas. Small rural groups are either ignored or considered only tangentially.[1] Thus, while they have enjoyed more visibility in the social sciences than groups like the sosyete-s, thorough descriptions of what GPs are and how they work are scarce.[2] The following case studies respond to that gap by providing a first-hand account of our interactions with several GPs and the organizations that work with them.

The "Shoulder-to-Shoulder" GP of Lakay

Benwa and I headed out of my lakou early on a Sunday afternoon in February. Crossing the creek below Madan Mèsidye's house, we made our way toward Lakay, an abitasyon several hills and valleys beyond Mòn Gagè, at the western edge of the Bamòn zone. As we climbed and descended, climbed and descended, the fruit trees and crops clinging to the dusty mountainsides became more and more sparse. The land around Lakay is dry and rocky, and renowned in the region for its merciless refusals to reward the women and men who till it with yields enough to sustain them. Yet as we descended finally into the heart of Lakay itself, we found ourselves weaving through a thick maze of branches dripping with the leaves of coffee, coconut, citrus, and palm trees. Against the surrounding landscape, these luscious groves gave the lakou-s of the area an oasislike character. At the center of one of these havens we found the home of Klesiyis, the president of the GP Zepòl Sou Zepòl (Shoulder-to-Shoulder) of Lakay.

While we were late according to "clock" time, we arrived before most of the group members. As they waited for the others to come, a few of the female members swept the ground in and around the meeting site, a simple thatch-covered shelter at the edge of the lakou's large packed-dirt yard.

A Kalfounò *gwoupman peyizan* meeting.

Klesiyis greeted us warmly and quickly seated us by the shelter, offering us thick, red-orange slices of a papaya his daughter-in-law had just picked nearby. As we sat and ate, Klesiyis and the others told us about the group. It had started in early 1991, Klesiyis said, when then-president Aristide had called on the population to "put our heads together to help the country change." Although it had stopped meeting for a while during the 1991–94 post-coup era due to widespread attacks on GPs, the group had been functioning fully again since the beginning of 1995 and now had thirty-two members—thirteen women and nineteen men.

They cited maintenance work on the footpaths in their neighborhood and on the Bamòn road as one of their main civic duties. They were interested in instigating other types of local development projects as well, they said, and had begun a community latrine project in 1991. However, because it was to be financed by the Aristide administration, this project fell through when the coup occurred in September of that year. In fact, a chronic shortage of funds was a central focus of many of the group's discussions. Although they had been able to amass eight hundred goud-s by regularly conducting kòve-s for nongroup members, they reported that they would need much more if they were going to complete a latrine project. They were hoping to be given such support by a large IGO that had funded some latrine projects closer to Jérémie.

We had not chatted long before the others began filing in. When the group reached a dozen people (six women and six men), Klesiyis gathered us all in a circle formation on the narrow wooden benches beneath the shelter. Beside Klesiyis sat a young man who, notebook in hand, was the group's secretary. We sang a couple of verses from a Catholic church song used often to convene GP meetings.

Kè:	Chorus:
Fò m di Bondye mèsi; mèsi	I must give the good Lord thanks; thank you
Pou tout sa l fè pou mwen	For all that he has done for me
Se nan fason map viv	It's in the way that I live
Chak jou map di mèsi.	That I daily thank him.
Mwen te dekouraje nan lavi	I had gotten discouraged with life
Pou jan m tap pase mizè	Because of the hardships I was going through
Men lè m rele bay Bondye	But when I called out to God
Li koute m, li pran ka m . . .	He listened to me, He took my needs to heart . . .

After welcoming Benwa and me as "family," Klesiyis began imploring his fellow members to deepen their commitment to the group, adding that they had been getting too dependent on him. He suggested that some of them needed to take more ownership so that when he dies, the group would not fall apart. Noting that many of the members were missing (four late arrivals had brought attendance to sixteen, just half of the group's membership), he said he understood that some of them had gotten discouraged with the group because it had not made much progress in getting funding for projects. "There were a lot of us," he pointed out, "who believed that as soon as the president [Aristide] came back, they were going to send us help." He told those present that while he understood their disappointment, they should not let this cause them to give up on the group.

A woman then spoke up and said that personally, she had gotten discouraged because one of the men had said he did not want to work kòve-s with women, because women do not work as hard as men. "He said that women don't do anything except sit around and talk!" Mumbles, sighs, and gestures of disapproval erupted among the other members. Soon a discussion ensued about the importance of women in the work of the group, in the home, and in the greater society. "Whoever said *that* must not have a mother or a wife," one man concluded. "You cannot be a part of a group,"

Klesiyis added, "if you are *regadan*, if you are always looking out to see if everyone is doing the same amount of work you are."

Klesiyis continued, "They [the Aristide government] have asked us to change, to change the country. . . . So what is change?" After a momentary lapse, one of the members responded:

> When there is food prepared at my house, and I have company, but don't have enough food for everybody; if I have them [the people cooking] prepare a big bowl and set it aside for me, and wait until everyone leaves, and then eat it all. . . . Instead of that, I should divide up the food and tell my guests, "Here's a little sweet potato for you." Then we would all eat. After that, if I am still hungry, I can go out to the fields and try to find something else.

"And what else is change?" Klesiyis asked. Someone offered, "When someone tells you she needs two goud-s, and you have ten on you, and you give that person the two goud-s." Then Klesiyis offered a response of his own: "It is not waiting on people from other places to come and do for us."

This prompted a conversation about the leadership of the Federasyon Peyizan Bamòn (FPB), a peasant group federation based in Nazon and one of several federations to which Zepòl Sou Zepòl belonged. As has been the case for most peasant group federations, the majority of FPB's leaders were not farmers or small commerçantes. They were, rather, residents of Nazon proper. Thus, they were considered townsfolk by many in other areas of Bamòn. Most, moreover, were schoolteachers, employees of Nazon's Catholic missionaries, or small-business owners, and were of a higher socioeconomic standing than the vast majority of the federation's members.

During the preceding few months, FPB had managed to secure from some international aid institutions and the Haitian government a good deal of money and materials for several community development projects. These projects, including a tools project, a fowl distribution project and a latrine project, were ostensibly designed to benefit the whole of FPB's membership. Yet Zepòl Sou Zepòl had benefited little, if at all. As was the case for many of the other GPs we visited in the area, its members felt that FPB leaders had intentionally neglected their concerns. Rather than serving their constituency, FPB officers, they felt, were hoarding the new-found resources for themselves and their *mounpa*-s (friends and family/relations). Benwa and I had seen little reason to dispute these accusations. We had watched a FPB latrine project birth dozens of new latrines in Nazon itself. A number went to the homes of some of the area's most prominent residents, most of whom already had latrines. Only a handful were left to be scattered throughout the rest of the Bamòn rural section. The chickens of the fowl distribution program had traveled much the same trajectory.

At the time of Zepòl Sou Zepòl's meeting, FPB was in the midst of administering its tools project, in which wheelbarrows, pickaxes, and other tools allocated for working on the Bamòn road and footpaths were to be spread throughout the zone. On several occasions, group representatives from Lakay and other outlying areas of the zone had gone to Nazon to request tools, only to be turned down because "they were checked out." FPB leaders, it seemed, were *kouto famasi*-s (pharmacy knives, meaning two-faced) and could not be trusted. "That group [FPB] was founded in 1991," Klesiyis continued, "and I have yet to see a single thing enter Nazon, to do us any good up here. . . . Those guys in Nazon leave me to sit outside while they crowd up next to the cook pot and eat. That's not democracy."

The terms *democracy* and *development* are used liberally in many sectors of the Haitian popular movement and came up repeatedly in our visits with GPs in Bamòn. Noting this, we had begun asking GP members to explain these terms to us, and I took the lead from Klesiyis' comment to do just that. This group's numerous responses were consistent with those we received from many others. Below are a few of the most representative ones:

> If you are going to have development, something new must happen, and it must be something that *everyone* agrees would make the community better. . . . And [it means that] you are advancing, moving forward from where you are, helping all people participate, so that we can all go forward together.
>
> A good literacy center—there are some young men and women who need to know how to read and write, but they have not had that opportunity. We are working at it, but it's as though we need help. We know what we need, what we need to do, but we need some help, help that would allow us to do these things well.
>
> If we had some agricultural [assistance], to show us how to cultivate our fields better, to help us make the earth produce, to get better harvests, that would be a democratic change. . . . Now all we are doing is breaking up the dirt and putting dirt back in its place.
>
> We have money for development projects in our treasury. But that little bit of money is too small to really do anything.
>
> It's the "big man," the one who has money, who can get a hold on all the rich land. . . . The poor folks, they cannot even get enough [land] to work. That's not democracy.
>
> I have to say that to speak truthfully about democracy, I must admit that I don't really understand what it means. It's not clear, because I see lots of people talking about democracy, and they are doing all kinds of things. . . .
>
> If a person, a stranger from Dame Marie [a port town in the Grand'Anse], came by here, and you welcome him, and give him food, and a good place to sleep, and if he needs a little money to get where he needs to go, you give it to him . . . and then when a person from your own neighborhood needs two

goud-s, and you have ten, and you tell him "go fend for yourself"—that is not democracy.

"If there is a person in the community who has a problem and needs to go to Port-au-Prince, if the whole community gets together and collects one hundred goud-s to give her—democracy.

As reflected here, GP members generally wove *democracy* and *development* together in analyzing these terms and often used them interchangeably in discussions about what a society should be. One group member described their interconnectedness this way: "They are different things, but you cannot have one without the other. Really, democracy is development. You cannot have development without democracy. You cannot have democracy without development."

Both, we were told, involve both political and economic rights, and both involve responsibilities as much as rights. For Haiti to be more democratic and in order for it to develop, these rights and responsibilities must be more evenly distributed among its citizens. One leader of the FPB federation said to me: "Do you know what the biggest problem we have in this country is, Djeni? If I can eat and another person can't eat, how are you supposed to build a democracy on that? How do you think we can *mete tèt ansanm* [put our heads together] like that? No, we have to be more uniform."

While many GP members agreed that "we ourselves, we know what needs to happen" in order to bring about democracy and development, they also readily acknowledged that they did not have the resources to realize these goals alone—without some assistance. Assistance was needed both in the form of education and training, as well as in the form of material and financial support. Still, many people were quick to point out that getting "handouts" from foreigners does not constitute a step toward democracy and development. "You open up your bellies and hand them over to the foreigners, and then what do you have to show for it? Nothing!," said a leader of a women's GP in Bamòn during a discussion on alimentary aid.

Conversations I have had about democracy and development with Haitian peasants both within and outside of the gwoupman context have often evolved into conversations about the importance of *respe* (respect) as a governing principle. As one group member put it, "If in a region, democracy hasn't lit the lamp of respect there, development cannot be done." As was the case during the group meeting cited in chapter 1, characterizing the mutual respect that citizens of a democratic country would have one for another often involved critiquing "American" (i.e., U.S.) democracy as a faux democracy—"without respe."

By the time Zepòl Sou Zepòl's discussion about democracy and development was wrapping up, the sun was beginning to set on Lakay, and people were getting concerned about getting their chores done before dark. Thus, after quickly going over their plans for the next couple of weeks, the meeting was concluded with a prayer and another verse of "I Must Give the Good Lord Thanks."

Historical Precedents of the *Gwoupman Peyizan*

In many ways, the history of the GP movement in the Grand'Anse began with the emergence of *konsèy kominotè*-s (literally, "community councils") in the 1960s. As Glenn Smucker reports, the Code Rurale put into place by François Duvalier in 1962 called for "the creation of local administrative councils to assume civilian governance over every rural section through principles of community action" (1983, 378–79). Encouraging such bodies may seem to have been a move toward giving local communities greater autonomy. Most likely Duvalier's objectives were quite the opposite. In fact, this initiative might be more accurately characterized as one among the many directed at securing greater surveillance and control in rural communities, while further centralizing power in the capital. Not insignificantly, it appeared just as Duvalier's infamous Volontaires de la Sécurité Nationale (National Security Volunteers) were beginning to proliferate throughout the countryside.[3]

According to members of some of Bamòn's original kominotè-s, the first task ever given these councils by Duvalier was to "clear brush from the footpaths." The reason, they said, was so his troops would be better able to drive out the *kamoken*-s (antigovernment rebels) he suspected to be lurking in the mountains, plotting revolution. *Gwoupman kominotè-s* (known in Bamòn simply as *kominotè*-s) evolved directly out of these councils. To this day, the kominotè-s of Bamòn regularly clear their local footpaths and often express a keen interest in obtaining better roadways for the areas where they are located.

The konsèy kominotè-s and gwoupman kominotè-s[4] did not begin to proliferate on a large scale until foreign-based organizations and the church got involved. As Smucker explains:

In 1963 the national planning council (CONADEP) stated that community development was a national policy devoted to integrating rural communities into the "rhythm of national progress". . . . In this plan the agency called ONEC was directed to conduct a mass literacy program, to construct rural social centers and potable water systems, to introduce modern agriculture, foster peasant crafts, improve local roads and footpaths. Throughout the 1960s Protestant and Catholic missions and private voluntary agencies organized numerous community councils in rural Haiti. These efforts were primarily of American origin. (G. Smucker 1983, 379)

This foreign involvement in organizing the early kominotè-s established a pattern of association between community-based groups and outside institutions that has become a central feature of the larger GP movement. Like sosyete members, kominotè members often highlight as their groups' "good old days" the period in which they served as local conduits for *manje sinistre*—the food aid sent by the U.S. government. This aid was often handed out to the kominotè-s in exchange for their labor in road-, school-, clinic-, and church-construction projects. Since the aid was administered through the Duvalier government, it is generally "Papa Doc," not the United States, who is gratefully remembered by kominotè members as the donor. "But he forgot about us again," they add with a sigh.

As the years went by, more and more of the aid the kominotè-s occasionally received was administered by foreign NGOs. In the critiques they make of those initiatives, kominotè members reveal that their own understandings of this aid often differed markedly with the understandings of the aiders themselves. What representatives of the sponsoring agencies generally called "collaborations" or instances of "promoting community volunteerism," kominotè members often described as exploitative short-term jobs for which they were not fairly compensated.[5] Citing past projects, Bamòn residents tended to claim that they were not offered just wages or, if the program involved "food for work," that they had not been given all the food they had earned. Again, former participants complained of being "forgotten" after the institutions got out of their sweating muscles what they had needed. Other complaints offered by long-term members focused on certain kominotè leaders who were known to "skim the cream off" much of the aid before it was distributed more widely.

Despite members' complaints about the assistance they have received, the kominotè-s are often criticized by others as being "gimme" groups. In fact, several GP educators and group leaders in Bamòn complained that the kominotè movement had done much to undermine their own efforts to motivate local residents to contribute to community development and social change initiatives as ends in themselves, without expecting "handouts" in return. Kominotè-s, like many sosyete-s, have also been criticized for being "available for sale" to the corrupt Duvalier regime and its political descendants. As Benwa described it:

> They used to call [kominotè-s] to come to meetings—the ones they did each year to preach the government, to make the people applaud and yell, "Long live Duvalier!" In the meetings, they gave them food and money. . . .

They used to hold meetings before elections and give them rum and bread with dried fish. And the candidates would pass by, and throw money on the ground, so the people would say, "There's the candidate with the money, that's the one we're going to elect."

Because of such legacies, Glenn Smucker (1983), along with certain Bamòn residents, feels that "as a rule, community councils do not mediate upwards the political interests of peasant farmers; rather, they serve primarily as channels for foreign social services to rural areas" (433). This perception may be accurate in many instances, yet Benwa and I encountered kominotè-s in Bamòn that had come a long way from the pro-Duvalier rallies of the 1970s. They had joined other gwoupman-s in helping to organize local voting booths for the country's first democratic elections in 1990. During the 1991–94 post-coup era, they had again worked with gwoupman-s in the area to set up underground networks for spreading political news, for organizing local resistance, and for providing support to those forced into hiding. Since the post-coup period, these kominotè-s have continued to be adamantly pro-Aristide. It is surely true that crying "Long live Duvalier!" and "Re-elect Aristide!" are not necessarily radically different stances. However, one of the things that stood out to me as Benwa and I visited kominotè-s in Bamòn was a commitment to political and social change that went well beyond a momentary devotion to particular parties and individuals. By the spring of 1996, for instance, many of them were working with other gwoupman-s in the area to establish *kolektivite teritoryal*-s. (Mandated by the 1987 constitution, these local governing structures are meant to decentralize governmental control.)

In Bamòn, the gwoupman kominotè may be seen as a bridge between more long-standing forms of organization such as the sosyete and the atribisyon, and more recently emergent GPs. At first, it was sometimes difficult for me to distinguish kominotè-s from sosyete-s and atribisyon-s for they carry out kòve-s in much the same way. Like those groups, kominotè-s work on a rotating basis in the fields of their members and sometimes sell their labor to others in the community. One also might find a kominotè conducting a house-roofing kòve, carrying a sick member to the hospital in Jérémie, or providing the coffin, rum, sugar, oil, and soap for the wake of one of their members. Some, though not all, kominotè-s have musical ensembles to "heat up" their processions and work sessions, and most have flags. None of these traits are consistently found in other GPs in Bamòn. Plus, the kominotè-s' memberships and rosters of officers tend to resemble those of sosyete-s more than most gwoupman-s, which rarely have more than thirty members. Benwa put it this way: "The kominotè-s is almost the same thing as the sosyete-s, except they are more concerned with development."

Adopting many of the priorities and principles of more recently established GPs seems to have enriched kominotè-s in many ways and increased their ability to influence and participate in positive social change in Haiti. At the same time, some of the advantages they have reaped from continuing "older" organizational practices should lead us to hesitate from accepting analyses such as Clerisme's. He characterizes the trajectory of contemporary kominotè-s (and the GP movement in general) as a movement away from outdated vestiges of "traditional peasant culture": "All objective and clear-sighted observers must admit that in the case of the Haitian peasantry, the apathy and mistrustfulness of the inhabitants are in the process of being transformed into a more constructive mode based on confidence" (1978, 15).

The history of the gwoupman kominotè features a myriad of mergers, compromises, and conflicts between what might be called "organic" philosophies, methodologies, and concerns, and externally inspired or directed ones. In this way it is both consistent with the larger political, economic, and cultural history of Haitian society—from its inception a "creolizing" one—and a precursor to later stages of the GP movement.

Consolidating a Movement

Whereas in the 1960s, foreign-sponsored community development programs targeting rural Haitians concentrated on material and technical assistance, the 1970s saw an increased concern with the underlying "root causes" of poverty. As Smucker and Noriac note, this shift had far reaching consequences (1996, 38) as it led to peasants questioning more boldly than ever before the social and economic injustices to which they had been subjected.

Among those leading the shift were various Catholic church-related institutions, such as the Justice and Peace Commission, an advocacy group comprised of clergy and lay church members, and CARITAS, an organization that had previously worked mostly in the area of relief aid.[6] Also central to the new movement were Catholic-sponsored Christian community development centers, the first of which had been founded in 1964 in Laborde. These centers focused on training grass-roots organizers called "animators." In general terms, training women and men to be, respectively, *animatris*-s and *animatè*-s involves equipping them to motivate residents of a locale to organize into small community groups; guide these groups in a process of reflecting together on social problems; and teach group members how to work together effectively for positive social, economic, or political change. Animators have been trained to educate groups and individuals in technical skills, too, such as sustainable agricultural techniques, preventative health strategies, income generation, literacy instruction, finance management, water purification, human rights, civic rights and responsibilities, and women's empowerment.

As animation work developed and spread, new GPs, TKLs (Little Church Communities),[7] and urban community groups like the neighborhood committees sprouted up all over the country, even as the konsèy kominotè-s and gwoupman kominotè-s of the 1960s and early 1970s began to decline. The GPs that have developed since then are often referred to in Bamòn as *gwoupman tètansanm*-s. Literally meaning "heads-together," *tètansanm* refers to a spirit of solidarity, cooperation, and unity. Following the lead of Bamòn residents, I use this label in discussing GPs that have been associated with the "animation" movement.

In the Grand'Anse

As previously suggested, the GPs and other elements of Haiti's popular movement played a central role in the countrywide explosion of protest and resistance that culminated in 1986 downfall of the Duvalier regime. In the months following Jean-Claude's flight, "*Baboukèt la tonbe!*" (The muzzle is off!) became a popular saying, as traditionally marginalized Haitian citizens proclaimed themselves free and worthy to speak, act, and organize in their own interests. Gwoupman tètansanm-s (GTs) multiplied rapidly in this context. Robert Maguire explains that they "surge[d] forward, initiating action programs designed to confront—and resolve—fundamental problems that kept them poor" (1990, 33).

At the center of this movement in the Grand'Anse region was a program I shall call the Project for Social Change (PSC). Although PSC had been founded in 1980, it did not have a great impact on rural communities in the Grand'Anse until the mid-1980s, when a new director moved its headquarters out of Jérémie to a village several kilometers away. This Haitian priest, determined to transform the project into one of empowerment for rural Haitians, set to work building from the ground up what is now one of the country's premiere animasyon training centers. He continued to run the center during my time in the region, along with a host of coworkers—foreign and Haitian, clergy and nonclergy, paid and volunteer, degreed and illiterate.

It was from the work of the PSC that many of the first Grand'Anse GTs emerged. By the time I moved to the area in 1995, PSC was working directly or indirectly with hundreds of GTs scattered throughout the Grand'Anse department, providing them with training and material assistance in such areas as:

sustainable agriculture
preventive health
women's empowerment
civic rights and responsibilities (education on the rights people do and do
    not have under the laws of the country, as well as voter education and
    motivation)
animal husbandry
financial management and accounting
Bible study (generally from a liberation theology perspective)
group formation, cooperative philosophies, and organizational skills

The project has also sponsored a wide array of small-scale development projects focused on social change that is sustainable and under autonomous local control, including:

a Creole pig (*kochon kreyòl*) repopulation project
a microlending project[8]
literacy centers
potable water projects
a rabbit distribution project
a reforestation project
homemaking projects, such as soap making
an economic cooperative and a community store, where the cooperative's
    bulk goods are sold at subsidized prices[9]

The Project for Social Change

Much of the education carried out at the PSC center reflects the pedagogical principles promoted by Brazilian educator Paulo Freire, including critical consciousness, co-investigation, community-based praxis, and collective self-empowerment (Freire 1983). One basic technique GT members have been taught, for example, is the praxis method, or in Creole "GRA,"[10] meaning *Gade* (Observe), *Reflechi* (Reflect), *Aji* (Act). An animatris specializing in women's empowerment summed up the work of the GTs in this way: "We have tied our umbilical cords together so that we can move our country forward . . . , so that we can live as humans were meant to live . . . so that we can have decent homes, health clinics, schools, roads, good hospitals, [so that] we can realize our rights as people, so that we can live as *humans*."

Among the different categories of GT representatives who have been trained at the center are *ajan chanjman*-s, or "change agents." This post was established in early 1991, as PSC realized the need to supplement the extension work of its staff by training group members themselves to be animators at the neighborhood level. According to their training materials, the change agents had as their calling "to bring the idea of change to the localities where they live. . . . To help people in the localities where they live understand the reasons for their suffering, to study them together, and to search for solutions to those problems."

Group representatives, such as the change agents who come to the center to be trained for working in their own communities, are not paid by PSC but are expected to carry out their work in the spirit of *bonvolonté* (goodwill/volunteerism). This stipulation has been as much a matter of principle as of PSC's very limited budget. Despite occasional pressures from some group representatives, the leaders of PSC have been resolute in their resistance to becoming a "handout" organization like so many of the NGOs, IGOs, and missions working in Haiti. (Many of these organizations, they sometimes complained, had undermined their own efforts to encourage development that is genuinely grass-roots, community-based, and sustainable.)

As we have seen, in rural Haiti music is commonly employed as a tie that binds and defines collectivities of people. The music of the GT movement is no exception. In fact, one of the best ways to get a sense of the philosophies and flavors of the sort of community organization promoted by PSC is to listen to the songs sung in PSC training sessions and during GT meetings. Following are some of the most popular (see also chapter 3):

Lit Chanjman	**The Struggle for Change**
Ké:	Chorus:
Lit pou pote yon chanjman	The struggle to bring about change
Se yon lit ki di anpil	Is a very hard struggle
Si n angage tout bon vre	But if we are truly committed
Se sèten na rive!	We're certain to succeed!
Poukisa nou rasanble?	Why have we come together?
Paske n wè nou twò gaye.	Because we are too dispersed.
E kisa nou vin cheche?	And what is it we're seeking?
Plis fòs pou n chanje peyi n.	More strength for changing our country.
Poukisa dwe gen chanjman?	Why does there have to be change?
Paske jan nap viv la pa bon.	Because the state we're in is no good.
E kisa pou nou chanje?	And what needs changing?

Tou sa k anpeche n viv byen.

Everything preventing us from living well.

Nèg Lakay, Kote Ou?
Kè:
Nèg lakay, kote nou ye?
Ann pote kole pou n fè lit la mache.

Lit la di, nou vle avanse

Annou ransanble pou wè si na rive.

Nap viv nan yon peyi kote nèg pa vle wè nèg
Nèg ap trayi zanmi l pou yo kap fè gwo lajan
Yo touye tout yon pèp kape chache libète

Nèg lakay, kote nou?

Fanm yo kote nou ye? Fòk nou di kisa nou ye!
Lit la gen anpil plas, fanm yo gen wòl an primyè
Mare tèt nou sere, kenbe men pou n avanse

Negès yo kote nou?

Home Folks, Where Are You?
Chorus:
Home folks, where are you?
Let us join together to advance the struggle
The struggle is hard, we must move forward
Let's get together to see if we can do it.

We're living in a country torn by animosity
People are betraying their friends for money
They're assassinating a population for seeking after liberty
Home folks, where are you?

Women, where are you? You must say where you stand!
The struggle has room for all, and women have a role at the helm
Tighten your headscarves, hold hands, and let's go forward
Where are you, women?

Si Bèf Te Konn Valè Li
Kè:
Si bèf te konn valè li
Se pa nenpòt ti gason
Ki tap vinn foure kòd nan tèt li
Si peyizan te konn valè li
Se pa nenpòt vò anyen

Ki ta vin chante kòk sou tèt li.

Abitan fòk nou konpran sa
Peyizan, fòk ou konpran sa
Si yo fin rich sou tèt nou
Se paske se nou k bay

Si yo fin eksplwate nou
Se paske se nou k vle.

If the Cow Knew Its Value
Chrous:
If the cow knew its value
It wouldn't let just any little guy
Come and tie a rope around its neck
If peasants knew their strength
They wouldn't let any old good-for-nothing
Come and climb all over them.

Country folk, we must understand this
Peasants, we have to understand this
If they've gotten rich at our expense
It's because we've provided them with everything they have

If they have exploited us
It's because we have let them.

Vini, Non

Vini non, vini non, wa wè kote n te ye

Vini non, vini non, wa wè kote nou ye

Vini non, vini non, wa wè kote n prale

*Vini non, vini non, wa wè sa n gen
   pou n fè*

Ké:
Woy, jounen sa, mesyedanm
Woy, se premye jou n wè sa

Woy, nou komanse lit la
E nape rive kanmen.

Lè nou gade peyi n, nou wè se divizyon

Lè nou chache lespwa, nou wè se kout baton

Lè nou chita koze, nou wè se tèt kole

Annou kole zepòl pou n wè si na rive.

Lezòt tonbe pale, nou menm nou vle travay

Lezòt tonbe kraze, nou menm nou vle bati.

Lè m gade fòmasyon, se li k pi gwo zouti

Avèk yon bon dyaloòg, na fin òganize n.

Lapli Demokrasi
Ke:
Lapli demokrasi tonbe
Lavalas espwa desann

Li lè pou n al òganize nou.

Nan tan pase, nou te gaye
Makout te divize n

Come Join Us

Come join us, come on, you'll see
   where we are

Come join us, come on, you'll see
   where we are

Come join us, come on, you'll see
   where we are heading

Come join us, come on, you'll see what
   we have to do.

Chorus:
Woy, today, ladies and gentlemen
Woy, this is the first time we've seen
   anything like it
Woy, we have started the struggle
And we are going to succeed despite
   everything.

When we look at the country, we see
   division

When we search for hope, we find the
   blows of batons

When we gather to talk, we discover
   togetherness

Let's put our shoulders together and
   see if we can arrive.

The others talk, but us, we want to
   work

The others beat on each other, but we
   want to built

When I look at training, I see it's the
   greatest tool

With real dialogue, we can get
   ourselves organized.

The Rain of Democracy
Chorus:
The rain of democracy is falling
The cleansing floods of hope are
   descending
The time has arrived to get organized.

In the past, we were dispersed
The [tonton] makout-s had divided us

Kounye a nou gen libète	But now we are liberated
Li lè pou n al òganize nou.	It's time to get organized.
Yon sèl nou fèb, ansanm nou fò	Alone we are weak, together we are strong
Ansanm ansanm, nou se lavalas	Together-together, we are a cleansing flood.
Pou n dechouke tout sa ki mal	We'll uproot all that is bad
Pou n plante tout sa ki bon	So we can plant all that is good
Li lè pou n al òganize nou.	The time has arrived to get organized.

With these songs, the PSC encourages peasants to unify and organize; to recognize and criticize the oppressions and injustices they have suffered; to take responsibility for bringing about social change; to challenge the status quo and the powers that be; to respect themselves and insist on better treatment; and to persevere in the belief that positive change is possible. These are hardly politically neutral ambitions. Indeed, if successful, they would turn Haiti's traditional social, political, and economic structures flat on their heads—something formal democracy has thus far been unable to do.

It is not surprising, then, that PSC's work has been challenged on occasion, and sometimes violently. The director and most of his staff have had to go into hiding repeatedly. During the 1991–94 post-coup era, many GTs and group leaders were also targeted. "We were like little sheep surrounded by rabid dogs," a GT member explained. Many fled the area. Some boarded one of the hundreds of rickety boats then leaving Grand'Anse's shores in an effort to make it to Miami. Others went to Port-au-Prince. But most of the change agents and nearly all of the PSC staff stuck it out. Many PSC-affiliated GTs and GT federations met secretly (gatherings of more than two people were forbidden at the time), disseminated resistance tracks throughout the zone, and collected food, money, and medicines to send to those in hiding. An expatriate nun living at the PSC center later told me as we talked about the population's perseverance through this hard, hungry, terrifying time, "This is a people that has resistance, that has courage. They plant, they don't harvest anything. They go back and they plant again."[11]

Gwoupman Fanm Vanyan-s

> When poor women are struggling to put food in their mouths they are actually doing much more than that—that is, . . . they are actively constructing a way of life, resisting forms of oppression, and dreaming of a better world. (Escobar and Alvarez 1992, 11)

One type of PSC-affiliated GT is the *gwoupman fanm vanyan* (GFV), or "strong women's grouping."[12] One of the most dynamic and resilient sectors of the GT movement, these groups—most of which are composed entirely of women—have many of the same trademark characteristics found in the other GTs. They have similar rosters of officers: president, vice-president, secretary, treasurer, and perhaps a councillor. Their memberships tend to range between twelve and thirty members. They meet weekly or biweekly. Their activities and discussions reflect a concern for carrying out community-development initiatives, as well as for promoting "critical consciousness" and challenging larger-scale societal injustices. But they are also distinct, for among their central objectives are promoting women's rights, addressing women's special needs, and empowering women to do those things themselves.

Due to their central place in Haiti's informal economy as well as their roles as traditional health care providers, spiritual leaders, and increasingly, heads of households, Haitian peasant women are commonly referred to as the *potomitan* (the center pillar, or backbone) of Haitian society. Yet, as in much of the world, Haiti's women are in general even poorer, less educated, more malnourished, more overworked, less well represented politically, and less protected by the law than the nation's men. Some women friends in Bamòn, in reflecting on their never-ending and ever more painstaking efforts to provide for their families, have told me that they were "beating water to make butter." There was no reason to think they were actually going to arrive at butter, they explained. But they had to keep beating and beating, because if they stopped, they would have given up hope; "and if you give up hope you are finished." The women in GFVs see themselves as searching for more promising alternatives to giving up than trying to "beat" out a better life.

Most of the women who join GFVs have already belonged to one or more "mixed" (mixed-gender) GTs. Unlike most sosyete-s and atribisyon-s, GTs often have as many female as male members, and sometimes more. Few male GT members hesitate to acknowledge the central importance of women in the movement, and many agree, as a regional GT coordinator put it, that "everything goes better if the women are helping to run it." However, GTs have not been immune from the effects of the male privilege that characterizes Haitian culture and the cultures of the aid organizations with which GTs have worked. Although there is significant integration of women into the leadership ranks of mixed groups, most of the highest positions tend to be held by men.[13] And as is the case worldwide, for the most part, the "meatiest" development projects, such as those involving income generation, have been placed by sponsoring agencies into the hands of men's groups or the male leaders of mixed groups and federations.

A Bamòn *gwoupman fanm vanyan* performs a service project (cleaning the home of a sick widower in the community and bringing him food, water, and firewood).

As GT women have been introduced at PSC training sessions and conferences to "critical consciousness" philosophies and, more specifically, to the field of "women's empowerment," many have become dissatisfied with such discriminations. More aware of their particular needs, more assured of their right to address them, and more confident of their capacities to do so, women have increasingly formed groups on their own. As one women's group member said, "When we look around, we see that the men get all the opportunities. But all the while, women are slaving away, without their value being recognized. Women are half, men are half. We must reclaim our rights as women."

While visiting GFVs, it was striking to observe many women, whom we knew to speak only rarely and timidly in mixed-up group meetings, be assertive, outspoken, and passionately opinionated in this context.

In discussing women's organizations in the South some scholars have distinguished between "feminine groups" and feminist groups. Haynes clarifies that whereas the former are "concerned with an array of material concerns, from consumption issues to questions of sociopolitical status," the latter "pursue what are known as 'strategic' objectives," for example, explicitly political women's rights agendas (Haynes 1997, 128–29; see also Baldez 1998). This distinction may prove useful in other regions, but in Haiti as well as in other Latin American and Caribbean societies, women's groups tend to fall somewhere between the two categories.[14]

While reclaiming their voices and their rights as women constitutes an important part of the agenda of most GFVs, the groups I knew in Bamòn insisted repeatedly that they had not formed in *opposition* to men or to the male leadership of the larger GT movement. They tended to see themselves instead as a necessary component of a whole, healthy, and strong GT movement. A PSC staff member working in the area of "women's promotion" put it this way: "The women's struggle is not a struggle by and for women only, but women and men, to change the face of society. . . . If you say 'that's a women's issue, it's not a national issue,' [that means] you do not yet understand."

She went on to draw connections and comparisons between the rape of women on the one hand and, on the other, abuses against poor people of both genders by the military during the post-coup era; between the subjugation and exploitation of Haitian women by Haitian men, and the subjugation and exploitation of the Haitian people by foreign powers; and between Haitian women's dependency on local patriarchal systems, and the dependency of all Haitians on international political and economic systems. She and most other GFV members with whom we spoke agreed wholeheartedly with Kaufman when he says:

> The underlying problem shaping differential participation is not inequality between men and women in the narrow sense but the very conception of power that has become hegemonic in patriarchal societies throughout the world. This is a definition in which power is understood as the capacity of certain humans to control and dominate other humans and control of social and natural resources. Such a conception of power is not simply a matter of ideology but is the organizing principle that is embedded in a vast range of political, social and economic relations. . . . Nevertheless . . . men's own capacities for participation are distorted and limited through this process. In other words, differential participation negatively affects men as well as women, although differentially of course and, in most cases, not as severely.[15]
> (1997, 154)

One of the GFVs Benwa and I came to know best was the Gwoupman Fanm Bwamari. This group was based in Bwamari, a village located in Anwomòn, a rural section bordering Bamòn to the south. I had first learned of this group while doing human rights work with the United Nations in 1993. As our Jérémie-based observer team tried to document human rights violations in the region, we were sometimes given invaluable help by citizens willing to take enormous risks to report violations to us. One of the groups that stood out in this way was Gwoupman Fanm Bwamari. At times, members would walk several hours to our Jérémie headquarters to report a violation. At other times, they would send notes with commerçantes on their way to the Jérémie market. Some of the women even met with us during our investigative visits to the Anwomòn zone (an especially risky move).

I rediscovered this group in December 1995 as they gathered for their weekly meeting on the porch of Bwamari's Catholic schoolhouse. Since the reinstatement of President Aristide to power in 1994, Gwoupman Fanm Bwamari has met there nearly every Sunday afternoon. This Sunday, twenty-six members had gathered.[16] As usual, the group launched the meeting with a GT song. The president, Madan Bris, pulled out of her bag a well-worn mimeographed song sheet she had gotten at a PSC conference the year before and chose "Òganizasyon," a song popular among both women's groups and mixed groups. After introducing it with a short pep talk on the importance of the women organizing together, she began:

Òganizasyon, òganizasyon	Organization, organization
Òganizasyon pèp la se li nou bezwen.	Popular organization, that's what we need.
Èske nou vle rete tout tan	Do we want to remain like this forever
Ap mache tout tan, tout tan sou dominasyon?	Plodding along all the time under domination?
Se nou ki konnen	We're the ones who must decide
Si n pa òganize n	If we don't get organized
Se nou ki konnen.	We're the ones who decide.

The group, already familiar with the tune and lyrics, took little prompting. Before we had finished the first round of the chorus, most of the women were standing and clapping hands. By the time we belted out the second verse, everyone was dancing.

Èske nou vle rete tout tan	Do we want to remain like this forever
Ap pase tout tan, tout tan ap di Bondye bon?	Passing away the time, always saying, "God is good."[17]
Se nou ki konnen	We're the ones who must decide
Si n pa òganize n	If we don't get organized
Se nou ki konnen.	We're the ones who decide.

Inspired and energized, members began to compose verses on the spot, drawing from the realities weighing on their minds.

Èske nou vle rete tout tan	Do we want to remain like this forever
Ap mache tout tan, tout tan	Trying to get by all the time, without
nan pwen lopital?	decent medical care?
Se nou ki konnen	We're the ones who must decide
Si n pa òganize n	If we don't get organized
Se nou ki konnen.	We're the ones who decide.
Èske nou vle rete tout tan	Do we want to remain like this forever.
Ap mache tout tan, tout tan	Struggling along all the time without
pa gen bon lekòl?	adequate schools?
Se nou ki konnen	We're the ones who must decide
Si n pa òganize n	If we don't get organized
Se nou ki konnen.	We're the ones who decide.

When the song ended and we caught our breath and retreated to our seats, the group's vice-president said a short prayer. Madan Bris then read to us from the Bible. The verses she had chosen for the day were from the Book of Proverbs. They contrasted people whose words and behaviors are wise with those who engage in backbiting and pettiness. When she finished, Madan Bris continued to follow a typical GT meeting pattern by asking simply, "What do you see in these verses?" Gradually, responses came forth. A woman said she heard "that we must have patience in all things." Another member talked about a "sister" who had been on good terms with her until "the works of an ignorant person" had caused a rift between them. Another added that her father had told her just before he died, "My child when you have a good friend, don't work kòve with her." When a couple of other members commented on how "just a little word" can break up a whole group of people, it began to dawn on me that they were all alluding to an actual conflict between two Gwoupman Fanm Bwamari members. What ensued was an exchange of confrontations, pacifications, defenses, and chastisements between the two disputing individuals and their fellow group members.

This discussion illustrates how the meetings of GPs (both kominotè-s and GTs) like the meetings of the sosyete-s, offer their members opportunities to regulate disagreements and tensions in a controlled, supportive environment where others may offer opinions or solutions. Group members might come to a consensual "judgment" on the case, or might advise the parties on what they should do to absolve themselves and put the dispute behind them. That day, however, the women never arrived at a final resolution. Instead, Madan Bris eventually closed the discussion by giving a short lecture to the women on the importance of working out their differences. She then moved on to the next item of business: the elections coming up in mid-December.

The centerpiece of those elections was to be the presidential race. Aristide, who was not constitutionally eligible to run for reelection, had encouraged his former prime minister, Rény Préval, to run. The Lavalas platform supporting Préval was Aristide's own and had taken its slogan, "*Rendevou bò tab la*" (Meeting around the table), directly from some of Aristide's public addresses. (Chapter 3 introduced the Aristide-inspired motto "Souke Tab La" [Shake the Table] from the 1980s.) Reflective of the changes that had since taken place on the national political scene and of the international community's push for "reconciliation" between the victims and perpetrators of past atrocities, this later slogan proposed that Lavalas and Préval would bring *all* Haitians, rich and poor, urban and rural, "around the table" to make decisions about the direction of their country. While there was a typically crowded roster of parties, platforms, and candidates (fourteen candidates appeared on the final ballot), the Lavalas platform—and candidate Préval—were the overwhelming favorites.[18]

"Are we voting?" Madan Bris asked the women. "Yes!" they responded in unison. But then some of the women reported that many of their acquaintances were saying they were not going to vote this time—a concern I had heard in several other gwoupman meetings.[19] Madan Bris responded that she wanted to make sure everyone in their group, at least, "has only one rendezvous." Spontaneously, the women began chanting "*bò tab la, bò tab la, bò tab la*" (at the table, at the table, at the table). Madan Bris then explained to them exactly where to "make the cross" on the ballot (right below "the table").[20] "*Menmsi n analfabèt, nou pa bèt!*" she exclaimed. Playing on the rhyme in the Haitian terms for illiterate (*analfabèt*) and beast (*bèt*), this phrase asserts, "We may be illiterate but we're not [dumb] beasts!" "I may be poor," someone added, "but I *never* eat under the table!"

Returning to the topic of the greater community's participation in the elections, one woman suggested that "there are a lot of people who are discouraged." She explained, "They say every other place has been benefiting and we never see anything [from assistance programs]," and then, "but we ourselves, we won't get discouraged." "People say they are tired of voting for nothing," another offered.[21] These comments prompted a heated conversation about how they had been betrayed by their government officials, particularly those at the departmental level. The Grand'Anse's departmental "delegate," an appointed position meant to be a liaison between the local population and the national government, was from the Bwamari-Anwomòn area. As was commonly the case in Anwomòn GTs, it was he who was most bitterly critiqued in this meeting. "He asks and asks and asks [for aid] in our name, but doesn't share with us any of what he gets." Their complaint echoed widespread suspicions that the delegate was using funds he had secured from governmental and international donors for his own enrichment and for that of his friends and family in Jérémie, rather than for developing the region's infrastructure or helping its neediest citizens. He had "forgotten that he came from the common folk."

The women also cited as a major cause for voter disinterest the failure of the economic situation to get any better: "Coffee prices have gone down, down, *down*. It was fifteen goud-s [per pound] and now I think it's six goud-s. Plus, everything else is getting more expensive, so you can't buy anything at all." That their money was buying less and less in the marketplace, even as the produce they tried to sell lost value, was a perception consistent with economic surveys confirming that the nation's economy, having suffered tremendously during the post-coup era, had failed to recover even to the desperately poor state it had been in before 1991. Moreover, there seemed to be no end in sight.[22]

That things were so bad, the women insisted, was not Aristide's fault. "His hands have been tied," they agreed, by "the international community." And by wealthy Haitians. They discussed reports they had heard that the business elite, threatened by the prospect of populist rule, had been stockpiling staple goods to drive up prices and foment discontent with the government and, as a consequence, disinterest in the democratic process. We cannot let this keep us from going to the polls, a younger woman insisted, offering this reasoning:

> For myself, I am a *machann* [market woman/commerçante], and it's true that when I do my calculations, I see a lot of things have gotten worse. . . . They are trying to discourage us—so that we won't vote "at the table" again. In other words, they are holding onto the flour, they are hiding the rice, so that we won't vote for Préval . . . [They know that] when the nose takes a lick, the eyes shed tears!

Repeating phrases like those I had heard many times during the 1991–94 post-coup period as poor Haitians asserted their willingness to suffer the hunger pangs of the embargo if it would lead to the return of their president, some of the women chimed in to say, "We've got coconuts, we'll *make* oil!" "We've got sour oranges, we'll make juice!" A member continued:

> If the "big men" in town have anything, it's because we provide it to them. If we don't carry our beans down to the cities, they won't eat beans. If we don't carry our oranges down there, they won't drink juice. But us, we don't need them. So we can't let them fool us into serving their interests! We can't let ourselves be trumped in this game.

The discussion ended as a member stood up and exclaimed, "*Mezanmi!* We've gotta heat ourselves up and get going on this! *Chofe! Chofe! Chofe!*"

The meeting wrapped up soon thereafter. Lasting just under an hour, it was shorter than usual, since several members we're to attend a *nevenn* funeral rite for a local resident who had died recently. The meeting was dismissed with a song popular among TKLs (little church communities) and GTs:

O Lespri Sen	Oh, Holy Spirit
Desann sou nou	Descend on us
Nou gen yon misyon pou Ayiti.	We have a mission for Haiti.
O Lespri Sen	Oh, Holy Spirit
Desann sou nou	Descend on us
Nou gen yon misyon pou latè a.	We have a mission for the Earth.

Just an hour's walk down the path, in the Bamòn neighborhood of Zamann, another gwoupman fanm vanyan discussed many of the same issues at their Sunday afternoon meeting. The Zamann group's president, Sè[23] Sara, often seemed to have a more difficult time than Madan Bris at eliciting the enthusiastic participation of her group's generally more timid membership. Having attended a number of sessions at the PSC center, Sè Sara was well versed in the principles of community organization, local activism, and women's rights, and was passionate about bringing this knowledge back to her group.[24] Discussions in the Zamann GFV, then, were often punctuated by animated mini-sermons from Sè Sara on the importance of women thinking for themselves, having confidence in themselves, reflecting critically on their society, and pulling together to change the way things are. Sometimes her members cheered her on, and sometimes they simply stared blankly back at her.

The week before (in late November), Benwa and I had arrived at their meeting to find Sè Sara asking the circle of women gathered about her on benches in the yard of Zamann's Catholic meetinghouse, "If someone is suffering next to you, and you give her a little corn, or a slice of breadfruit, or some rice, have you truly helped that person?" "No!" the women responded, taking her lead. To really help a person, Sè Sara continued, "You have to work for *justice*, for a society where one person doesn't weigh more on the scales than anybody else." She went on to expound upon the importance of the upcoming elections, eliciting assurance from the group members that they were going to vote and to urge their friends and family members to do the same.

As she talked about the importance of taking responsibility for the well-being of one's community, this prompted her to begin singing a GFV song, "Si N Pa Pale Wòch Ap Pale" (If We Don't Speak Out the Rocks Will Speak Out). The rest of the women gradually joined in.

Kè:	Chorus:
Fanm yo si n pa pale wòch va pale	Women, if we don't speak out, the rocks will speak out
Pou di tout maswife fanm ap monte	To tell of the persecutions we confront
Fanm yo si n pa rele mouton va rele	Women, if we don't cry out, the sheep will cry out
Pou di tout enjistis fanm ap sipòte.	To tell of the injustices we are bearing.
Enjistis sosyete a sou nou	Social injustices, they bear down on us
Enjistis lafanmi lan sou do n pi rèd	Injustices in the family, a heavier burden still
Enjistis gwo zouzoun yo, tonnè!	The injustices of the ruling class— enough!
Nap rele anmwe! Anmwe! Kote fanm yo?	We're calling out for help! Help! Where are you, women?
Bourike nan jaden an se nou	Laboring hard in the fields, that's us
Tchitchile nan komès la sou nou pi rèd	Slaving away in the markets, an even greater task
Pèseptè chifonnen nou, tonnè!	Meanwhile, the rich merchants tear us apart—enough!
Nap rele anmwe! Anmwe! Kote fanm yo?	We're calling out for help! Help! Where are you, women?
Tout travay domestik yo se nou	All the domestic chores, they are ours
Edikasyon timoun yo sou nou pi rèd	The education of the children, on us too
Vye mouche pa konprann, tonnè!	Our old men don't understand— enough!
Nap rele anmwe! Anmwe! Kote fanm yo?	We're calling out for help. Help! Where are you, women?

Sè Sara then began to stress the connection between larger social injustices and the abuse of women in the context of the home and family. She talked about the women of irresponsible husbands having to take full responsibility for child care, as well as for generating the income needed to put food on the table. "And then he comes home and grabs his bowl of food and devours it with no gratitude." Women must look these common, everyday events in the face, she suggested, and name them. "What do you call that?: EN-JI- . . ." "TIS!" the others shouted back, "Injustice!" "And who was it," Sè Sara asked at one point, "who put Aristide in as president?" "Women!" they cried. She said that even though it was not a well-known fact, women had also given invaluable support to some of their country's first heroic leaders, such as Toussaint, Dessalines, and Christophe.

Later, during one of the group's December meetings, she offered a short but equally impassioned lecture on the importance of knowing the history of the revolution and the founding of Haiti. "But are we liberated, women?" she demanded, when she finished that talk. "No!" they replied. "And what do we lack?" After a moment of hesitation, one woman replied, "We're not willing to live as brother and sister." Others added that the population lacked brotherly love and *tètansanm* (solidarity/unity). "*Linyon fè lafòs!*" (Unity is strength!) a member offered, repeating the motto on the nation's flag. "If we don't take our liberation into our own hands," Sè Sara insisted, "nobody's going to do it for us!" This discussion led to the singing of another GFV song, "Aba Polemik Ant Gason Ak Fanm!" (Down With the Battle between the Sexes!).

Kè:	Chorus:
Revolisyon pèp la pa kap avanse	The revolution of the people cannot succeed
Lè fanm ak gason chita nan polemik antre yo	If men and women are fighting among themselves
Gason deklare mwen siperyè a fanm	The man declares he's superior to the woman
Fanm menm deklare mwen pap ret ak gason	The woman herself declares, "I'm finished with men!"
Mezanmi! Ann sere kole	C'mon, friends! We've got to get together
Fòk pèp la libere!	The people must be liberated!
Baton k sou do fanm yo	The same batons beating the backs of women
Li sou do gason tou	Are beating on men's backs, too
Ann nou rekonèt, nou genyen menm pwoblèm	We must recognize that we all have the same problems
Nou gen menm lenmi	That we have the same enemies.
Anpil vye pwoblèm ki fè nou dozado	The problems that make us turn our backs on each other
Sa se konsekans konplo yo fè sou do n	They are actually caused by the plots
San nou pa konprann.	Of those who want us all to fail.
Ni fanm ni gason pran reskonsablite n	Women and men alike have to take responsibility
Lite pou chanje tout sosyete pinèz	For struggling to change this society
Kap simen lanmò.	Where parasites are sucking out our life.

Like the Bwamari GFV and many other GTs, the Zamann group often utilized the Christian scriptures for illustration and inspiration. During the

December meeting, the passage 2 Timothy 1:7 fueled a discussion on the importance of women taking responsibility to change their situation. Members found the last two verses especially inspiring: "Hence I remind you to rekindle the gift of God that is within you through the laying on of my hands; for God did not give us a spirit of timidity but a spirit of power and love and self-control."[25]

As in kominotè and sosyete meetings, well-known proverbs and sayings are also drawn on heavily in GT meetings. During the November meeting, Sè Sara had used "*De vye tach pa kouvri kay*" (A couple of worn-out old pieces of palm tree bark can't cover a house) and "*Lè marengwen ap vole, ou pa konn kiyès ki mal, kiyès ki fimèl*" (When mosquitoes fly, you can't tell the males from the females) to emphasize that it will take both women and men giving their all for the situation of Haitian women to get better. If a man is conscientious, she explained, he will take responsibility for making things change. At that point, Benwa offered another common saying, "*Direktè kreten, pwofesè kreten, elèv kreten, lekòl kraze*" (The principal's negligent, the teacher's negligent, the student's negligent—school falls apart). A member added, "Women *always* take *their* responsibilities seriously. . . . Even if the man beats her, curses her, the woman keeps reaching out and offering him his plate [of food] with respect." "*Mezanmi*, sisters!" the woman sitting next to her sighed.

Soon someone added that they should work with other groups of women and called on still another proverb, "*Yon sèl dwèt pa manje kalalou*" (One finger on its own can't eat stew). Other topics the group discussed during those two meetings included the poor state of schooling in the area and how it constituted yet another injustice. They talked about making plans to meet with a few other GPs in the area about getting the latrine at the Savanèt school repaired, but they set no dates. They would either have to find a source of funding, Sè Sara pointed out, or take up a collection in order to fund such a project. They also discussed the group's recent enrollment in PSC's microcredit project and planned times to travel to the center's store to buy bulk goods to divide among themselves and sell.

The GFV songs, like the songs of other GTs, provide a window into the central concerns of the groups that sing them. These are some of the most popular among the GFVs Benwa and I visited.

Im Nasyonal Fanm Ayisyen	The Haitian Women's National Anthem
Nou menm fanm peyizan, nou jire devan Bondye	We women of Haiti, we swear before the Lord
Nap goumen jouk sa kaba pou peyi nou kab libere	We'll struggle until this crisis is past us and our country is liberated

Nou di devan lemonn nou pa vle e
  sklav ankò
Toupatou sou toutlatè, nan pwen ti
  pèp nan pwen gwo pèp.

We declare before the world that we
  are finished with being slaves!
There is no nation of people in all the
  earth that is superior to another.

Kè:
Ann fè yon sèl chemen, men si nou diferan

Pa gen yon lòt sinas ki pi klere pou
  fè n konnen
Se sinas lamizè, konplo, imilyasyon

Ki rann nou kokobe depi ayè jouk jodya.

Chorus:
Let us choose the same path, even
  though we're different
We could not ask for reasons more
  clear than those that surround us
The poverty, the political plots, the
  humiliations
That have been crippling us
  throughout our history.

Ann fè yon blok solid, ann mache men
  dan lamen
Tras zansèt yo te make fò n pa kite
  yo disparèt
Ayiti se pou nou fò n pa di nou pa mele

Okontrè si n libere se yon viktwa
  se yon lonè.

Let us form a solid coalition, let us
  walk hand in hand
Let us not allow the visions of our
  ancestors to disappear
Haiti is our own, we cannot remain
  uninvolved
If we are liberated, it will be a victory
  and honor for us all.

Fanm kou gason, jèn kou timoun

Ann mete vanyan sou nou
Pou tout nasyon kab respekte n
Se pa vye sinistre ni se pa vye zagribay

Ki pou fè n pa rekonnèt ki vye sistèm kap
  toupizi n.

Women and men alike, teenagers and
  children
Let us consolidate our strengths
So that all nations will respect us
We can't let that lousy food aid and
  political double-talk
Keep us from recognizing the systems
  that are stepping all over us.

Kote Fanm Yo?
Kote nou, fanm dayiti, fanm vanyan, fanm
  peyizan yo?
Èske nou la e e e? Nou la!
Men kote nou fanm kat kwen peyi a?

Nan nò, nan sid, nan lès, nan lwès

Fè m wè nou la e e e!

Where Are You, Women?
Where are you, women of Haiti, strong
  women, peasant women?
Are you here with us? We're here!
Where are you, women from all four
  corners of Haiti?
From the north, from the south, from
  the east, from the west
Let me know you're here!

Kè:
Nou la anba tonèl la

Chorus:
We've gathered under one roof

Nap degaje nou, nap louvri je nou

We're moving forward, we're opening our eyes

Nap plenyen mizè nou

We're making our problems known

Men nap òganize nou pou revolisyon an vanse

We're organizing to advance the revolution

Jouk nan viktwa final la.

Until we win the final victory.

Nou menm fanm ki rekonèt

Women who recognize

Nou dwe met men ak tout gason, tout bon patriyòt

That we have to work together with men, with *all* true patriots

Pou bati yon lòt sosyete

To build a better society

Èske nou la e e e?

Are you with us?

Nou menm fanm ki rekonèt fò n kale je n

Women who recognize we must open our eyes

Pou chache konprann sa kap pase

And learn to analyze what is going on

Ni nan leta, ni nan legliz, nan òganizasyon toupatou

In the state, the church and in all types of organizations

Fè m wè nou la e e e!

Let me know you're here!

Fanm Ayisyen, Kanpe!

Haitian Women, Rise Up!

Kè:

Chorus:

Fanm ayisyen kanpe pou n òganize nou

Haitian women, rise up! Let's organize ourselves

Men n pap bliye tout fanm ki poko òganize

But we can't give up on the women who have not joined us

Gen bèl pwovèb nou tout nou leve nou trape

One of the proverbs we were raised on and grasped well

Pwovèb ki di nou, "Men anpil, chay pa lou."

Is the proverb that tells us, "When the hands are many the load is light!"

Nou gen gwo reskonsablite

We have a huge responsibility

Pou nou chanje mòd sosyete sa a

To change the ways of our society

Se pa you mirak kap sòti nan syèl

We can't wait on miracles from heaven

Se tout ti fòs pou met ansanm.

We have to consolidate our modest powers.

Chanjman nou swaf nou vle pote a

The changes we are so thirsty for

Lè depase pou 1 te rive

The time has passed for their arrival

Si n pa santi nou anreta

It's clear that we have fallen behind

Kijan pou n deside longè pa?

There's no way of knowing the length of the road ahead.

Pandan n chita nap reflechi

While we sit here reflecting on the situation

Men fòs lanmò yo sou biwo yo	The forces of death are at their desks working
Yap diskite sou fineray	Making arrangements for our funeral
Yap fè sèvo pou pete je nou.	They are brainwashing and blinding us.
Nou gen konfyans nan tètansanm	We have confidence in our solidarity
Nou ki se yon fòs ki pa gen parèy	We who would be an unstoppable movement
Jou n deside sove peyi a	The day we decide to save our country
Tout fòs lanmò blije disparèt.	The forces of death will inevitably disintegrate.

Reflections on the *Gwoupman Peyizan*

Merrill Singer points out that it is important to distinguish between com-
munity-*based* organizations and community-*placed* organizations (1994,
340). Gwoupman peyizan-s have been both. We have seen that one trademark of GPs (both gwoupman tètansanm-s and gwoupman kominotè-s) is
their association with outside institutions. This association has had come
about with trends in the international development industry that have involved trying to move away from top-down aid programs and toward programs that incorporate philosophies of "community participation," "felt
needs," "bottom-up social change," "local ownership," "participatory democracy," and "team-building with local populations."[26]

The women's groups discussed above were closely linked with PSC. But
PSC was hardly the only game in town. Other NGOs, missions, government
offices, and IGOs working in the Grand'Anse department during the past
few years have also sought to carry out their objectives by forming, training,
and funding GPs. The impact on community organization in the region has
been dramatic. Many GPs have been formed for the sole purpose of securing "a project" from one of these institutions.[27] Examples include the
planters' groups formed by extensionists from agricultural development
programs; the mother's circles created by health educators working for a
U.S.-based foundation concerned with maternal and child health; community governance committees promoted by OTI/IOM staff; and community
water groups convened by CARE International as part of a potable water
initiative. GPs especially successful at such pursuits might carry out projects
sponsored by several different organizations simultaneously. Like many
kominotè-s, such groups are sometimes marked by others as *gwoupman
mandyan*-s (beggar groups). This negative image is due partly to the short

life span of many groups, often lasting only as long as the duration of the aid projects around which they coalesced. I found myself continually erasing lines I had filled out on my GP chart during my fieldwork in Bamòn, as groups emerged, changed form, and disappeared with sporadic project starts and suspensions, with the transfer of project technicians and educators, with the comings and goings of NGO staff, with the pullout of organizations and missions from the area, and with funding delays caused by arguments among congressional delegates in the United States.

Despite the vulnerability of certain gwoupman-s to the whims of aid, overall GPs have proved surprisingly resilient. Many managed to survive during the 1991–94 post-coup era despite harsh persecution, for example. Robert Maguire notes that this reflects an impressive reserve of "determination and resourcefulness" (1990, 5) not dependent on their sponsors, many of which pulled out of the country altogether during that period. Indeed, while some GPs have been quite beholden to their sponsoring institutions' ideologies and agendas and have relied heavily on the training and material assistance they have received from them, other gwoupman-s have demonstrated remarkable degrees of self-direction and autonomy. While the members of Zepòl Sou Zepòl, Gwoupman Fanm Bwamari, and Gwoupman Fanm Zamann have expressed a keen interest in securing outside resources, they have nonetheless managed to continue meeting, working, and providing services to their members throughout numerous project "pull-outs" and severe political and economic crises. A GP song popular among the gwoupman-s in Bamòn affirms and celebrates this strength:

Peyizan malere, nou se wozo,	Poor peasants, we are *wozo*,[28] we
nou se wozo, se wozo nou ye. . . .	are *wozo*, we are *wozo* . . .
Yo met boule nou, yo met koupe rasin	They can burn us, they can cut at
nou, lè lapli a tonbe nap boujonnen.	our roots, but when the rain falls,
	we'll sprout again.

Although perpetually facing overwhelming odds posed by the economic, social, and political situation in which they exist, and though often somewhat less securely rooted than the wozo reeds they admire, as a whole, Haiti's GPs show no signs of "lying down under the torrents." Rather, they continue to multiply both within and beyond the reaches of aid throughout even the most remote regions of the country's rugged terrain.

As previously noted, GPs and other elements of the contemporary Haitian popular movement have been understood by many as representing a movement away from outdated vestiges of traditional peasant civic culture, and as having "little similarity to traditional groups" (Smarth 1997,

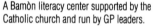

A Bamòn literacy center supported by the Catholic church and run by GP leaders.

106). In fact, the tendency to "picture 'new and old' political spaces as 'totally sundered from each other, instead of elucidating the manifold connections that exist among them'" (Escobar, as quoted in Starn 1992) is found in much of the literature on contemporary civic organizations and social movements. This view—a very popular one among development agents—is sometimes expressed by Haitian peasants themselves. On several occasions, we heard GP members critique the structures and ideologies of more traditional groups, particularly the sosyete-s,[29] and emphasize distinctions between the latter and their own, more "modern" organizations.

Yet Benwa and I found that the gwoupman kominotè-s and gwoupman tètansanm-s draw liberally on the discursive, behavioral, organizational, material, ethical, spiritual, artistic, and philosophical resources of the "Old Testament" groups. They have often done so, moreover, even when those priorities and behaviors have conflicted with regulations imposed on them by their sponsors. Bamòn GPs commonly carry out kòve-s or konbit-s, for example; they integrate music, singing, and dancing into their meetings and workdays; and many add to their roster of officers positions like the konsèy. Such practices make clear that they have not by any means

A Bamòn group federation meeting.

simply absorbed or unquestioningly incorporated outside influences.[30] Indeed, our research indicates that it is not a break from traditional habits and objectives that should be credited with the GP movement's impressive growth and tenacity, so much as the tendency of these groups to selectively combine long-standing traditions of rural community organization with concerns promoted by contemporary development and democratization initiatives.

8

Beyond "Democracy" and "Development"

But I do believe that those clearsighted Europeans who struggle, here as well, for a more just and humane homeland, could help us far better if they reconsidered their way of seeing us. Solidarity with our dreams will not make us feel less alone, as long as it is not translated into concrete acts of legitimate support for all the peoples that assume the illusion of having a life of their own in the distribution of the world. (Márquez 1995, 135)

Outside (though not completely so) the circuit of the *international* division of labor, there are people whose consciousness we cannot grasp if we close off our benevolence by constructing a homogeneous other referring only to our own place in the seat of the Same or the Self. Here are subsistence farmers, unorganized peasant labor, the tribals, and the communities of zero workers on the street or in the countryside. To confront them is not to represent (*vertreten*) them but to learn to represent (*darstellen*) ourselves. (Spivak 1988, 288–289, italics in the original).

People are persons, knots in nets of concrete relations. They want to continue being persons (people cannot be otherwise), and to organize society in a way in which they can be treated as such, not as individuals or masses. This personalized treatment is a normal condition among the "poor" in their own contexts. (Esteva 1999, 156)

The failure of Post–World War II development and democratization initiatives to make the world a more decent, livable place for most of its poorest citizens presents us with the challenge of developing alternative ways of thinking and acting. In order to succeed, the search for these alternatives must begin with the practices and visions of the poor themselves—not preformulated social theories or economic models. Reflecting Donna Haraway's assertion that "the only way to find a larger vision is to be somewhere in particular" (1988, 590), Benwa and I grounded our search in discursive and organizational practices found in the rural communities of Haiti's countryside. What we found is that Haitian peasants have developed their chante pwen-s, atribisyon-s, sosyete-s, and gwoupman peyizan-s by drawing selectively, if not always consciously, from a wide variety of organic and non-organic traditions and influences. In the process, they have been simultaneously acting from, transforming, and producing a series of shared convictions about what a good society would be and how it can (and cannot) be brought about. These convictions, which call into question more dominant North-Western ideologies of social progress, also suggest needed changes in how we understand and contribute to the struggles for survival and social change instigated by the poor and disempowered.

Reconsidering Democracy and Development

Haitian peasants oftentimes talk about what a truly civil society would look like using the terms *developed* and *democratic*. In fact, according to group members, a central objective of the atribisyon-s, sosyete-s, kominotè-s, and gwoupman-s is to redress the chronic failure of the Haitian government to develop their communities. A kominotè member stated during one of his group's meetings:

> From the point of view of the Haitian government, it has never had a system in advantage of the people. . . . They have never done what they should do for the nation, either in terms of agriculture, or schooling. . . . And then they look at you, at the state you're in, and they say you aren't development material! . . . If it wasn't for kominotè-s we wouldn't have *anything* here.

Some analysts claim that by conceptualizing their situation and their future in terms of development and democracy, the poor demonstrate their internalization of North-Western values and ideologies. Gustavo Esteva, notes, for example, that

> for those who make up two-thirds of the world's population today, to think of development—any kind of development—requires first the perception of themselves as underdeveloped, with the whole burden of connotations that this carries.
> Today, for two-thirds of the peoples of the world, underdevelopment is a threat that has already been carried out; a life experience of subordination and of being led astray, of discrimination and subjugation. Given that precondition, *the simple fact of associating with development one's own intention tends to annul the intention, to contradict it, to enslave it. It impedes thinking of one's own culture* (1993, 8, italics mine).

Esteva is hardly alone in pointing out the overwhelming hegemonic force of the discourse of development. Escobar asserts that by the 1970s, "Development had achieved the status of a certainty in the social imaginary. Indeed, it seemed impossible to conceptualize social reality in other terms" (1995, 5). As a result, "Many in the Third World began to think of themselves as inferior, underdeveloped, and ignorant and to doubt the value of their own culture, deciding instead to pledge allegiance to the banners of reason and progress" (52).

The arguments of these critics are compelling. Indeed, it is imperative that scholars and other analysts continue to disclose and confront both the ideological and the material violence done by certain aid industry efforts to democratize and develop the world. It is equally essential that we question the facile employment of these two great call words of the late twentieth- and early twenty-first century as we evaluate the realities and potentialities of the world's social, political, and economic systems. But in the process, we must not reduce those who have suffered the injustices of this era to simple victimhood. The stories presented in the previous chapters demonstrate that Haitian peasants, like many others throughout the South, have revealed the ideological reign of the democracy and development paradigms to be as incomplete as it is far-reaching.

We have seen that rural Haitians have some very particular sorts of ideas about what democracy is. Many of these ideas are far from synonymous with definitions of democracy being promoted by the powers to their north. Here, as Lara and Molina and others have found while working with community organizations in Latin America, democracy has less to do with voting rights and formal political structures than it does with "the satisfaction of common needs and the concrete benefits to be derived from it" (1997, 46). Haitian peasant groups, like Casteñeda, insist that "until the gaps between rich and poor are reduced . . . , democracy will simply not work. It is not so much a question of the *desirability* of having inequalities and democracy coexist, but of the *impossibility* of that coexistence" (1996, 49–50; see also Lummis 1996).

Haitian peasants also have taken issue with dominant North-Western assumptions about the nature and prerequisites of development. During group meetings, UNDERDEVELOPMENT was employed to critique situations in which the few exploit the many at least as often as it was used to refer to the conditions in which "the many" live, what they do, or how they think. The gwoupman peyizan-s are particularly prone to liberally employ the terms *democracy* and *development* while simultaneously contesting dominant First World definitions of them.

That they use these and other concepts claimed by "the discourse of development," then, does not mean that Haitian peasants have simply annulled, contradicted, and enslaved their intentions, as Esteva concludes in the excerpt above. Rather, they have based their understandings of democracy and development first and foremost on their own experiences in regulating community life, organizing work, engaging with the past, and grappling with their place in the world.

Moreover, because Haitian peasants—like Márquez's Latin Americans alluded to in the epigraph to this chapter—base their reality on "the illusion of having a life of their own in the distribution of the world," democracy and development are only two among many concepts they call on in thinking and talking about their aspirations for their society. That sosyete-s and atribisyon-s talk about democracy and development more rarely than gwoupman peyizan-s should not tempt us to think that members of the latter groups have had less to say in the realm of sociopolitical analysis. But as the chante pwen-s aptly demonstrate, we must sometimes tuck away the yardsticks with which we generally measure progressive and nonprogressive, promising and hopeless, and re-sensitize our ears to recognize the sounds of their analyses.

Visualizing the Future

During the first weeks of fieldwork, I began to notice patterns and themes emerging in notes taken during encounters with atribisyon-s, sosyete-s, kominotè-s, and gwoupman tètansanm-s: certain concerns voiced repeatedly, certain styles of organization being practiced, certain issues discussed, certain opinions expressed, certain tensions reappearing, certain types of lyrics sung. At first, I was surprised by these continuities, given the numerous distinctions between the different types of groups. My surprise quickly diminished, though, as I got to know the groups better and became more aware of the connections between them.

Throughout the remainder of the fieldwork period, I offered Benwa and group members my perceptions, and elicited their help in teasing out and defining just what those patterns and themes meant. The result was a collection of common values, concerns, objectives, perceptions, struggles, and aspirations. Through careful thought and discussion with my tutors in the field, I eventually saw that emerging from this stew was a multifaceted vision about what a good society should be and how such a society might be brought about. *Demokrasi* and *devlopman* were sometimes utilized when people commented directly on what elements they thought would form the foundation of a truly civil society. In general, though, other terms and concepts dominated. Among the most prominent elements that Benwa and I, together with group members, identified were these:

relative economic parity
a certain type of sociopolitical hierarchy
respe (respect)

a recognition of the citizenry's full humanity
the right of all citizens to speak and to be heard
consistency with the desires of ancestral and spiritual guides
opportunities for collective play and performance
access of citizens to basic social services
the provision of personal and collective security.

As mediated through our interpretations and translations, these generalizations reflect only some of what we saw and heard, and thus invite skeptical evaluation. Nor should they be assumed to constitute some sort of seamless image of a good society shared universally by Haitian peasants, or even by all the residents of Bamòn. The Haitian peasantry is far from being a homogenous, undifferentiated mass of like-minded people but, like Gavin Smith's subjects in rural Peru, is "shot through with differences among themselves" (1991, 8). Yet the vision that emerges from the discussion below does reflect the "partial views and halting voices" of the individuals and groups with whom we worked. Thus, it presents "a collective subject position that promises a vision of the means of ongoing finite embodiment, of living within limits and contradictions" (Haraway 1988, 590). As such, it can offer valuable insight to those interested in assisting populations like Haiti's majority poor to make their world a more hospitable place.

Each constitutive element of this vision has been embodied, practiced, and expressed differentially—in distinct ways and to varying degrees—among the different types of groups. Some elements are intertwined, and their realization is mutually dependent. Others are in tension and, at times, competition with one another and have to be balanced.

Elements of a Good Society

In peasant-group discussions about positive social change, a common subject was the need for relative economic parity among all members of a society. Parity here does not mean absolute equity. Group members seemed to be envisioning, rather, a situation in which levels of wealth and power would not be so disparate that a few would have the means to "suck out" the resources of the rest of the citizenry; in which everyone would have a certain degree of financial and material security; where a few people would not "get *ice* in their glasses every day" while the majority "have to walk miles to get cruddy water."[1] Without such parity, they insisted, the attainment of a just or stable political system remains elusive. It is no coincidence that people in Tisous considered the malicious *baka*[2] beast—whose raison d'être was the unashamed and unbridled accumulation of wealth—to be among the most reprehensible of all evildoers and the most dangerous of all social threats.

Inherent in this first element are a number of prescriptions for relationships between citizens. A conviction consistently expressed in group meetings and work sessions was that everyone should work, and everyone should benefit from the work that is done. A common proverb asserts that in Haiti, the donkey does the labor so the horse can neigh (*"Bourik travay pou chwal garyonnen,"* that is, those who do their society's hard labor are not the ones who get credited or rewarded for it).[3] It was pointed out repeatedly that this was still the rule in their "newly democratized" nation, a disappointment also expressed by many social movement participants in other areas of the Latin American and Caribbean region (see Munroe 1996). In a good society, this would not be the case. In a good society, both labor and the rewards it brings would be shared. (Recall the coffee-processing kòve at Sesa's house.) This does not mean that all must either contribute or benefit in precisely equal measure. Group members repeatedly pointed out that "not everyone has the same strength"; neither, they insisted, does everyone have the same needs.

This first principle and its social prescriptions have been embodied and expressed in the structures, discourses, and activities of peasant groups in a number of ways, and were manifested in nearly all of the group meetings and work sessions Benwa and I attended. It was most poignantly advocated in the January 1 celebrations of the atribisyon. There, participants insist that every member must get a share of the meat and that no one should miss out on the delicacy of the animal's head, "even if they only get to taste the eyeball." Even among the most hierarchically structured and "class-stratified" of the groups, the sosyete-s, group discussions were filled with rhetoric about economic parity.

The sosyete's supplier (*founisè*) system also reflects a commitment to this principle. It was manifested clearly in my discussions with GTs about their understandings of democracy and development. "Do you know what the biggest problem we have in this country is, Djeni? If I can eat and another person can't eat, how are you supposed to build a democracy on that? How do you think we can *mete tètansanm* [put our heads together, develop solidarity] like that? No, we have to be more uniform" (a leader of the GT federation FPB).

Many of the proverbs I have cited in this book (proverbs commonly used outside as well as within the group context) also reflect this aspiration—albeit very often in indirect or negatively constructed ways. Among numerous other examples are:

Grangou chen pa gade karang.
What concern is the dog's hunger to the lice?

Boutèy la manke plen, tèt la pa jwenn anyen.
The bottle is almost full, but the cap can't even get a taste.

Depi ou malere, tout bagay sanble ou.
When you're poor, everything resembles you.
(When something is stolen, it is you who are accused, not the "big guy" who took it.)

The prioritizing of relative economic parity has been a source of tension between community groups and aid organizations. Part of the reason is that such prioritizing tends to be perceived by aid agents as counter-conducive to peasants progressing.[4] The systems of communal agricultural labor practiced by many groups, for instance, do not seem to encourage individuals to make innovations that might increase the productivity of their own fields. Aiders perceive, rather, that these systems level agricultural production. With their networks of mutual aid, the groups (particularly the "Old Testament" ones) spend their time, energy, and resources not on getting ahead but on getting by—and on worshipping, playing, and celebrating in the process.

Through the lens of current development ideology, such collaborations constitute yet another instance of Haitian peasants pulling each other down. In the words of Glenn Smucker, theirs is "an egalitarian impulse where poverty is best shared . . . [of] crab antics, social pressures on one's peers, and subtle forms of sabotage" (1983, 450). An expatriate Catholic priest working in Bamòn, whose personal mission was to "launch an initiative to . . . show them [the peasants in the area] that if they organize themselves well, they can accomplish many things," explained to me that they must first learn to draw boundaries around their personal space, their property, and their families. If they fail to do this, he suggested, they will remain forever within the confines of their "crab basket."

> The people don't respect limits at all. They are all over each other. You could say that is because they see the importance of solidarity. But this is not an advantageous solidarity. It is not a real sharing. It is a poverty mentality. . . . Why do the women never buy in bulk, for instance, so that they can maximize their profits? Because they will have to share it with everybody—all the neighbors, family members, they'll all have to take some of it. . . . Their idea of solidarity is that when one person begins to get ahead, the rest of them try to take him down . . . so none of them ever progress.

Another reason that the prioritizing of relative economic parity has led to tension between local groups and aid agencies is that it calls into question the appropriateness of prominent aid practices—sometimes explicitly. This is apparent in more than a few of the chante pwen-s sung by the gwoupman peyizan-s (see chapters 3 and 7). Recognizing that aid programs have not increased economic parity between Haitians but, instead, have exaggerated disparities in wealth, group members complain that "the people who benefit from development are those who sit with their big vests, big neckties in the city,"—the members of the local elite who get hired by the agencies to be their local intermediaries. One of my neighbors perceived this contradiction to be epitomized by an IOM representative who "rides up this way on his big pretty motorcycle, with his wallet bulging out of his pants' pocket, says '*Bonjou*,' and then rides back down to Jérémie again to get his [pay] check."

The ideal of relative economic parity has also contributed to certain problems among group members. Benwa and I spoke with many former members whose groups were no longer meeting. One of the most common reasons they gave for their groups' "discouragement" or "death" was *divizyon* (division). In many cases, troubles among the membership had arisen when a few members were charged with benefiting disproportionately from the labor or resources of the rest of the group. Tellingly, we found such complaints to be most common among GTs, whose discourses were most explicitly egalitarian. We traced this ironic discrepancy to the fact that most divizyon-s had occurred during periods when the groups were receiving support from outside agencies. GT officers, who generally acted as liaisons with sponsoring organizations, were commonly targeted for critique, as they had more opportunities to "skim off the cream." This tendency of external material aid to catalyze fissures in local civic groups has been noted by various scholars of Latin America, the Caribbean, and other areas of the South. A good example of such work is Laura Macdonald's study of NGOs in Central America. She finds that rather than "strengthening civil society" (an increasingly popular objective within the aid industry), NGOs tend to perpetuate "imbalances and distortions in civil society" (1997, 4).

Another component of a good society that emerged from the organizational and discursive practices of the groups is the existence of a certain kind of sociopolitical hierarchy. Although this second component might initially appear to contradict the first, in reality, it arises from it. As already suggested, that peasant group members consider themselves "one and the same we" does not mean they profess a desire for an absolutely equal sharing of wealth or power. They insist, rather, that for a group or society to function well, it must possess individuals who are willing and able to lead the others, to "care for" them, and to "stand for" them. This is evident in the way people talk about their groups as "families" and "bodies," and their leaders as "mothers," "fathers," and "uncles."[5] "Yes, we are one body, but we have to have a head." "If a group has no head, it cannot function. It was in the head that the Lord put the eyes." That "head" should demonstrate a genuine concern for defending the interests of those situated at all the body's levels, just as she or he would the interests of sons, sisters, and cousins.

This priority is aptly demonstrated in the structure of the sosyete-s.

Humor, performance, and aesthetic concerns imbue the multiple ranks and elaborate titles of sosyete officers, but these titles also demarcate distinct roles and real divisions of authority and status. This is obvious in the ways the positions are invoked to get members to work in the fields, for example, or carry out funeral rites. It is also obvious in the gestures of respect officers are offered. Yet the sosyete hierarchy is a tempered one. Here, officers are accessible, subject to critique, and can be overridden in group meetings—all things that they do not share either with full-fledged "big men" or, for that matter, with the leadership structures of many of the aid organizations criticizing them for not being more democratic.

Among the sosyete-s officers who receive the most respect are the members of the konsèy-s, or councillor teams. The teams generally comprise men or women more aged than most of the other members. We were told repeatedly by Bamòn group members that the experience and wisdom of their konsèy-s (councillors) were invaluable, and that these individuals were always consulted when major decisions needed to be made. As the proverb goes, "*Bouch gran moun yo santi men pawòl yo dous*" (The mouths of old folks may stink, but their words are sweet).[6] Although the GTs also esteem older members, they are not as prone to give them leadership roles. This is likely because the priorities of the external organizations with which they associate tend to place greater value on traits more common to younger, more "cosmopolitan" men and women: literacy, mobility, and professionalism, as opposed to spiritual and social wisdom, knowledge of the community, musical talents, and a prominent place in kin relations.

Even though sponsoring agencies themselves generally comprise complex hierarchies, many of them insist that members of the local groups with which they work share power and responsibilities as equally as possible. Thus, at animation training centers such as PSCs, group leaders are taught to gather the members of their groups in a circle. No one should sit in a more prominent position than the others. Everybody should have a chance to talk. Everyone's opinion is to be equally valued. No one should be considered or treated as "higher" than another. And although it is necessary to have a modest array of officers, these positions and responsibilities should not be held by individuals for long periods of time but rather be redistributed regularly among the membership.

We found many of these principles being upheld in GT meetings. However, most of the GTs actually had one or two strong leaders who served as their top officer(s) and who possessed marked degrees of status and authority. If a group did not have a leader or leaders of this sort, it was generally looking for someone to take up that role. Again, the complaint that their groups were "discouraged" or weak because "*nou manke chèf*" (we lack a chief [leader]) was especially common among GTs. Like sosyete members,

GT members told us that they needed someone to organize them, to speak for them, somebody to believe in.

Yet, the GTs insisted on portraying themselves as more "egalitarian" (*egalego*) than the sosyete-s kominotè-s, and atribisyon-s. As Smarth notes in discussing Haitian popular organizations in general, "From their inception, they defined themselves as spreading and defending the rights and claims of the popular classes." This was used as evidence that they had "little similarity to traditional groups, which they dismissed as part of the existing political system"(1997, 106). At several of the PSC training sessions I attended, animators and GT members criticized more "traditional" groups, and sosyete-s in particular, for their lack of egalitarianism. Sosyete-like distinctions were labeled as expressions of a mentality of dependency and paternalism, and opportunities for exploitation among members and, thus, were to be avoided. GTs were different, participants were told. "Our groups are *gwoupman tètansanm*-s" (heads-*together* groups).

Next to the eskwad-s, which generally had no officers at all, the atribisyon-s were the least hierarchically structured of the civic organizations we studied. In many of those groups, distinctions between officers and lay members were rarely visible. Yet even atribisyon members affirmed a certain amount of stratification. One group in Tisous had nearly ceased to function when I first arrived there. Only after they finally convinced one of the older men in the area to be their konsèy was the group able to rekindle its enthusiasm and revive itself.

Aid practitioners and scholars alike have critiqued the insistence of Haitain civic groups on strong leadership as "undemocratic" (see Smarth 1997). Members of all the categories of groups, however, were quick to insist that the value they placed on having solid, directive leaders is not inconsistent with democratic principles. It is, rather, what allows them to function as "one family," "one hand," or "one body." Still, their attempt to fuse hierarchy and egalitarian principles did seem to generate a distinctive sort of tension in many groups. This tension we came to call the *chèf-tèt-ansanm* (head honcho-heads together) dilemma. It seemed especially common in gwoupman federations, where increases in size and distance among members have been accompanied by greater bureaucratization and more complex hierarchical structures.[7] In meetings of the Federasyon Peyizan Bamòn (FPB, one of the region's several peasant group federations), officers often preached passionately about "participation" and "equality" while simultaneously "passing on" decisions to the federation's membership without involving them in decision-making processes. Challenges leveled by group representatives attending the meetings tended to be dismissed as ridiculous or ignored altogether by the officers.

Zepòl Sou Zepòl of Lakay is an example of a group that dealt significantly more effectively than FPB with the chèf-tètansanm dilemma. As
Benwa and I walked back to Tisous following a meeting, I commented on
how well-loved among the membership Zepòl's president, Klesiyis, seemed
to be. Benwa responded that Klesiyis was known in the area as being a *pi
gwo demokrat* (an ultimate democrat), the ideal group president. Although
he could not read or write very well, Benwa explained, he was wise, dignified, and fair, and a "father figure" to many. (This image seemed to be enhanced by the fact that he was in his late forties or early fifties, a fairly old
age among the peasantry.) He was therefore able to represent the group
(e.g., speak in its interest at the meetings of gwoupman federations and in
negotiations with NGOs or governmental representatives). Klesiyis took initiative and guided his group, but he also demonstrated respect for its members. "He never does anything that's not in [line with] the opinion of the
group." Perhaps most important, he insisted on transparency in matters of
governance and money, and thus encouraged his group to hold him and
the other leaders accountable for their actions.

In talking about Klesiyis and other group leaders known to be especially
"democratic," people sometimes described them as *moun respè*. *Respe* (respect), it turns out, is not only a key to integrating chèf and tètansanm together in a constructive way. It is also another of the major social ideals embodied in the groups' discourses and activities. As observed in chapters 1
and 7, when GTs described to Benwa and me how they understood democracy and development, they very often used the term *respe* to characterize
the social fiber with which the fabric of a democratic and developed society
would have to be woven. Respe was consistently discussed and promoted in
the meetings and work sessions of other groups as well. Put simply, to act according to the principle of respe means properly acknowledging certain
distinctions between people (e.g., bowing to the sosyete president during
the salitasyon); at the same time, it means affirming the humanity and
worth of all, regardless of social status (e.g., by offering everyone equal
quantities of rum during the work party, or giving weight to the opinions of
all at group meetings).

A society of respect would be a society in which people come to one another's aid not out of charity but out of a recognition of its members' profound interdependence. Sosyete members made this clear when they explained to me their reasons for instituting the practice of offering help
during times of death and sickness: "It's because we are family, brothers
and sisters, . . . because we are all one and the same 'we.'" When a sosyete
sponsors a wake for a member, the group is not aiding the person's family,
but simply offering her what she deserves, and what others will be offered

when it is their turn. Not incidentally, the group is also making possible a social event they will all take pleasure in, a time of visiting with others, singing and praying, playing games, eating and drinking.

The groups' prioritizing of respe may be understood in part as an effort to address the difficulties that too often color Haitian peasants' relationships—the jealousies, family rivalries, destructive competition, and so forth. By setting up systems of exchange and cooperation, by promoting shared interests, and by forging a collective identity, peasant groups have sought to inhibit the proliferation of social relationships lacking respe.

Consistent with the value they place on respe is the group members' insistence that their full humanity be recognized, by others as well as by themselves. Haitian peasants are well aware that in this increasingly interconnected world, if they fail to gain the respect of those outside their communities, their hopes for a better society are in vain. A number of gwoupman peyizan songs declare that in order for others to affirm their humanity, peasants must first affirm it themselves. Recall the following lines:

> If the cow knew its strength
> It wouldn't let just any little guy
> Come and tie a rope around its neck
> If peasants knew their strength
> They wouldn't let any old good-for-nothing
> Come and climb all over them.

> Country folk, we must understand this
> Peasants, we have to understand this . . .
>
> *　*　*　*　*　*
>
> We women of Haiti, we swear before the Lord
> We'll struggle until this crisis is past us and our country is liberated.
> We declare before the world that we are finished with being slaves!
> There is no nation of people in all the earth that is superior to another.

> Women and men alike, teenagers and children
> Let us consolidate our strengths, so all nations will respect us.
> We can't let that lousy food aid and political double-talk
> Keep us from recognizing the systems that are stepping all over us . . .

The issue of how they have been constructed in the imagination of outsiders was discussed in many of the group meetings we attended, oftentimes passionately. Group members revealed an awareness not only that "because we are small, they take us for bits of grain"[8] but also that such perceptions matter in material and political terms:

When foreigners come here, they take pictures of people doing all kinds of things, as if to show how poor we are. After that, they go back over there and pass us off as old dogs. There were some [Catholic] sisters who used to come to the homes of school children and make them take off their shoes and their good clothes, their school clothes, and put on old rags, and then climb up mango trees. They would take their pictures so they could send them [the photos] overseas and ask for money. When the money came, they [the sisters] bought pretty beds for themselves. . . . But now that doesn't happen as much anymore, people around here have opened their eyes more. (a woman who was the president of a large *gwoupman tètansanm* outside Nazon, speaking as we walked together to a meeting of a "strong women's group" above Tisous)

There is a story the people of Nazon will never forget, Djeni. That is the time Brother Michael [a Catholic missionary] said to the class he was teaching at the [secondary] school here, "When a *blan* (foreign, white) baby is born, it is born head-first, but when a Haitian baby is born, it is born with its hands like this [hands outstretched and cupped]." (a school student in Nazon)[9]

When the *blan*-s disembarked at the Jérémie wharf [for the September 1994 U.S.-led military intervention], everybody seemed to be clapping their hands for them, without yet seeing what they were going to do. . . . As for me, I now see they've deceived us again. . . . They said they were coming to help all Haitians—*makout*-s [local elites sympathetic to the junta regime] and poor people alike. But I see they are only helping the *makout*-s. They are living in the *makout*-s' houses, aren't they? For us, they see we are black. Yes, we are black, but our hearts are not black. (a teenage boy, at a retreat for youth groups)

We have to go show the *blan*-s that we are *adults*! We are not children! We've got to demand to be treated like adults! (a group federation officer, during a meeting in which members were accusing a foreign priest of trying to seize control of the region's popular movement and take over its projects)

Many such statements came from Bamòn residents who had dealt extensively with aid agencies. Significantly, some of the most harsh and pointed judgments we heard were uttered by people who were actually employed full time by such agencies. Many of those individuals had heard a great deal of rhetoric about mutual respect, collaboration, teamwork, and equality from their foreign bosses and supervisors yet had repeatedly experienced condescension and one-upmanship. Their talk about respect, like their talk about collaboration and equality, is an elaborate lie the foreigners construct for themselves, we were told repeatedly. In reality, it means little.

When the *blan*-s come, they always tell you that there's equality between Haitians and *blan*-s, but never! Everything is decided by the will of the *blan*. It is he who decides what each person makes. . . . He's the one who has [re-sources], so he is the boss. . . . As long as [Haitians] are not autonomous, this problem won't get any better. Do you think we would get away with going to the United States and taking authority over the *blan*-s? They come here and do what they want! (a community educator working with a health outreach program run by a USAID-sponsored development foundation)

Of course, Haitian peasants have also been confronted with a variety of dehumanizing stereotypes from sectors of their own society. One of the most vivid demonstrations of the awareness of these stereotypes occurred during a conversation with Dyebeni and Elifèt, co-directors of the Tèwouj Catholic chapel. These two men had stopped by my house for a drink of water as they made their way home from a training session at the Catholic church in Nazon. As we discussed some of the difficulties they were having in trying to run a literacy project out of the Tèwouj chapel, Dyebeni noted that it was hard for people to take time away from marketing and farming chores in the middle of the afternoon. As he spoke, I noticed something that had troubled me in previous conversations with him: every time he said the word *kòve*, he followed it with *eskize* (excuse me), and added once, "but I know you understand the reality of the country, Djeni." Confused by this, I asked him about it. "Ah, well," he said, "the reason I say that is be-cause there are a lot of people, people who are from a higher place, who are offended by that word—in other words, they don't understand it." "Yes," Elifèt seconded. They went on to talk about how city people in Haiti tend to view the kòve as a shameful thing. "And so," Dyebeni explained:

> the *kòve* guy feels ashamed when he is walking home from the fields and sees a nicely dressed person, or a person who speaks many languages. . . . Their hands [of the *kòve* participant] are dirty and they're barefoot, and they've been working in the dirt. . . . If I'm on the road to Jérémie in pretty clothes, and I meet up with someone I know who's just come from a *kòve*, and he holds out his hand to me, I may not want to take it . . . so that person's ashamed of what he's been doing.

Elifèt reasoned, "Peasants wouldn't be ashamed of this work, but they're made to feel that way in the society," adding that he knew a man who had been told by a Jérémie resident that he "smelled of kòve." Experiences of interclass shaming occurred even within the peasant group,movement. At several of the federation assemblies I attended, salient tensions emerged when group members perceived they were being disrespected or insulted by federation leaders.

An important reason for earning the respect of others is that respect is a prerequisite for acquiring a voice in larger spheres. Through chante pwen-s and other customarily legitimate modes of expression (poetry, proverbs, artwork), rural Haitians both within and outside the peasant group movement have crafted remarkably effective ways of permitting even the most humble individual's voice to be heard. This underlines the shared conviction that to have a decent and just society, all citizens must be allowed to speak—and to be heard. "Having a voice," we were told, depends not only on the absence of persecution but also on the establishment of mechanisms through which one's input would be given weight. It would involve, in other words, the institutionalization of the participation of the marginalized in spheres of influence.

In talking about the political and economic situation during our fieldwork, many group members noted that although they were not muzzled, as they had been under most other governments, they still remained "silenced" because few avenues existed for them to have an impact on the way their society was governed. Again, like many other citizens of the "newly democratic" Americas, they expressed a desire for more than the opportunity to occasionally vote for a president, a parliamentarian, or a regional assembly member. They wanted to ensure that those representatives knew their needs and were committed to addressing them. The "democracy" they had seen thus far had failed as miserably to meet this desire as it had to meet the desire for increased economic parity.

A good society, the peasant groups also demonstrated, is one that is consistent with the desires of their ancestral and spiritual guides. When Atribisyon Kay Mano members explained the reasons they have continued to practice the rachòt, when Sosyete Solèy Leve members offered libations to the founders of their group, when the Zamann women's group discussed the importance of realizing Dessalines' dreams, they all expressed the conviction that people are not meant to live only for themselves and generations to come but also in honor of those who have come before them. A society whose citizens fail to do this pushes from under itself the very foundation on which it was built and, along with its past, loses much of its contemporary relevance and vibrancy.

Permeating the objectives and practices of Haitian peasant groups is a myriad of religious concerns as well. Recall the dance of the sosyete kongo Solèy Leve; the songs, scripture readings, and prayers during gwoupman peyizan meetings[10] the involvement of many groups in wakes and ceremonies for the deceased; and how certain groups have lay priests to conduct these services. Whereas many GPs are directly affiliated with Protestant or Catholic missions or church-sponsored NGOs (e.g., the Program for Social Change), the kominotè-s sosyete-s, and atribisyon-s regularly honor and interact with the lwa-s. It is not uncommon for the discourses and practices of individual groups in each of these categories to reflect the traditions of Protestantism, Catholicism, and Vodou alike. In their studies of Latin American social movements, Bryan Froele (1994) and Susan Eckstein (1989) emphasize the centrality of religious belief. According to Froele, "Religion is perhaps the most powerful force in the creation of community life at the grassroots in Latin America today" (145). For Eckstein, the importance of belief in this context lies not only in its "manifest content but— as Weber argued—on the predispositions it inspires" (32). This is true for peasant groups in rural Haiti as well, where faith and social practice constantly presuppose and inform each other (see Desmangles 1992).

The value peasants place on cooperative work means that in the countryside, the grueling rhythms of hard labor are frequently punctuated by laughter, jokes, dramatized performances, swigs from the bottle, singing, and games. These practices are not seen as either inconsistent with or threatening to getting work done. Rather, play and performance are generally understood as fuel that "heats up" and encourages laborers. Collective play and performance, then, compose yet another element of a good society and, once again, reveal the peasantry's resistance to the compartmentalization of different facets of life, a common phenomenon in late capitalist societies.

This element also constitutes a source of tension between local groups and aid agencies. In several of our conversations with development program staff, the rowdy parties that the sosyete-s and kominotè-s were known to throw at the end of their workdays were highlighted as evidence of the counterprogressive nature of these traditional groups. Peasants must learn to be more responsible with their money and serious about their work, the argument went, if they are going to get anywhere. To this end, GTs were often instructed to refrain from integrating the inefficient or whimsical cultural practices of more "traditional" groups into their agendas.

Despite the bias against it, most GTs managed to fit "distraction" into their meetings and workdays. A few sponsors even encouraged a limited amount of this. At PSC training sessions, for instance, group leaders were taught how to guide GT members in putting on impromptu skits. Designed to provoke reflection and discussion about difficult topics (like domestic abuse), these skits generally worked brilliantly. More often than not, they concluded with nearly everyone participating in one way or another and, frequently, to roars of laughter from all. The songs of the GTs would also become occasions for animated performances and partying. Song seminars were highlights of all the training sessions I attended at the PSC center. Oftentimes those present spontaneously broke into dances. Talent shows generally held on the final night of each session also elicited eager participation and elaborate embellishment.

Prominent in conversations among groups of all sectors about what a good society would look like was the idea that all citizens would have access to basic social services. This would mean having access to resources well beyond the reach of most group members: adequate schooling (primary and secondary schools with competent teachers, regular hours of operation, and supplies such as paper, pencils, and books); literacy training for adults; decent transportation (no one ever mentioned wanting an automobile but rather wanting a road that comes within a reasonable distance of one's house, "so that when people are really sick, they could get a ride to the hospital"); agricultural equipment (sturdy hoes and machetes, and ideally, plows, fertilizers, and pesticides); occupational training (for farmers, this might be in sustainable farming practices, pesticide use, "garden vegetable" cultivation, and animal husbandry); "Western" health care (an adequate but financially accessible health clinic within an easy walking distance); a fair judicial system (that would provide equal justice to the wealthy and the poor); enough land to live on (and land redistribution); and a healthier environment.

Nearly all the groups we visited had either tried to provide one or more of these services to their communities or had sought to obtain them from aid organizations. (More rare were efforts to seek them from the state.) Cases in point were the sosyete-s "holding court" as an alternative to the notoriously corrupt judicial system, the kominotè-s working on the roads and footpaths, and nearly all the groups contributing to the construction or maintenance of local school buildings. The group federations in the Bamòn area (and the Grand 'Anse in general) were especially active in making demands of government officials and aid organizations for support in all these areas, and others. By the time I left Bamòn, several of them had succeeded in some of their efforts. One of the smaller group federations in the zone, for example, had managed to acquire from an NGO a school-lunch program for a primary school in its community.[11] With funds from several different institutions, another federation had begun implementing a major road construction project that was to cover several miles of territory.

The need for personal and collective security beyond the economic security already discussed was another necessity mentioned often. As my fieldwork progressed, and Haiti's population became progressively disenchanted by the failures of the new government to make things better for them, crime gradually worsened. While particularly visible in the escalation of robberies and street crimes in Port-au-Prince and major provincial towns, the growing crime rate was felt in the countryside as well. This troubled people greatly. Benwa and I began to hear more and more often group discussions about the need to feel safe. Lamenting that the terrorizing fears of the post-coup era had been replaced by disconcerting feelings of vulnerability in contexts that had previously felt fairly secure (in the local marketplaces, during trips to Port-au-Prince, and even in their own neighborhoods), they discussed what might be done. A number of groups from the upper region of Bamòn "put their heads together" at one point to strategize ways to maintain security in their area. They decided to elect neighborhood security agents to ensure the safety of people within their abitasyon-s.[12] Some GTs and group federations also worked at tracking the work of the "new police force,"[13] which was becoming known for its neglect of rural areas and its excessive use of force in the areas it did patrol.

The collection of prerequisites for a good society delineated by the peasant group members of Bamòn, Haiti, makes clear that the ways Haitian peasants understand their world, and the hopes they have for its future, often differ markedly from the understandings of those who have sought to develop and democratize them. The vision that emerges from this collection celebrates not market liberalization but local subsistence. It offers little praise for voting rights if those rights are not accompanied by broader political—and economic—rights. It does not value efficiency over pleasure or profit over relationship. Its telos is not the United States of America. It is not Europe, Japan, or the eastern "Tigers." Like the visions embedded in many other social movements in the South, it advances "an alternative conception of citizenship [which] would view democratic struggles as encompassing a redefinition not only of the political system but also of economic, social, and cultural practices that might engender a democratic ordering for society as a whole" (Alvarez, Dagnino, and Escobar 1998b, 2).

Shiva has noted that "the worst of the damage" done by contemporary international development activities in the "underdeveloped" world has resulted from activities that have "superimpose[d] the scientific and economic paradigms created by western, gender-based ideology on communities in other cultures." In doing so, these activities have discredited and undermined the strategies and technologies of the people in the communities where they have occurred (Shiva 1988, 1–14). With her studies of Indian women engaged in ecological struggles, Shiva stresses that poor people do not mobilize solely to gain economic resources or political power but for other reasons as well.

The truth of Shiva's claim is lived out daily by the atribisyon-s, sosyete-s, kominotè-s and gwoupman tètansanm-s. With the songs they sing, the kòve-s they carry out, the ceremonies they host, the discussions they craft, and the goals they aspire to, they demonstrate over and again that civic coalitions and initiatives aimed in part at economic and political ends may also (1) be powerfully evocative of collective historical memories; (2) involve elements of worship, performance, community governance, play, engagement with ancestral spirits, and politico-social reflection and critique; and (3) be deeply marked by cultural mores, ethical principles, and a sense of kinship based on a profound sense of interconnectivity.

The dominant aid industry calculus has little room for such a complex mix of qualities, orientations, and priorities, and thus little chance of seeing the "deeply cultural character" (Escobar 1992, 82) of such groups. The result is that the aid-intervention interface is a site of tension-filled encounters between discontinuous and contradictory knowledges. The outcome of such encounters has often been that more indigenous sets of knowledge are dismissed while those of the aiders are promoted (see Vander Zaag 1999, 35, 283).

Despite recent efforts within the aid sector to take into account the concerns of local organizations and to work more collaboratively with them, for the most part, populations like the peasants of Haiti continue to be regarded and treated as targets for economic assistance and political enlightenment, not as members of a partnership. Thus, when incongruencies arise between peasant group members' ways of seeing and doing things, on the one hand, and the objectives, assumptions, regulations, and practices of democratization and development programs, on the other, those incongruencies continue to be understood within the aid community as signs that Haitian peasants have underdeveloped values, habits, and aspirations. I would propose that these incongruencies reveal instead that North-Western institutions too often come into areas of the South with an impoverished sense of what social change can and should mean.

I am not suggesting that Haitian peasants or the organizations they form be idealized as something they are not. Members of atribisyon-s, sosyete-s, kominotè-s and gwoupman tètansanm-s are quick to acknowledge that they have repeatedly failed to live up to the vision they express. Rather, in order for North-Westerners to do work that truly benefits populations such as Haiti's peasantry, it is essential to recognize that those populations are made up of people who have ways of thinking about things that differ from—and challenge—North-Western conceptual parameters, and people who know how to work and how to organize in ways that many North-Westerners do not. It is essential to recognize that, as the Haitian proverb puts it, "the big branch at the top of the tree thinks it has the best view, but it fails to see the sights enjoyed by the little bud tossed about by the wind." Changing ways of seeing is not enough, however. What is needed is not only a transformation of analytical practices but also a new ethic of relating across the boundaries of the Brandt line.

A Movement toward the Future

The goal of sustainable development cannot be reduced to a sort of splendid self-sufficiency and to a belief that we can reproduce atavistic patterns of social life. This is all the more true when we consider that the globalization of the world economy is an ongoing design of a "market colonialism" affecting the livelihoods of more than 80 percent of the world's population. (Alfonso 1997, 184)

NGOs, ethnic groups, private associations and corporations alike must recognize that society can no longer afford for them to operate according to the narrow, self-interested rights-oriented calculus of classical liberalism. Instead, they need to join in creating a new global ethic of responsibility. (Clough 1999)

We have to start down here where we are, and we can't just be looking out to help ourselves, but to help others who are in the same situation. (a Haitian animatris during a women's group meeting)

. . . *Jah, tande rel klas travayè a*	Jah, hear the cry of the working class
Kap mande yo ale miyè	Asking for an end to their suffering
Jah, tande rel tout malere yo	Jah, hear the cry of all the world's poor
Kap mande yo ale miyè.	Asking for a better life.
Wi, se frè nou yo ye	Yes, they are our brothers
Kèlkanswa koulè yo	Whatever their color
Se yon sèl la nou ye	We are all one
Ede nou met tèt ansanm.	Help us put our heads together
Yon sèl lin la nou ye	We are all one family
Annou yonn pa manje lòt	Let's not eat each other alive
Se yon sèl la nou ye	We are all one
Ann ale soude!	Let's join ourselves together!
Jah, vire je ou sou Ayiti	Jah, turn your eyes toward Haiti
Kenbe pèp la mobilize	Keep the people together
Pou Dye desann ann Ayiti	So God will come down to Haiti
Annou chante libète pou yo . . .	Let us sing for their liberty . . .
. . . *Jah, voye kèk lanmou ann Amerik*	. . . Jah, send some love to America
Pout tout fanm, timoun e nonm	For every woman, child and man
Voye kèk jistis ann Amerik	Send some justice to America
Libere san tè a	Liberate the blood of the land.
Se san mwen ki la, nan resèvasyon yo	That's my blood down there, on the reservations
Se san mwen ki la, tout nasyon endyen yo	That's my blood down there, all the Indian nations
Se san mwen ki la, premye ameriken yo	That's my blood down there, the first Americans
Se san mwen ki la, m pral ede yo si mwen kapab kounyeya	That's my blood down there, I'm gonna help them if I can now
Se san mwen ki la, toupatou nan lemonn	That's my blood down there, all over the world
Se san mwen ki la, tipitit, gason e fi	That's my blood down there, little bitty boys and girls

Se san mwen ki la, nan Nikaragwa	That's my blood down there, in Nicaragua
Se san mwen ki la, nan El Salvadò	That's my blood down there, in El Salvador
Se san mwen ki la, nan Bèlfas.	That's my blood down there, in Belfast, Ireland.[14]

Developed in very particular historical circumstances but not in isolation from global economic, political, social, and ideological influences, the vision Benwa and I found embodied in the organizational and discursive practices of the peasant groups we studied is striking for the ways it speaks to issues and concerns that expand far beyond the boundaries of Haiti. Smarth characterizes Haiti's contemporary popular movement as part of a "political current flowing through Latin America and much of the world" (1997, 107). Indeed, related movements are currently sprouting up in rural hamlets, urban neighborhoods, universities, churches, and organizations all over the globe as people gather in attempts to confront the systems and agendas responsible for the disparities in wealth and power that now cripple the human community.[15] Some have called this trend a "quiet revolution," others an "organizational explosion"; some have placed it "at the cutting edge of a democratic revolution whose central themes are liberty, equality and autonomy" (Haynes 1997, 5).

Not all portraits are so enthusiastic. During the past several years, the optimistic projections scholars made in the 1980s and the early 1990s concerning the new social movements and burgeoning civil societies in the South have been tempered by a growing recognition that these movements are not immune to replicating many of the injustices against which they have struggled. As Alvarez points out, in the Latin American context.

> difficult questions regarding representation, accountability, and internal democracy *within* the social movement sector are far from resolved. And relations among the various strands and nodal points of intra- and intersocial movement webs are far from smooth. Indeed, movement fields are themselves mined by unequal power relations among individual participants, organizations and strands that have obtained differential access to material and cultural resources and gained uneven avenues of influence in and interlocution with official publics (1997, 105).

All too many illustrations of this are found in the patriarchal structures and gender-based inequities that characterized many of the groups Benwa and I worked with.[16] Despite the rapid growth of the gwoupman fanm peyizan movement, as Starn found among the *rondas* of Peru, much about Haitian peasant groups "recycles the all-too-familiar concept . . . of the male right to rule public affairs" (1992, 106). Yet, as group members themselves are prone to say, "They [the groups] may be ugly, but they are our own" and, therefore, immensely valuable. Alvarez, Dagnino, and Escobar agree. They acknowledge that many contemporary social movements are "riddled with unequal power relations." But they also assert that "however contradictory, the sustained public presence and proliferation of social movement webs and alternative publics has been a positive development for existing democracy" (1998b, 20; also see Haynes 1997, 170).

Change at the local level cannot be sustainable unless larger changes are also enacted. The ability of locally based social improvements to bring about large-scale changes will depend on their ability to identify the common visions among them and on finding ways of mobilizing their particular strengths in service of these visions. Esteva puts it this way:

> Globalised phenomena are real. Identifiable actors are promoting them. There are thus reasons to create coalitions of discontents of very different peoples and cultures, sharing a common opposition to those phenomena and lacking enough force to struggle against them at the local, regional or national level. (1999, 162)

. . . and beyond. During the past several decades, we have witnessed the rapid growth of transnational corporate enterprises and the proliferation of intergovernmental institutions. In general, such coalitions have exaggerated rather than challenged global disparities. Ironically, however, a key to the future success of grass-roots organizations and movements aimed at bringing about more just redistributions of wealth and power is whether they can follow the example of those institutions—specifically in developing networks and partnerships that traverse national boundaries, including those between the nations of the North and the nations of the South (see Alvarez, Dagnino, and Escobar 1998a, 1998b; Ching and Creed 1997). This effort will be very difficult for organizations in Haiti, most of which are in dire financial straits and have little or no access to telecommunications facilities. There are some notable exceptions, the most far-reaching of which is the Papaye Peasant Movement.[17] At present, however, Haiti has only very weak and incomplete "associative networks" (Chamers, Martin, and Piester 1997) among peasant groups themselves, and only rare communication with similar movements in other countries (see also R. Maguire 1990, 34). Still, such North–South coalitions are not impossible; many have been developed by Latin American movements in recent years despite serious infrastructural political and economic barriers. Fisher, for example, cites a virtual "explosion" of networking between Northern human rights and environmental organizations, and Southern grass-roots groups (1997, 452–53).

But these new coalitions must be radically different from the translational partnerships of the governmental and corporate world. They must also distinguish themselves from many previous established relationships between NGOs of the North-West and civil societies of the South—collaborations that, however well meaning, have very often continued to perpetuate dependency and subordination rather than liberation.

Where do such coalitions begin? First, a practiced respe must be developed between prospective partners. This sort of respe can be nurtured by acknowledging the common concerns and needs shared by individuals and communities on both sides of the Brandt line, while also honoring the many differences. For North-Westerners, it would mean actively challenging the idea that First Worlders have, know, and can, while Third Worlders lack resources, knowledge, and skills. It would mean opening ourselves to the possibility that the sort of subjectivity forwarded by group members who speak of being "fingers on a hand," "sticks in a bundle," and "one and the same we" is a sort of subjectivity many of us could stand to learn from. It would mean not only learning to "hear the voices of the disempowered" but also radically opening ourselves to the possibility of those voices transforming us.

It would mean, moreover, turning around the lens that looks for shortcomings and limitations exclusively in the communities of the impoverished and focusing instead on communities of the wealthy and the powerful. It would mean, as Spivak says, relearning "to represent ourselves" (1988, 289). The participants in these coalitions would have to replace dominant patterns of giving and receiving between the wealthy and the poor with patterns of reciprocal exchange, and acknowledge beyond a superficial level our mutual dependence on each other for liberation. Indeed, if we are to develop transnational social movements that can bring about true change, either on a large or small scale, we must radically redefine our "we's" and our "they's." We must recognize that it *is* "my blood down there" and act in the realization of that truth.

But of course, true respe and genuine coalitions cannot be generated simply by changes of heart. And they may well be impossible as long as the gulfs in material wealth and economic power that separate the affluent and the nonaffluent among us remain unchallenged. Consider once again the federation leader's analysis of impediments to collaboration among Haitians themselves. "Do you know what the biggest problem we have in this country is, Djeni? If I can eat and another person can't eat, how are you supposed to build a democracy on that? How do you think we can *mete tè-tansanm* [put our heads together, develop solidarity] like that? No, we have to be more uniform."

Real solidarity is impossible if the interests of those joining together are at odds. To call up an image from the countryside, in order to walk shoulder to shoulder, your feet have to be on the same path and be heading in the same direction. This has rarely been the case for North–South collaborations. Whether or not the potable water project is a success has generally had completely different implications for local residents and for the outsiders funding it or studying its impacts. It was obvious in our conversations with disgruntled Haitian employees of NGOs that they credited the failure of blan-s to work with them as colleagues not to the blan-s' mindsets or levels of goodwill, but rather to their inability to loosen their grasp on the resources, status, and decision-making powers granted them by their organizations. It will surely be impossible to get rid of illusions about the (in) capacities of the poor and the essential differences between those who aid and those who are aided as long as those illusions (to recall Chomsky's phrase) are "necessary," that is, as long as the pocketbooks and occupational status of the North-Westerners depends on the maintenance of those gaps. Any meaningful ideological restructuring must be accompanied by political and economic restructuring.

A Call for Undoing Ourselves

One must then resist the desire to formulate alternatives at an abstract, macro level; one must also resist the idea that the articulation of alternatives will take place in intellectual and academic circles, without meaning by this that academic knowledge has no role in the politics of alternative thinking. . . .

The crisis in the regimes of representation of the Third World . . . calls for new theories and research strategies; the crisis is a real conjunctional moment in the reconstruction of the connection between truth and reality, between words and things, one that demands new practices of seeing, knowing, and being. (Escobar 1995, 223–23)

We are not being asked, nor are we needed, to control or direct local efforts of change. We are being challenged, however, to respond to them on their own terms and to work in helping to find new and sustainable solutions of age-old problems. (Maguire 1990, 43)

Because challenging the gulfs that separate "First World" and "Third World" citizens, fostering mutual respe, and building coalitions between us means integrating differences, detecting commonalities, acting and thinking both globally and locally at once, and combining theoretical innovations with practical strategies, anthropologists have unique opportunities to make a contribution. Because this challenge will involve the recruitment of financial and material resources, and a wide variety of technical skills and knowledge, NGOs, IGOs, and transnational professionals also stand to make essential contributions. But to do so, these parties must be willing to push our professions beyond their limits, to undo them and recreate them.

David Lewis (1999) rightly points out that anthropologists have thus far failed to take full advantage of our profession's particular skills in building the sorts of transnational coalitions envisioned here. Yet we have extensive experience in serving as liaisons between sectors in the South and sectors in the North. Neither are anthropologists unfamiliar with trying to "widen the discussions of what constitutes the global public good" (Jackie Smith 1998, 102). Many of us do that daily in our classrooms. The challenge is to move that discussion beyond the classroom walls, peer-reviewed journals, and conference dates, and into arenas populated by publics—and the political and economic powers—of both the North and the South. Made ever more feasible (and imperative) by technological changes taking place around the globe, such dialectical exchanges may well be the future role or "place" for which the field of anthropology now seems to be searching.

Anthropologists might also do well to more intentionally invite the examples and philosophies of those with whom we have worked to interrupt the pursuit of our professional and personal agendas, and guide us toward new ways of thinking and acting. As anthropologists have learned many times, this can sometimes mean having to restructure our lives: redefine job descriptions, reformulate identities, and reconstitute lifestyles. Taking ethically informed positions that challenge practically as well as theoretically some of the very privileges on which we stand can involve taking messy risks indeed. We have little choice, however, if we hope to contribute in meaningful ways to the efforts of the people of Bamòn and Kalfounò to bring about a world in which we can all finally "live as humans were meant to live."

Notes

Chapter 1. Introduction

1. See Castañeda 1996; Escobar 1995; Esteva 1993; Haynes 1997; Lummis 1996; Sachs 1993.

2. See Elie 1992; G. Smucker 1996, 1983; Smucker and Noriac 1996, Vander Zaag 1999; A. White 1994, 1992.

3. Such portrayals are found in Conway 1989; Elie 1992; Erasmus 1952, 1956; Laguerre 1975; Lundahl 1983; Murray 1977; Smucker 1983; and S.A.C.A.D.-F.A.M.V. 1993.

4. Kayayo, like the names of all the communities and individuals cited in the text (except for major cities and towns, and nationally known figures), is fictional.

5. In the countryside, older men are often titled *Ton*, meaning "Uncle," to indicate respect.

6. Here the speaker was playing on the semi-rhyming sound produced by pronouncing the last two syllables of the Haitian Creole term for *democracy* (*demokrasi*) and the term for *spit* (*krache*).

7. For critical assessments of U.S.-sponsored democracy-enhancement initiatives in Haiti, see IHERC 1992; CHA and IHERC 1990; Aristide and Richardson 1994b, 35.

8. I continued my engagement with Haiti as a graduate student in a number of ways, among them working as a Haitian Creole-English translator in Guantánamo Bay, Cuba on several occasions between January 1991 and the spring of 1993 (first with the U.S. Immigration and Naturalization Service and then with a coalition of lawyers working on behalf of the refugees); as a U.N. human rights observer in Haiti (between June and November 1993); and in several other capacities as a volunteer, both in the United States and during trips to Haiti.

9. Also on this subject, see Comaroff 1985; Cooper et al. 1993; Dirks 1992b; Roseberry 1993; Scott 1990, 1985; Shanin 1990; G. Smith 1991, 1989.

10. Most notably, Herskovits 1971 [1937]; Leyburn 1941; Lundahl 1979; Moral 1978; Mintz 1973, 1974, 1990; Trouillot 1990.

11. As Dupuy notes, this system grew in large part out of the rural population's chronic resistance to forced plantation labor in the early to mid-nineteenth century (1989, 98).

12. Though dated, see Mintz 1964, 1961; Murray and Alvarez 1975; J. Smucker 1981; and Underwood 1960 for good discussions of this marketing system.

13. Women's *'ti komès,'* or small marketing activities, commonly provide rural households with the majority of their cash income.

14. See Dupuy 1989, 99–102, for a concise but detailed overview of stratifications and fragmentations within both the elite and the peasantry. An especially rich discussion on class in the countryside is offered by Woodson 1990, 279–305.

15. This is true of peasantries in general. Orin Starn makes a similar point in his study on peasants in Peru (1992, 94).

16. *Abitasyon-s*, sometimes translated as "rural hamlets" or "scattered rural settlement," is the term used to describe the loosely defined residential neighborhoods in which most rural Haitians reside. An abitasyon may include anywhere from a handful to over a hundred residences.

17. The *seksyon riral* is the smallest rural administrative district in Haiti. Each section joins several others in comprising a commune, which may be loosely compared to a county in the United States.

18. This calculated guess is based on statistics from the Jérémie office of the Ministry of Public Health and Sanitation (MSPP) and a population survey conducted by a large foreign-based NGO in Jérémie.

19. Jérémie, which is reported to have around 35,000 inhabitants (Devin 1995, 40), lies approximately 120 kilometers (290 km by road) from Port-au-Prince. It can be reached from Port-au-Prince via an 8–12 hour jeep or public-bus ride, a 45-minute flight on a twelve-seater airplane, or a 12–15 hour ferry trip.

20. Literally, "stepped-over clothes," these are items sent to Haiti from the Salvation Army and other charities, and sold on the black market. They are found piled in heaps on the ground in even the most out-of-the-way outdoor marketplaces of the country. They are very inexpensive and have thus both provided poor Haitians with more variety in clothing than they would otherwise have, and simultaneously devastated the local tailoring industry.

21. The deities of the Vodou religion.

Chapter 2. Persistent Legacies

1. Beginning in January 1, 1804, Dessalines ruled the nation (first as president and later as self-proclaimed emperor) until his assassination on October 17, 1806.

2. In this way, Trouillot accounts for the rise and reign of the notorious Duvalier regime. He suggests the success of the Duvaliers was not so much an exceptional phenomenon as it was the nearly inevitable outcome of a long list of social, economic, and political strategies employed by Haiti's ruling elite since the first days of the country's independence (see also Dupuy 1989; Fick 1990; Heinl and Heinl 1978; Leyburn 1941; Mintz 1974; Moral 1978; Nicholls 1979)

3. A senk kòb piece, worth 5/100 goud, is roughly equivalent to one third of a penny. In fact, U.S. pennies circulate in great numbers on the Haiti market as substitutes for Haitian-minted senk kòb pieces.

4. Fass reports that in 1979, "Port-au-Prince received 83 percent of all public expenditures, including 79 percent of salaries, 95 percent of other operating expenditures, and 80 percent of subsidies" (1988, 8).

5. This term was derived from the locally made popsicle of the same name. To consume it, one "presses down" at one end and "sucks out" the frozen sweetness at the other, until the plastic wrapper is left empty and dry.

6. As Mintz notes, between 1807 and 1915, "of Haiti's twenty-four executives . . . only eight were in office for a period equal to their elected terms, and seventeen were deposed by revolution" (quoted in Leyburn 1941, ix).

7. Elsewhere (in J. M. Smith 1993) I have written in detail about what happened to these refugees once they were intercepted by the U.S. Coast Guard.

8. These policies ranged from amnesty for the perpetrators of the coup to land redistribution, "free-trade" economic initiatives, and the privatization of state industries.

9. Statistics on Haiti are difficult both to acquire and substantiate and, thus, should be taken with more than a small grain of salt. The statistics cited are taken from a number of sources, including annual profiles prepared by the UNDP; The Economist Intelligence Unit and Business International, 1991–92; Gagnon 1986; the Institute for Agriculture and Trade Policy 1996; Kovaleski 1999; PAHO 1990; Schutt-Ainé 1994; WOH-PAPDA 1996; the World Bank; and USAID.

10. All dollar amounts presented here represent U.S. dollars.

11. When I told several Bamòn residents about the $100 figure, they reacted with surprise and quickly informed me that most people do not earn any amount close to that.

12. Only 162, Meme (1996) reports, are recognized officially by the state.

13. This item has been pouring into Haiti during the past few years. Because most Haitian do not have access to refrigeration, these hotdogs, like turkey wings and other imported perishables, are generally sold on the streets of Haiti's major towns in unrefrigerated boxes, thus presenting the population with yet another serious public health threat.

14. Unfortunately, Haitians are not the only ones familiar with such experiences. Similar stories are legion in Africa, Asia, and the larger Latin American and Caribbean region. See Macdonald (1997) for an informative study of the impact of aid on Latin American communities.

15. CIVPOL, the civilian police force of the United Nations, was in charge of supervising and training the new Haitian police force, which was founded in 1995 to replace the previous, infamously corrupt and abusive, one.

16. IOM/OTI 1994, "Initial Field Interview Guidelines," 1.

17. IOM is an IGO based in Geneva. Before receiving funding for this project, IOM's work in Haiti had been largely confined to migration issues. In collaboration with the U.S. INS, for instance, it ran a highly controversial asylum screening program during the post-coup era. Its communal governance and development program, as well as another program through which it offered compensatory salaries and professional training to ex-military employees, became equally contested by Haitians, particularly those active in popular movements.

18. The initial grant, provided by USAID, amounted to $14 million.

19. As quoted in Kovaleski 1999; see also Arthur 1995; Chomsky 1994; Cooley-Proust 1995; Deshommes 1995; Dewind and McKinley 1986; Diederich 1985; Farmer 1994a, 1994b; Haïti Progrès 1996; HIB 1994; IHERC 1992; Izmery 1994; Matenowska 1996; McGowan 1997; NLC 1994, 1996; Regan 1994; Richardson and Chery 1997; Ridgeway 1994; Trouillot 1990; Voices for Haiti 1995; R. White 1997; WOH-PAPDA 1996.

20. The USAID official is quoted in WOH-PAPDA 1996. Also see DeWind and Kinley 1986, and Lappé, Collins and Kinley 1981. Ransom (1996, 9) reports that the situation is similar in the case of aid from ODA (Great Britain's Official Development Assistance).

21. This occurred, for example, during Aristide's first administration (1991), when he proposed raising the daily wage from 25 goud-s (around $1.65) to 75 goud-s ($5.00). A compromise of 36 goud-s ($2.40) was eventually reached (a figure that still falls well below a living wage).

22. It is now well documented how much of the food aid itself leads to more hunger in the long run, primarily by undercutting local market prices, reducing demand for locally produced goods, increasing dependency on imported items, and eventually driving small farmers out of business—and often, out of the countryside and into urban slums. In a 1995 special report, the Washington Office on Haiti details how one particular food security program, supported by USAID and the U.S. Department of Agriculture, has actively undermined the wellbeing of rural Haitians while generating millions of dollars for the U.S.-based Comet Rice Company (WOH 1995). See Richardson and Chery 1997 for a more general but rigorous critique of U.S.-sponsored food aid in Haiti during the past several decades; also see McGowan 1997, and DeWind and Kinley 1986.

23. See Aristide and Richardson 1994a; Kennedy and Tilly 1996; Richardson and Chery 1995–96; WOH 1995.

24. In fact, some rural Haitians have become quite adept at figuring out ways to get something of value out of that water. As Vander Zaag notes:

Rural people have developed quite pragmatic knowledges concerning "development". They have learned how to exploit, divert, and comply with project intentions according to their own short term interests. Even though the practices of development may be ill-suited to the actual conditions and requirements of rural Haitians, to a large degree they have adopted the discourse, identified themselves with it, and learned to utilize it to gain whatever benefits they can from its agents. (1999, 265)

25. This song is sung by GP community organizations (see chapter 7). The *wozo* is a reed that grows near the water. It is renowned for its tenacious resistance against floods, fire, machetes, and other enemies bent on destroying it.

26. When referring to "Vodou," I am pointing to a myriad of beliefs and practices centered on the lwa-s, the deities of the Haitian people. Vodou was developed initially in the context of slavery, and on the foundation of the religious memories, spiritual needs, and cultural resources of the slaves. It is a dynamic, syncretic, and complex religion that draws from many traditions, most notably the religions of the slaves' African homelands and the European Catholicism of their captors.

27. It is said that the first leaders of the Saint Domingue Revolution used the lanbi to summon their enslaved and runaway followers to fight against the colonists. The lanbi's use as a means of calling people together continues to this day in rural Haiti, and its value as both a tool and a symbol of liberation remains widely recognized among the population.

28. At the time (fall of 1993), diplomatic talks concerning the return of the coup-ousted government were faltering, the country's economy was deteriorating rapidly, and human rights abuses executed by the ruling junta and its allies were increasing in number and kind.

29. Holland and Eisenhart 1990, see also Abu-Lughod 1990; Comaroff 1985, 260; Levinson and Holland 1996; Willis 1977, 1981.

Chapter 3. Melodic Machetes

1. This song, called "Raraman," is recorded by the Mini All Stars on the collection *Konbit: Burning Rhythms of Haiti.*

2. The lwa-s are the deities of the Vodou religion.

3. See Richman (1987) for a discussion of other media.

4. *Chante pwen* may also be written *chan pwent, chante pwen,* or *chante pwent,* the spelling of both words varying according to geographical region or context. (Although *chante* means both "song" and "to sing," *chan* is strictly used as a noun.).

5. In enlisting the services of Vodou practitioners (the *ougan,* the *manbo,* and the *bokò*) and appealing to certain lwa-s, these pwen-s are given the power to cast spells, charm, lend protection, or otherwise act on the world in a supernatural manner. The same chante pwen might be laden with magic powers in some contexts and not in others—just as "Panama M Tonbe" might be used either for launching political critiques or simply goofing off. This chapter concentrates on the social rather than the spiritual affectivity of chante pwen-s.

6. During my time in Bamòn, the standard wage for a day of work was 5 goud-s (US $0.33). People were sometimes paid as much as 8 goud-s ($0.53) or as little as 3 goud-s ($0.20).

7. Adapted from Courlander 1973 [1960], 143.

8. Recorded in Courlander 1973 [1960], 153. Sam ruled Haiti between 1896 and 1902.

9. The gwoupman peyizan is the subject of chapter 8.

10. Community Relations Service, the branch of the U.S. State Department in charge of resettling refugees admitted into the United States.

11. I heard it sung on several occasions in Miami and Washington, D.C., during marches protesting the junta rulers and U.S. policies toward Haitian refugees.

12. These lyrics are excerpts of "Tande M Tande," from the Boukman Eksperyans album *Kalfou Danjere* (1992).

Chapter 4. Hoes Striking in Unison

1. Blaike's term, as cited in Blaike and Brookfield 1987, 13.

2. Hunter estimated the population density at 244 persons per square kilometer in 1996 (1996–97, 608).

3. Recent research reveals that most peasants own less than a quarter of a hectare (Institute for Agriculture and Trade 1996). In 1951, Bastien claims, 94 percent of residents of the southern village of Marbial held less than 3 *kawo*-s (<3.87 hectares), and 70 percent less than 1 kawo (<1.29 hectares) (1985 [1951], 40–41). Murray found that in the 1970s, the average holding in the northern village he calls "Kinabwa" was "slightly less than 2 hectares" (1977, 208). Lundahl (1983) estimated in the early 1980s that rural landholdings averaged 1–1.5 hectares. Participants in A. White's 1994 study in the Central Plateau averaged 2.5 hectares in landholdings (1994, 24), which would have been quite high for the nearby zone of Kalfounò. Neighbors in Bamòn estimated in 1996 that few people in the area held more than one-half hectare.

4. For good discussions of land-tenure patterns in rural Haiti, see Dupuy 1989, Murray 1977, and Woodson 1990.

5. In most rural settlements, at least one family would also have a *kouto digo* or a *louchèt* (a spade made of a short wooden handle to which a single blade is attached); and perhaps a *pens* (a heavy iron gig with which larger and deeper holes may be made). More rarely found are tools such as the *pikwa* (pickax), the *derapin* (a type of double-bladed hoe with a long, flat rectangular blade on one side and a pickax blade on the other), and the *rach* and *rachòt* (ax and hatchet, respectively). As well adapted as such tools are to the rugged landscape, utilizing them nonetheless involves an incredible amount of painstakingly slow and back-breaking effort.

6. Only 7 percent of cultivated land is irrigated (McGowan 1997, 4).

7. Significant rainfall is limited in most areas of the country to a couple of brief seasons, each lasting only a few weeks. As I noted in chapter 1, in Bamòn this generally occurs in April and May, and again beginning in October or November and lasting through most of December. The longest dry season tends to fall between January and early April. (See Anglade 1977; Lundahl 1983; A. Métraux 1951; R. Métraux 1952; Moral 1978; Murray 1977; S.A.C.A.D. and F.A.M.V. 1993 for detailed descriptions of agricultural seasons in different areas of the country and their effects on agricultural practices.)

8. This common phrase, meaning "one helping another" is used to talk about mutual assistance, cooperation, and reciprocal sharing.

9. This term, commonly translated as *yard* or *courtyard*, is used to refer to the extended-family or nuclear-family residential compounds in which Haitian peasants reside. Lakou-s are comprised of a packed-dirt yard, one or more house(s), one or more outdoor kitchen(s), and the grove of fruit trees and plants that surrounds all this. Many such groves contain a latrine or other structures, such as a small cane press and an animal pen. When a lakou contains two or more houses, the sharing of material items, chores, food, space, and child care between its residents is extensive. It is therefore more accurate to say that the lakou, and not any one of the discrete physical structures comprising it, is the "home" of those who live there. In discussing the lakou and describing its history, Smucker says, "If the *habitation* was the fundamental unit of the colonial regime, the *lakou* is the essential social unit of peasant society" (1983, 112–21). See also Woodson 1990, 195–206, for another detailed discussion of the meaning and significance of lakou-s.

10. Literally, "Mrs." When a woman in the countryside marries, it is proper to address her by this title, followed by the first name, or common nickname, of her husband. Even close family members, including parents and siblings, will regularly address a woman as "Madan——" once she marries. In fact, even if she and her husband part (through death, migration, or a rift in the relationship), and she later partners with someone else, most acquaintances will likely continue to call her "Madan [*her first husband's name*]." Usually, people do not refer to a woman in a common-law marriage with the title "Madan——," though that sort of union is widely accepted as a legitimate. She would be addressed, rather, by her first name or nickname, which might be preceded by another respect-denoting familial title such as "Aunt," or "Sister."

11. A backyard grove in Bamòn might include any number of the following trees: orange, lime, mango, a variety of palm trees, cocoa, coconut, banana and plantain, breadfruit, *labapen* and *djaka* (both related to the breadfruit), grapefruit, shaddock, avocado, almond, cashew, papaya, pomegranate, ackee, custard apple, star apple, guava, sapodilla, and corossol.

12. Also common are plants such as passionfruit, pineapple, ginger, tropical pumpkin, patches of sugar cane, peanuts, sesame, mushrooms, *toto* (an edible fungus), and jicama. (See Smucker 1983, 112–17, for a discussion of still more resources found within and around the peasant lakou.)

13. "*Men, Djeni, non tout, se nou menm nou menm nan.*" By this phrase they did not mean that they are all just alike, but rather, that they are inextricably interconnected and, therefore, interdependent.

14. See chapter 1.

15. Dry seasons are also called *sezon grangou* (hungry seasons) or *sezon chèch* (lean seasons).

16. "In all rural areas, but especially the more backward ones, there is a strong social pressure among the farmers to maintain the status quo through what might be called the 'jealousy pattern,'" and thus an accompanying predominance of "black magic" (Erasmus 1952, 23 1956).

17. These societies are said to comprise either djab-s or lougawou-s. *Djab* is often translated literally as "devil," and *lougawou* as "werewolf," but neither of those definitions fits just right. They are malleable terms, sometimes used interchangeably to refer to people who can become invisible or turn into any of an assortment of creatures in order to carry out malevolent tasks, such as cursing and killing others. Groups of these demonic characters, I was told, meet at the region's crossroads at midnight or one- or two o'clock in the morning. When out at night, one may see their fires burning or hear their voices in the distance. "They turn other people into djab-s by inviting them to come [to their meetings]," I was told. "[If you refuse] they can go ask a bòkò to put a curse on you."

18. Lakou-s are nuclear-family or extended-family residential compounds. (See note 9, above, for a detailed description.)

19. Murray (1977) offers a detailed discussion on "domestic labor" recruitment. While it is helpful in general, his estimation of women's low degree of participation in agricultural labor is not accurate for Bamòn, where women play a greater role. For more accurate portrayals, see Vander Zaag 1999 and A. White 1993.

20. This hybridity has characterized the Haitian peasantry since its inception. Of Haiti's nineteenth-century peasantry, Dupuy says, "In addition to being peasants with access to land, the poor peasants were also partial wage-laborers and must therefore be included among the rural proletariat" (1989, 102).

21. Though unofficially sanctioned by local convention as a just wage for agricultural labor, this sum was significantly lower than the nation's legal minimum wage during the same period. That wage was 25 goud-s per day when I first began my fieldwork and then rose to 36 goud-s per day—an amount still well below a living wage.

22. A type of sharecropping system (*demwatye*) commonly practiced in the Haitian country-side involves a landowner renting out a plot of land to a tenant for a specified time. That time may consist of one or two seasons, or several years (often via extension of a shorter "contract"). The sharecropper is obliged to give a certain percentage of the crop to the landowner as payment. Sharecroppers are often required to part with more than one half of their produce, though many take advantage of having control over the means of production to reduce this amount significantly (see Dupuy 1989, 91).

23. See G. Smucker 1983, A. Métraux 1951, and Murray 1977 for details on the wage labor systems in the areas where they studied.

24. For additional perspectives on this issue, see Murray (1977, 293–94) and Martínez (1996, 75–76); for a discussion of similar labor preferences among Latin American peasants, see Eckstein (1989, 18). See also Barthélemy 1989; R. Métraux 1952; G. Smucker 1983.

25. "*You sèl wou pa fè mizik*" is a familiar proverb in rural Haiti.

26. For a detailed discussion of the konbit and the kòve, and a chart of scholarly references to them, see J.M. Smith 1998.

27. The owner might be male or female. While their participation is often understated in the literature, women as well as men participate in konbit-s and kòve-s, both as hosts and work-

ers. Owing to the large (and increasing) number of women-headed households, land-tenure patterns that ensure female ownership, and the participation of women in the marketing system (which provides many women with capital while also taking them away from work close to home), it is not unusual for women to own and administer landholdings. In terms of participants, most konbit-s and kòve-s are mixed. While all-female ones are found in some areas of the country, all-male konbit-s and kòve-s are more common. Neither situation is regarded as ideal, however. Although men generally outnumber women participants in mixed konbit-s and hold most of the leadership positions among the guests, the contributions of women workers are nonetheless regarded as crucial.

28. Some of these are described in detail by Herskovitz 1971 [1937]; Laguerre 1975; A. Métraux 1951; and S.A.C.A.D.-F.A.M.V. 1993.

29. A musician and a composer, the *sanba* is also commonly referred to as a *simidor.*

30. Called *kleren, tafya,* or *gwòg,* the liquor consumed at konbit-s and kòve-s is a locally produced unrefined white rum distilled from sugar cane.

31. Herskovitz notes that a konbit of fifty to seventy-five workers can clear a field of several acres in a single day "without undue effort" (1971, 72).

32. R.B. Hall 1929, Herskovitz 1971, A. Métraux 1951, Wirkus and Dudley 1931, as well as many older Haitians, recall such feasts. Following chronic increases in the costs of food and livestock, nowadays the final meal generally consists simply of a large bowl of rice and beans or, more commonly in the mountains, ground-corn porridge with beans. (Corn is less expensive than rice and is known to "lend strength" to the workers.) The meal may or may not be topped off with a small piece of goat meat, pork, or beef, or a sauce made with the less-expensive *aran,* an imported dried, salted fish.

33. This is true except in exceptional cases and for certain tasks. The people of Bamòn, for instance, told me that a simple meal of ground corn porridge and beans is often served at bean-planting kòve-s, since planting beans generally takes longer and is more tedious than other tasks. Food is also sometimes served at the more konbit-like "invitational" kòve.

34. This utilization of *corvée* labor to carry out public works projects was hardly unprecedented in Haiti. The Haitian state had orchestrated such systems in the nineteenth century (Dupuy 1989, 104). During the eighteenth century, the French had organized slaves into work teams or "gangs" (Lundahl 1983, 215). For this reason, Lundahl suggests that the konbit (and therefore the kòve) has "a 'double' origin," in both the plantations of Saint Domingue and certain collective African practices.

35. Rare voices of dissent on this issue are found in Clerisme (1978) and Smucker and Noriac (1996). It is notable that these authors imply that such groups continue to survive not because of but in spite of their immersion in "traditional" peasant culture: "They are able to thrive despite a peasant social context which is otherwise class stratified and individualistic—defined by self-interest, family ties, patron-client relations, and factions rather than the wider, general interest of the rural community" (Smucker and Noriac 1996, 36).

36. See chapter 1.

Chapter 5. The *Atribisyon*

1. In this case, *fèt* could be interpreted as "feast," "celebration," or "holiday."

2. A person who heals others through a combination of therapeutic touch and other physical and supraphysical techniques.

3. Many atribisyon members, in talking with me about their groups, stressed over and again the principle that at the end-of-year rachòt, no atribisyon member should receive any more meat than another. Women and men, officers and lay members, old and young, those who worked forty days during the year and those who worked fifty—everyone gets the same allotment. No worker, they would repeat, gets more than another.

Chapter 6. The *Sosyete*

1. Generally, the lists of cadences employed by the different types of sosyete-s are both extensive and fluid. Although each type of group claims certain ones as trademarks, many are shared with most of the other sosyete-s in the area.

2. See J.M. Smith 1993 for a detailed description of the signature instruments, cadences, and songs of each type of sosyete.

3. Anglade reports to have known sosyete-s with more than three hundred members (1977, 71).

4. For more descriptions of some of the above offices, and lists of others, refer to R.B. Hall 1929; Laguerre 1975; A. Métraux 1960, 1971; R. Métraux 1952; Vallès 1967; Wirkus and Dudley 1931.

5. Drill sergeants are described by R.B. Hall as having been in charge of advising defendants during trials held by the sosyete-s, as well as performing the sword work at ceremonies (1929, 695).

6. Intended for disaster relief, this assistance was provided mostly by the U.S. government.

7. See Chomsky 1994; Cooley-Proust 1995; Farmer 1996; Richardson and Chery 1997.

8. In general, exemptions from manual labor are based either on physical health or on a recognition of valuable contributions made. I was told that in Bamòn, for example, if some monitors were not expected to labor with their groups, it was because they were elderly, or because the rituals they performed for the group free of charge were considered to be of great value.

9. I have yet to discover in texts written between the 1920s and 1950s, for example, a reference to any of the founisè positions I found in Bamòn. The founisè-s, it seems, have adopted the responsibility of material support (and some of the privileges that come from providing it) that used to be assumed by queens, kings, and emperors.

10. At several points during the meeting, participants discussed others who had come to work in their neighborhoods. Although no foreigner had lived in the immediate area before I arrived, many initiatives had been promoted there by visiting blan-s and Haitians from the cities. People talked about programs carried out as far back as under Papa Doc Duvalier's reign, and about many of those sponsored by the Catholic church. They became most animated and passionate when discussing those of late. Tempers flared as people spoke passionately about the many times they had been deceived and disappointed ("Yo fè n desepyon, twòp!"). I took this in part as a pwen of sorts, an indirect but salient warning alerting me that they were not anxious to be taken for another ride.

11. Like many sosyete flags, Prankè's flag is red. Flags may feature group names and elaborate designs, but Prankè's consisted simply of a rectangular piece of cloth attached to a long wooden pole. Some groups use a flag like this for kòve-s and reserve a fancier one for special ceremonies or feasts.

12. "Master" is a title bestowed liberally by rural Haitians on men of stature, such as teachers, pastors, judges, and prosperous farmers and businessmen. While the title denotes respect and at times a certain degree of subservience on the part of the speaker, it does not mean "master" in a literal sense.

13. A small fire built by the laplas with sticks and bits of fodder, it serves as a lighter for members' pipes and hand-rolled cigaretts.

14. Probably first performed between 1991 and 1994, this song had an uncannily peppy beat.

15. Given that the memberships of sosyete-s are both significantly larger and more geographically dispersed than those of the atribisyon-s, it is not surprising that sosyete leaders tend to have greater difficulty ordering and mobilizing participation in their groups' events. Most sosyete-s, therefore, have a set of definitive, if generally unwritten, rules of conduct and attendance. The strictest of these are the rules of attendance. While it seems that in most cases, members are quick to accept an excuse such as sickness or an urgent family need, still, the

truth of A. Métraux's assertion that "the gravest lapse of which a member can be guilty is to absent himself without good reason from work" (1951, 81) was clear in Bamòn. Absenteeism is thus the lapse for which penalties are most readily handed out.

16. This member, I was told, was dying of *maladi kat 'h'*, the "four h's disease." This way of referring to AIDS by people in a remote area underscores the remarkable scope of the ramifications of the U.S. Center for Disease Control's 1983 classification of Haitians (along with hemophiliacs, heroin addicts, and homosexuals) as one of the epidemic's four high-risk groups, that is, one of the "4 h's." For an excellent discussion of the impact on Haitians of this CDC proclamation—which was widely criticized and later changed—the spread of the virus itself, and some of the causes and effects of both, see Paul Farmer's work *Aids and Accusation: Haiti and the Geography of Blame* (1992).

17. To do this, they construct a *branka*, a makeshift stretcher made of long poles and slabs of wood.

18. Generally, the coffin is not ready until the wake is well underway. In fact, burials are often delayed because of the time taken to construct the coffin.

19. Along with other texts, prèt savann-s are generally equipped with the voluminous hymn-book known as the *Masay*, the full title of which is *Canticles of the Religious Soul, Said to Originate from Marseilles, Adapted to Common Tunes*. As A. Métraux puts it, "The tunes which form the basis of the Marseilles are of European origin and derive from Church music and the Cantilena, but rhythm and register are certainly African in tradition" (1972 [1959], 249). Texts also often utilized by the prèt savann-s of Bamòn include the *Bouke Finèb*, the *Rekèy*, and "the *kreyòl* book" (a Creole-language Catholic hymnbook). Few of the bush priests, so well versed in thousands of lines from such texts, speak or read either French or Latin with great proficiency. Indeed, many are functionally illiterate.

20. Usually, either a kerosene-filled *lanp gridap*, made from a small tin can, or one half of a calabash gourd into which castor oil is poured and a piece of cotton immersed.

21. Because the lime lanp and nevenn rites involve a considerable amount of expense, many families are not able to arrange them immediately after a death. In some cases, these rites are held years later, after family members have either become more economically secure or, on the contrary, have suffered so many trials and tribulations that they begin to suspect the deceased is showing his or her displeasure with their disloyalty.

22. This closely resembles dancing in the Vodou temple, where the priest or priestess's female assistants (*ounsi-s*) are commonly robed in the white dresses and lead attendees in dancing and singing.

23. Here "Ginen," which is associated geographically with West Africa, refers to the ancestral homeland of the Haitian people. It is said that when Africans were captured and transported on European ships to the slave plantations of the New World, their deities (*vodou-s* or *lwa-s*) passed under the water, accompanying them. Some Haitians believe that when they themselves die, they will go back to the original home of their lwa-s. "Ginen" may also mean more generally the dwelling place of the lwa-s, or refer "to a more general state of spiritual development and awareness for Haitians who practice traditional religion (Vodou)" (Boukman Eksperyans 1992).

24. This song is a chante pwen. One of the dancers explained, "There are people who come to the dances, but they don't dance. They don't even sing. They come to watch, so that afterwards, they can go ridicule others."

25. This song, I was told, calls on the three kings of the Kongo nation. Nelswa, Gaspa, and Baltaza.

Chapter 7. The *Gwoupman Peyizan*

1. See, for example, Luc Smarth's otherwise thorough study, "Popular Organizations and the Transition to Democracy in Haiti" (1997).

2. An exception is found in the work of American anthropologist Glenn Smucker and Haitian researcher and agronomist Dathis Noriac. Smucker and Noriac studied over the course of several years a variety of GPs in different areas of the country. From this work they generated two papers that outline the history and nature of GPs (G. Smucker 1996; Smucker and Noriac 1996; also see G. Smucker 1983, 1986).

. 3. Alvarez (1997, 93) and other scholars note that the pattern of authoritarian rulers using neighborhood-based associations to control and co-opt the poor is found in Latin America as well.

4. Clerisme (1978) explains that konsèy kominotè-s and gwoupman kominotè-s are two distinct group types, the former being more engaged in local governance and development, and the latter in agricultural labor exchange. In Bamòn, however, all of these priorities are combined in a single type of organization, which, as I have pointed out, is generally referred to as "kominotè."

5. Vander Zaag offers a rich study of "the encounter of discontinuous 'knowledge' and 'identities' at the development interface" (1999, 135).

6. See Anne Greene's *The Catholic Church in Haiti: Political and Social Change* (1993) for a description of these organizations and their work.

7. Small groups of lay Catholic church members concerned with studying the Bible together from a liberation theology perspective, they resemble the Christian base communities of Latin America in many ways.

8. Set up along with "small commerce" groups for women, it was patterned in large part on the Grameen Bank model. The project has aimed to help members build up enough capital to profit from their marketing activities.

9. This saved the small commerçantes in the area considerable amounts of money and time as well as energy, since they often walked many miles, either to Jérémie or the region's other commercial centers, in search of produce that might be selling at a few pennies less per pound than what was available in their home communities.

10. In Haitian Creole, *gra* means "fat."

11. Even under the "democratic" regimes of the late 1990s, repression of the peasant group movement has not been unknown. The March 25–31, 1998, issue of *Haïti Progrès*, for instance, reports that CIMO, the heavily armed rapid intervention force of the Haitian National Police (PNH), invaded the northern towns of Milo and Limonad, and attacked peasant group members and others who had been involved in recent land redistribution initiatives. Several people were beaten or wounded by gunfire, and two were killed. The offices and equipment of the radio station Peasants' Voice were destroyed. Peasant groups have continued to meet and work despite such oppressions.

12. Haynes suggests that "women's groups—both development and empowerment oriented—are probably the most rapidly proliferating types of groups in the Third World" (1997, 130). These groups, Baldez claims, "have played a very important role in the process of strengthening civil society, especially in the past ten to twenty years" (1998, 785).

13. Such contradictions are also found among community organizations in Latin America. Kaufman records a community association president in Costa Rica as admitting that while "women are better leaders in the community . . . 'because they are closer to the problems of everyday life' . . . many men try to keep their wives from getting too active" (1997, 152).

14. For characterizations of women's groups in the Americas region, see Baldez 1998; Kaufman 1997; Lind 1992, Mainwaring and Viola 1994, 39; and Schild 1997.

15. For more on this topic in the context of women's groups in Haiti, see Vander Zaag 1999, 206–19.

16. As is the case for the memberships of most other GFVs in the area, most of these women were in their mid-twenties or older, and had spouses and children. Teenage girls rarely participated in GFVs, though by the end of my fieldwork, PSC was beginning to encourage the formation of groups specifically for teenage girls.

17. This phrase implies, "He'll take care of us."

18. Préval won, earning nearly 90 percent of the votes cast.

19. Tallies revealed that under 30 percent of the 3.7 million eligible voters went to the polls (Farah 1995).

20. Such direct promotion of particular parties and candidates in gwoupman meetings has not been uncommon. I first noticed the conflation of voter education with campaigning during the 1990 election season that put Aristide in the presidency. I attended many GT meetings during that era which, ostensibly aimed at promoting the ideals of the democratic process and teaching gwoupman members the mechanics of how to vote, were largely dominated by members being instructed on why and how to vote for *him.*

21. There had been a round of local and parliamentary elections the past summer.

22. See *Monitoring Reports,* a monthly and bimonthly series published by USAID between November 1994 and January 1996.

23. This title, meaning "Sister," is a polite way to refer to unmarried women.

24. As Schild notes in her study of NGOs in Latin America (1997, 136–37), the "intangible aid" NGOs offer to local organizations has received much less attention than material aid, yet in many cases, it has been at least— or even more—highly valued by locals themselves.

25. This translation is from *The New Oxford Annotated Bible* (1977).

26. See chapter 2 for a critique of the overall effect of such trends.

27. In his study of GPs in a Central Plateau community, Vander Zaag suggests that a concern with getting "development" resources was the central priority of virtually all the groups: "*Groupman* and women's clubs were largely reinterpreted in terms of dominant local knowledges concerning how to gain access to development project resources. Thus membership and local group 'activity' were maintained in an informal and 'loose' manner, in order to sustain ascending social relations to more 'powerful' social actors represented by the . . . development program" (1999, 164).

28. The *wozo* is a reed that grows near the water. It is known for its tenacious resistance to floods, fire, machetes, and other attackers bent on destroying it.

29. Scholars of new social movements in Latin America have noted the same thing (see Alvarez 1997, 94).

30. This is surely due partly to the memberships of the "Old Testament" groups and the newer gwoupman tètansanm-s, which overlap extensively. (Many individuals belong to several different organizations at once, and many families contribute members to each group type.) Their members, therefore, are continually bringing the objectives, philosophies, technologies, and experiences they acquire in one group to others.

Chapter 8. Beyond "Democracy" and "Development"

1. This quotation is from the group meeting cited in chapter 1.

2. See chapter 4 for an explanation of *baka*-s.

3. A similar proverb states that "the needle sews the dress, only to send the pin off to the wedding."

4. Clerisme suggests that aid organizations should capitalize on "the patterns of accumulation that already exist in these groups" and discourage "less rational" ways of utilizing their resources (1978, 31).

5. These metaphors are consistent with group members' characterizations of themselves as "fingers on a hand" (as seen in chapter 4).

6. Another version of this proverb states, "*Dan gran moun yo gate men pawòl yo bon*" (The teeth of old folks are rotten, but their words are good).

7. This pattern is not uncommon in popular movements. Lara and Molina, for example, found that whereas members of smaller Costa Rican housing committees had a good deal of "sanctioning power" over leaders, in larger committees, "leaders gradually gain autonomy from the collective will; administration and decision-making are concentrated in the hands of a few" (1997, 45).

8. *Paske nou se piti, yo pran n pou pitimi.*

9. By asserting that white foreign people are thinkers and Haitian people are beggars, the missionary had launched one of the most shaming insults possible in Haitian culture. This insult was emblazoned in the local collective memory and had come to signify more broadly the lack of respect given rural Haitians by outsiders. I was told about the event, which had occurred many years earlier, at least five or six times by young people in Nazon.

10. Many GPs have been closely associated with Catholic and, less frequently, Protestant institutions. Even those that have not been (e.g., Zepòl Sou Zepòl) generally begin and end their meetings with a Christian prayer or song. Ideas about Vodou that have been prominent within the hierarchies of the Catholic and Protestant churches (which, along with the Haitian state, have orchestrated numerous anti-Vodou campaigns [see Hurbon 1995]) have meant that many GP groups have been encouraged by Catholic or Protestant sponsors to distance themselves from Vodou traditions. This is being challenged, however, as more and more gwoupmans become involved in a larger, nationwide campaign to challenge prejudices against Vodou and to eradicate oppression against its practitioners. As this occurs, acknowledgements of the lwa-s and practices from the ounfò have been showing up more often at GP events, particularly the large peasant-group congresses. There are annual meetings bringing together group representatives throughout a region or throughout the country.

11. Most rural Haitian schools provide no nourishment at all for their students during the day. Children whose parents cannot afford to give them enough change with which to buy a piece of bread or some peanuts from a local merchant during their breaks must wait until they return home in the evenings to eat. Because walks to school can range anywhere for a few minutes to several hours one way, this may mean going for eight, ten, or twelve hours without nourishment.

12. Although we learned that Klesiyis had been chosen for the Lakay abitasyon and had agreed to take the job, I was not able to follow how this strategy developed after my departure.

13. This force, called the National Haitian Police (PNH), was initiated, trained, and deployed by the CIVPOL, a UN civilian police force.

14. This song, "San Nou Ki La" (It's My Blood Down There), is recorded by the Neville Brothers and Les Frères Parents on the collection *Konbit: Burning Rhythms of Haiti.*

15. See Escobar 1995; Giri 1992; Haynes 1997; R. Maguire 1990; Sachs 1993; Verhelst 1990.

16. See Smarth 1997 for a glimpse at inequalities within more urban-based popular movements in Haiti; see also Ehrenberg 1999, Kaufman 1997, McIlwaine 1998, and Schild 1997 for illustrations from Latin America.

17. The Papaye Peasant Movement (Mouvman Peyizan Papay) was organizing a national, annual peasant congress, the National Movement of the Papaye Congress, as early as the late 1980s and has become a very important voice in national politics. It has also established partnerships with organizations in other regions of North, South, and Central America, as well as in Europe.

Bibliography

Abbott, Elizabeth. 1988. *Haiti: The Duvaliers and Their Legacy.* New York: McGraw-Hill.

Abu-Lughod, Lila. 1990. The Romance of Resistance: Tracing Transformations of Power through Bedouin Women. *American Ethnologist* 17(1): 41–55.

Alfonso, Haroldo Dilla. 1997. "Political Decentralization and Popular Alternatives: A View from the South." In *Community Power and Grassroots Democracy: The Transformation of Social Life,* edited by M. Kaufman and H. Alfonso, 170–88. London: Zed Books.

Alvarez, Sonia E. 1997. "Reweaving the Fabric of Collective Action: Social Movements and Challenges to 'Actually Existing Democracy' in Brazil." In *Between Resistance and Revolution: Cultural Politics and Social Protest,* edited by R. Fox and O. Starn, 83–117. New Brunswick, N.J.: Rutgers University Press.

Alvarez, Sonia E., Evelina Dagnino, and Arturo Escobar, eds. 1998a. *Cultures of Politics, Politics of Cultures: Re-visioning Latin American Social Movements.* Boulder, Colo.: Westview Press.

———. 1998b. "Introduction: The Cultural and Political in Latin American Social Movements." In *Cultures of Politics, Politics of Cultures: Re-visioning Latin American Social Movements,* edited by S. Alvarez, E. Dagnino, and A. Escobar, 1–32. Boulder, Colo.: Westview Press.

Anglade, Georges. 1977. *Mon Pays D'Haïti.* Port-au-Prince: Les Éditions de L'Action Sociale.

Aristide, Marx V., and Laurie Richardson. 1994a. "Haiti's Popular Resistance." *NACLA Report on the Americas* (January-February) 37 (4):30–36.

———. 1994b. " 'Democracy Enhancements'—U.S. Style." *NACLA Report on the Americas* (January-February) 37(4):35.

Arthur, Charles. 1995. *After the Dance, the Drum Is Heavy: Haiti One Year after the Invasion.* London: Haiti Support Group.

Averill, Gage. 1997. *A Day for the Hunter, A Day for the Prey: Popular Music and Power in Haiti.* Chicago: University of Chicago Press.

Bajeaux, Jean-Claude. 1994. "An Embarrassing Presence." *New York Review of Books* (November 3):37–38.

Baldez, Lisa. 1998. "Women's Organizations and the Development of Civil Society." *American Anthropologist* 100 (3):785–88.

Barthélemy, Gérard. 1989. *Le Pays en Dehors: Essai sur l'Univers Rural Haïtien.* Port-au-Prince: Henri Deschamps.

Bastien, Rémy. 1985 [1951]. *Le paysan Haïtien et Sa Famille: Vallée de Marbial.* Paris: A.C.C.T. and Karthala.

213

Bellegarde-Smith, Patrick. 1990. *Haiti: The Breached Citadel.* Boulder, Colo.: Westview Press.

Bilby, Kenneth M. 1985. *The Caribbean as a Musical Region.* Washington, D.C.: Woodrow Wilson International Center for Scholars, Latin American Program.

Blaike, Piers, and Harold Brookfield. 1987. "Defining and Debating the Problem." In *Land Degradation and Society*, edited by P. Blaike and H. Brookfield, 1–26. New York: Methuen.

Boff, Leonardo, and Clovodis Boff. 1987. *Introducing Liberation Theology.* Translated by Paul Burns. Maryknoll, N.Y.: Orbis Press.

Boukman Eksperyans. 1992. Liner notes to *Kalfou Danjere.* Mango Records 162–539–927–2. Compact disc.

Bourdieu, Pierre. 1990. *The Logic of Practice.* Translated by Richard Nice. Stanford: Standford University Press.

Brown, Karen McCarthy. 1991. *Mama Lola: A Vodou Priestess in Brooklyn.* Berkeley: University of California Press.

Burton, Richard D.E. 1997. *Afro-Creole: Power, Opposition, and Play in the Caribbean.* Ithaca: Cornell University Press.

Castañeda, Jorje G. 1996. "Democracy and Inequality in Latin America: A Tension of the Times." In *Constructing Democratic Governance: Latin America and the Caribbean in the 1990s*, edited by J.I. Domínguez and A.F. Lowenthal, 42–63. Baltimore: Johns Hopkins University Press.

Castor, Suzy. 1988. *L'Occupation Americaine d'Haïti.* Port-au-Prince: Henri Deschamps.

Chalmers, Douglas A., Scott B. Martin, and Kerianne Piester. 1997. "Associative Networks: New Structures of Representation for the Popular Sectors?" In *The New Politics of Inequality in Latin America: Rethinking Participation and Representation*, edited by D.A. Chalmers, S.B. Martin, and K. Piester, 543–87. New York: Oxford University Press.

Ching, Barbara, and Gerald W. Creed, eds. 1997. *Knowing Your Place: Rural Identity and Cultural Hierarchy.* New York: Routledge.

Chomsky, Noam. 1994. Introduction to *The Uses of Haiti* by Paul Farmer, 13–44. Monroe, Maine: Common Courage Press.

Clerisme, Calixte. 1978. "Organizations Paysannes dans le Developpement Rural." *Conjonction* 140:5–45.

Cliff, Michelle. 1984. *Abeng.* New York: Penguin Books.

Clough, Michael. 1999. "Reflections on Civil Society." *The Nation* February 22:16–18.

Comaroff, Jean. 1985. *Body of Power, Spirit of Resistance: The Culture and History of a South African People.* Chicago: University of Chicago Press.

Comaroff, Jean, and John Comaroff. 1991. *Of Revelation and Revolution: Christianity, Colonialism and Consciousness in South Africa.* Vol. 1. Chicago: University of Chicago Press.

Conway, Frederick J. 1989. "Haiti: The Society and Its Environment." In *Dominican Republic and Haiti: Country Studies*, edited by R.A. Haggerty, 239–78. Washington, D.C.: Library of Congress Federal Research Division.

Cooley-Proust, Worth. 1995. "Reflections on Learning Washington from Haiti." *Haiti News* 11(1):5–13.

Cooper, Frederick, F.E. Mallon, S.J. Stern, A.F. Isaacman, and W. Roseberry. 1993. *Confronting Historical Paradigms: Peasants, Labor, and the Capitalist World System in Africa and Latin America.* Madison: University of Wisconsin Press.

Coplan, David B. 1987. "Eloquent Knowledge: Lesotho Migrants' Songs and the Anthropology of Experience." *American Ethnologist* 14(3):413–33.

Council on Hemispheric Affairs (CHA) and Inter-Hemispheric Education Resource Center (IHERC). 1990. *National Endowment for Democracy (NED): A Foreign Policy Branch Gone Awry.* Washington, D.C.:CHA and IHERC.

Courlander, Harold. 1973 [1960]. *The Drum and the Hoe: Life and Lore of the Haitian People.* Berkeley: University of California Press.

Dalton, Harlon L. 1995. *Racial Healing: Confronting the Fear Between Blacks and Whites.* New York: Doubleday.

Deren, Maya. 1970 [1953]. *Divine Horsemen: The Living Gods of Haiti.* Kingston, N.Y.: McPherson and Company.

Deshommes, Fritz. 1995. *Neolibéralisme: Crise Economique et Alternative de Développement.* Port-au-Prince: Imprimer II.

Desmangles, Leslie G. 1992. *The Faces of the Gods: Vodou and Roman Catholicism in Haiti.* Chapel Hill: University of North Carolina Press.

Devin, Robin Block. 1995. "Women's Work and Child Health in Rural Haiti." Ph.D. dissertation, University of Connecticut.

DeWind, Josh, and David H. Kinley III. 1986. *Aiding Migration: The Impact of International Development Assistance on Haiti.* Boulder, Colo.: Westview Press.

Diederich, Bernard. 1985. "Swine Fever Ironies: The Slaughter of the Haitian Black Pig." *Caribbean Review* 14 (1): 16–17, 41.

Dirks, Nicholas B. 1992. "Ritual and Resistance: Subversion as a Social Fact." In *Contesting Power: Resistance and Everyday Relations in South Asia,* edited by D. Haynes and G. Haynes, 213–38. Berkeley: University of California Press.

Dupuy, Alex. 1989. *Haiti in the World Economy: Class, Race and Underdevelopment Since 1700.* Boulder, Colo.: Westview Press.

Eckstein, Susan. 1989. "Power and Popular Protest in Latin America." In *Power and Popular Protest: Latin American Social Movements,* edited by Susan Eckstein, 1–60. Berkeley: University of California Press.

Economist Intelligence Unit (EIU), and Business International. 1991–92. "Haiti." In *Dominican Republic, Haiti, Puerto Rico Country Profile: Annual Survey of Political and Economic Background.* London: EIU.

Ehrenberg, John. 1999. *Civil Society: The Critical History of an Idea.* New York: New York University Press.

Elie, Jean Rénol. 1992. *Òganizasyon Peyizan Yo nan Kalfou 92 la.* Port-au-Prince: L'Imperimeur II.

Epstein, Robin. 1996. Barbara Kingsolver (interview). *The Progressive* 60 (February): 33–37.

Erasmus, Charles John. 1952. "Agricultural Changes in Haiti: Patterns of Resistance and Acceptance." *Human Organization* 11: 20–26,

———. 1956. "Culture, Structure and Process: The Occurrence and Disappearance of Reciprocal Farm Labor." *Southwestern Journal of Anthropology* 12: 444–69.

Escobar, Arturo. 1992. "Culture, Economics and Politics in Latin American Social Movements: Theory and Research." In *The Making of Social Movements in Latin America,* edited by A. Escobar and S. E. Alvarez, 62–85. Boulder, Colo.: Westview Press.

———. 1995. *Encountering Development: The Making and Unmaking of the Third World.* Princeton: Princeton University Press.

Escobar, Arturo, and Sonia E. Alvarez. 1992. "Introduction: Theory and Protest in Latin America Today." In *The Making of Social Movements in Latin America: Identity,*

Strategy, and Democracy, edited by A. Escobar and S. E. Alvarez, 1–15. Boulder, Colo.: Westview Press.

Esteva, Gustavo. 1993. "Development." In *The Development Dictionary: A Guide to Knowledge as Power*, edited by W. Sachs, 6–25. Johannesburg: Witwatersrand University Press.

———. 1999. "The Zapatistas and People's Power." *Capital and Class* 68: 153–82.

Fabian, Johannes. 1983. *Time and the Other: How Anthropology Makes Its Object.* New York: Columbia University Press.

Fanon, Frantz. 1963. *The Wretched of the Earth.* Translated by C. Farrington. New York: Grove Weidenfeld.

Farah, Douglas. 1995. "Haitians Turnout Light in Vote for President: Wish for Aristide to Stay on Cited as Factor." *Washington Post* (December 18): A1.

Farmer, Paul. 1992. *AIDS and Accusation: Haiti and the Geography of Blame.* Berkeley: University of California Press.

———. 1994a. *The Uses of Haiti.* Monroe, Maine: Common Courage Press.

———. 1994b. "Swine Aid." In *The Haiti Files: Decoding the Crisis*, edited by J. Ridgeway, 130–33. Washington, D.C.: Essential Books/Azul Editions.

———. 1996. "On Suffering and Structural Violence: A View from Below." *Daedalus* 125 (1); 261–83.

Fass, Simon M. 1988. *Political Economy in Haiti: The Drama of Survival.* New Brunswick, N.J.: Transaction Books.

Fick, Carolyn E. 1990. *The Making of Haiti.: The Saint Domingue Revolution from Below.* Knoxville: University of Tennessee Press.

Fisher, William F. 1997. "Doing Good? The Politics and Antipolitics of NGO Practices." *Annual Review of Anthropology* 26: 439–64.

Freeman, Bryant, and Jowel Laguerre. 1996. *Haitian-English Dictionary.* Lawrence, Kans.: Institute of Haitian Studies.

Freire, Paulo. 1983. *Pedagogy of the Oppressed*, 2nd ed. Translated by M. B. Ramos. New York: Continuum.

Froele, Bryan T. 1994. "Religious Competition, Community Building, and Democracy in Latin America: Grassroots Religious Organizations in Venezuela." *Sociology of Religion* 55 (2): 145–62.

Gagnon, Anita J. 1986. "Health for All in Montrouis, Haiti." *International Nursing Review* 33(5): 135–139.

Gardner, Katy, and David Lewis. 1996. *Anthropology, Development and the Postmodern Challenge.* Chicago: Pluto.

Geertz, Clifford. 1973. *The Interpretation of Cultures.* New York: Basic Books.

Gillis, Verna, and Gage Averill. 1991. Liner notes to *Caribbean Revels: Haitian Rara and Dominican Gaga.* Washington, D.C.: Smithsonian/Folkways SF CD 40402.

Gilroy, Paul. 1991. *There Ain't No Black in the Union Jack: The Cultural Politics of Race and Nation.* Chicago: University of Chicago Press.

Giri, Ananta. 1992. "Understanding Contemporary Social Movements." *Dialectical Anthropology* 17: 35–49.

Glick Schiller, Nina, and Georges E. Fouron. 1990. " 'Everywhere we go, we are in danger': Ti Manno and the Emergence of a Haitian Transnational Identity." *American Ethnologist* 17 (2): 329–47.

Gramsci, Antonio. 1991. *Prison Notebooks.* New York: Columbia University Press.

Greene, Anne. 1993. *The Catholic Church in Haiti: Political and Social Change.* East Lansing: Michigan State University Press.

Haiti Information Bureau (HIB). 1994. "Subverting Democracy." In *The Haiti Files:*

Decoding the Crisis, edited by J. Ridgeway, 157–62. Washington, D.C.: Essential Books/ Azul Editions.

Haïti Progrès. 1996. "Plan Américain Qui en Est Complice?" Editorial. *Haïti Progrès* (May 3–9) 13 (6): 6, 16–17.

Hall, Robert Burnett. 1929. "The Société Congo of the Ile À Gonave." *American Anthropologist* 31: 685–700.

Haraway, Donna J. 1988. "Situated Knowledges: The Science Question in Feminism and the Privilege of Partial Perspective." *Feminist Studies* 14(3): 575–99.

Harvey, David. 1996. *Justice, Nature and the Geography of Difference.* Malden, Mass.: Blackwell Publishers.

Haynes, Jeff. 1997. *Democracy and Civil Society in the Third World: Politics and New Political Movements.* Cambridge, U.K.: Polity.

Heinl, Robert D., and Nancy G. Heinl. 1978. *Written in Blood: The Story of the Haitian People, 1492–1971.* Boston: Houghton Mifflin.

Herskovits, Melville J. 1971 [1937]. *Life in a Haitian Valley.* Garden City, N.Y.: Anchor Books.

Holland, Dorothy, and Margaret Eisenhart. 1990. *Educated in Romance: Women, Achievement, and College Culture.* Chicago: University of Chicago.

Holland, Dorothy, and Debra Skinner. 1995. "Contested Ritual, Contested Femininities: (Re)Forming Self and Society in a Nepali Women's Festival." *American Ethnologist* 22 (2): 279–305.

Hunter, Brian, ed. 1996–97. *The Statesman's Year-Book: A Statistical, Political and Economic Account of the States of the World.* 133rd ed. New York: St. Martin's Press.

Hurbon, Laënnec. 1995. *Voodoo: Search for the Spirit.* Translated by L. Frankel. New York: Harry N. Abrams.

Institute for Agriculture and Trade Policy. 1996. "Haitian Agriculture: Exports, Imports and Food." *NAFTA and Inter-American Trade Monitor* (March 22) 3 (6).

Inter-Hemispheric Education Resource Center (IHERC). 1992. "Populism, Conservativism, and Civil Society in Haiti." *The NED Backgrounder* 1(2).

International Organization for Migration (IOM), and the USAID Office of Transition Initiatives (OTI). 1994. *Initial Field Interview Guidelines.* Distributed to the staff of the IOM Community Governance Program.

Isaacman, Allen F. 1993. "Peasants and Rural Social Protest in Africa." In *Confronting Historical Paradigms: Peasants, Labor, and the Capitalist World System in Africa and Latin America,* edited by F. Cooper, F.E. Mallon, S.J. Stern, A.F. Isaacman, and W. Roseberry, 205–317. Madison: University of Wisconsin Press.

Izmery, Antoine. 1994. A "Fake Kind of Development: An Interview with Antoine Izmery." In *The Haiti Files: Decoding the Crisis,* J. Ridgeway, 155–56. Washington, D.C.: Essential Books/Azul Editions.

James, C.L.R. 1989 [1963]. *The Black Jacobins: Toussaint L'Ouverture and the San Domingo Revolution.* 2nd rev. ed. New York: Vintage Books.

Kaufman, Michael. 1997. "Differential Participation: Men, Women and Popular Power." In *Community Power and Grassroots Democracy: The Transformation of Social Life,* edited by M. Kaufman and H.D. Alfonso, 151–69. London: Zed Books.

Kearney, Michael. 1996. *Reconceptualizing the Peasantry: Anthropology in Global Perspective.* Boulder, Colo.: Westview Press.

Kennedy, Marie, and Chris Tilly. 1996. "Up against the 'Death Plan': Haitians Resist U.S.-Imposed Economic Restructuring." *Dollars and Sense* (April): 8–11, 43–45.

Kleymeyer, Charles David. 1994. "Cultural Expression and Grassroots Development."

In *Cultural Expression and Grassroots Development: Cases from Latin America and the Caribbean*, edited by C. D. Kleymeyer, 195–214. Boulder, Colo.: Lynne Rienner.

Kovaleski, Serge. 1999. "A Nation in Need: After 5-Year U.S. Intervention, Democracy in Haiti Looks Bleak." *Washington Post Foreign Service* (September 21): A13.

LaClau, Ernesto, and Chantal Mouffe. 1985. *Hegemony and Socialist Strategy: Towards a Radical Democratic Politics.* London: Verso.

Laguerre, Michel. 1975. "Les Associations Traditionnelles de Travail dans la Paysannerie Haïtienne." Paper for Institut Interamericain de Sciences Agricoles de l'OEA (IICA), Port-au-Prince, Haiti.

Lappé, Frances Moore, Joseph Collins, and David Kinley. 1981. *Aid as Obstacle: Twenty Questions about Our Foreign Aid and the Hungry.* San Francisco: Institute for Food and Development Policy.

Lara, Silvia, and Eugenia Molina. 1997. "Participation and Popular Democracy in Committees for the Struggle for Housing in Costa Rica." In *Community Power and Grassroots Democracy: The Transformation of Social Life*, edited by M. Kaufman and H. D. Alfonso, 27–54. London: Zed Books.

Levinson, Bradley A., and Dorothy Holland. 1996. "The Cultural Production of the Educated Person: An Introduction." In *The Cultural Production of the Educated Person: Critical Ethnographies of Schooling and Local Practice*, edited by B. A. Levinson, D. E. Foley, and D. C. Holland. New York: SUNY Press.

Lewis, David. 1999. "Revealing, Widening, Deepening? A Review of the Existing and Potential Contribution of Anthropological Approaches to 'Third-Sector' Research." *Human Organization* 58 (1): 73–81.

Leyburn, James G. 1941. *The Haitian People.* New Haven: Yale University Press.

Lind, Amy Conger. 1992. "Power, Gender, and Development: Popular Women's Organizations and the Politics of Needs in Ecuador." In *The Making of Social Movements in Latin America: Identity, Strategy, and Democracy*, edited by A. Escobar and S. E. Alvarez, 134–49. Boulder, Colo.: Westview Press.

Lummis C. Douglas. 1996. *Radical Democracy.* Ithaca: Cornell University Press.

Lundahl, Mats. 1979. *Peasants and Poverty: A Study of Haiti.* London: Croom Helm.

———. 1983. *The Haitian Economy: Man, Land, and Markets.* New York: St. Martin's Press.

Macdonald, Laura. 1997. *Supporting Civil Society: The Political Role of Non-Governmental Organizations in Central America.* New York: St. Martins Press.

Maguire, Robert. 1990. "The Peasantry and Political Change in Haiti." *Caribbean Affairs* 4(2): 1–18.

Mainwaring, Scott, and Eduardo Viola. 1994. "New Social Movements, Political Culture, and Democracy: Brazil and Argentina in the 1980s." in *Social Movements in Latin America: The Experience of Peasants, Worker: Women, the Urban Poor, and the Middle Sectors* vol. 4 the series *Essays on Mexico, Central and South America: Scholarly Debates from the 1950s to the 1990s.* Jorge Dominguez, series editor 17–52. New York: Garland Publishing.

Márquez, Gabriel García. 1995. "The Solitude of Latin America" (Nobel Lecture, December 8, 1982). *Georgia Review* 45(1): 133–36.

Martínez, Samuel. 1996. *Peripheral Migrants: Haitians and Dominican Republic Sugar Plantations.* Knoxville: University of Tennessee Press.

Maternowska, Catherine. 1996. "Coups d'Etat and Contraceptives: A Political Economy Analysis of Family Planning in Haiti." Ph.D. dissertation, Columbia University.

May, Herbert G., and Bruce M. Metzger, eds. 1977. *New Oxford Annotated Bible with the Apocrypha*, revised standard version. New York: Oxford Univeristy Press.

McGowan, Lisa. 1997. *Democracy Undermined, Economic Justice Denied: Structural Adjustment and the Aid Juggernaut in Haiti.* Washington, D.C.: Development Group for Alternative Policies.

McIlwaine, Cathy. 1998. "Contesting Civil Society: Reflections from El Salvador." *Third World Quarterly* 19 (4): 651–72.

Meme, Antoni. 1996. "ONG ak Lit Popilè: Ki Danjè?" *Libète* (December 11): 6.

Métraux, Alfred. 1951. "Making a Living in the Marbial Valley (Haiti)." Occasional Papers in Education. Paris: UNESCO.

———. 1960. *Haiti: Black Peasants and Their Religion.* Transalted by P. Verger and A. Métraux. London: George G. Harrap and Co.

———. 1971. "Cooperative Labor Groups in Haiti." *In Peoples and Cultures of the Caribbean*, edited by M. Horowitz, 318–39. Garden City, N.Y.: Natural History Press.

———. 1972 [1959]. *Voodoo in Haiti.* Translated by H. Charteris. New York: Schocken Books.

Métraux, Rhoda. 1952. "Affiliations through Work in Marbial, Haiti." *Primitive Man* 25(1–2): 1–22.

Mintz, Sidney W. 1961. "Pratik: Haitian Personal Economic Relationships." In *Symposium: Patterns of Land Utilization and Other Papers*, edited by V. E. Garfield, 54–63. Seattle: American Ethnological Society (c/o University of Washington Press).

———. 1964. "The Employment of Capital by Market Women in Haiti." In *Capital, Saving and Credit in Peasant Societies: Studies from Asia, Oceania, the Caribbean and Middle America*, edited by R. Frith and B. Yamey, 256–86. Chicago: Aldine Publishing.

———. 1973. "A Note on the Definition of Peasantries." *Journal of Peasant Studies* 1(1): 91–106.

———. 1974. *Caribbean Transformations.* Baltimore: Johns Hopkins University Press.

———. 1985. "From Plantations to Peasantries in the Caribbean." In *Caribbean Contours*, edited by S. W. Mintz and S. Price. Baltimore: Johns Hopkins University Press.

———. 1990. "The Peasantry as a Sociohistorical Category: Examples from the Caribbean Region." In *Agrarian Society in History*, edited by M. Lundahl and T. Svensson, 31–40. New York: Routledge.

———. 1995. "Can Haiti Change?" *Foreign Affairs* 74(1): 3–86.

Mintz, Sidney W., and Richard Price. 1992 [1976]. *The Birth of African-American Culture.* Boston: Beacon Press.

Moral, Paul. 1978. *Le Paysan Haïtien: Étude sur la Vie Rurale en Haïti.* Port-au-Prince: Édition Fardin.

Munroe, Trevor. 1996. "Caribbean Democracy: Decay or Renewal?" In *Constructing Democratic Governance: Latin America and the Caribbean in the 1990s*, edited by J. I. Domínguez and A. F. Lowenthal, 104–117. Baltimore: Johns Hopkins University Press.

Murray, Gerald F. 1977. "The Evolution of Haitian Peasant Land Tenure: A Case Study in Agrarian Adaptation to Population Growth." Vols. 1 and 2. Ph.D. dissertation, Columbia University.

Murray, Gerald F., and Maria Alvarez. 1975. "Haitian Bean Circuits: Cropping and Trading Maneuvers among a Cash-Oriented Peasantry." In *Working Papers in Haitian Society and Culture*, edited by S. Mintz. New Haven: Yale University, Antilles Research Program.

Nash, June. 1992. "Interpreting Social Movements: Bolivian Resistance to Economic Conditions Imposed by the International Monetary Fund." *American Ethnologist* 19(2): 257–93.

National Labor Committee (NLC). 1994. "Sweatshop Development." In *The Haiti Files: Decoding the Crisis*, edited by J. Ridgeway, 134–54. Washington, D.C.: Essential Books/Azul Edition.

——. 1996. *The U.S. in Haiti: How to Get Rich on 11¢ an Hour.* Washington, D.C.: National Labor Committee Education Fund.

Nicholls, David. 1979. *From Dessalines to Duvalier: Race, Colour and National Independence in Haiti.* New York: Cambridge University Press.

Nonini, Donald M. 1992. *British Colonial Rule and the Resistance of the Malay Peasantry, 1900–1957.* New Haven: Yale University South East Asia Studies.

Pan American Health Organization (PAHO). 1990. *Health Conditions in the Americas.* Vols. 1 and 2. Washington, D.C.: World Health Organization.

Price-Mars, Jean. 1983 [1928]. *So Spoke the Uncle (Ainsi Parla l'Oncle).* Translated by M. W. Shannon. Washington, D.C.: Three Continents Press.

Ranemah, Majid. 1993. "Participation." In *The Development Dictionary: A Guide to Knowledge as Power*, edited by W. Sachs, 116–32. Johannesburg: Witwatersrand University Press.

Ransom, David. 1996. "The Poverty of Aid." *The New Internationalist* (November): 7–10.

Regan, Jane. 1994. "Haiti on the Brink." *The Progressive* (September): 20–24.

Richardson, Laurie, and Jean-Roland Chery. 1995–96. "Haiti's Not for Sale." *CovertAction Quarterly* (Winter) 55: 30–37.

——. 1997. *Feeding Dependency, Starving Democracy: USAID Policies in Haiti.* Boston: Grassroots International.

Richman, Karen. 1987. "They Will Remember Me in the House: The Song-*pwen* of Haitian Cassette-Discourse." Society for Latin American Anthropology Symposium, "Change and Continuity," 86th Meeting of the American Anthropological Association. Chicago.

——. 1992. "'A *Lavalas* at Home/A *Lavalas* for Home': Inflections of Transnationalism in the Discourse of Haitian President Aristide." In *Towards a Transnational Perspective on Migration: Race, Class, Ethnicity, and Nationalism Revisited*, edited by N. Glick Schiller, L. Basch, and C. Blanc-Szanton, 189–200. New York: New York Academy of Sciences.

Ridgeway, James. 1994. *The Haiti Files: Decoding the Crisis.* Washington, D.C.: Essential Books/Azul Editions.

Robertson; Roland. 1990. "Mapping the Global Condition: Globalization as the Central Concept." In *Global Culture: Nationalism, Globalization and Modernity*, edited by M. Featherstone, 15–30. London: Sage.

Robinson, Kathryn May. 1986. *Stepchildren of Progress: The Political Economy of Development in an Indonesian Mining Town.* New York: State University of New York Press.

Romain, Jacques. 1978 [1944]. *Masters of the Dew.* Translated by L. Hughes and M. Cook. London: Heinemann.

Roseberry, William. 1993. "Beyond the Agrarian Question in Latin America." In *Confronting Historical Paradigms: Peasants, Labor, and the Capitalist World System in Africa and Latin America*, edited by F. Cooper, F. E. Mallon, S. J. Stern, A. F. Isaacman and W. Roseberry, 318–68. Madison: University of Wisconsin Press.

Sachs, Wolfgang, ed. 1993. *The Development Dictionary: A Guide to Knowledge as Power.* Johannesburg: Witwatersrand University Press.

Sachs, Wolfgang. 1993. Introduction to *The Development Dictionary: A Guide to Knowledge as Power*, edited by W. Sachs, 1–5. Johannesburg: Witwatersrand University Press.

Schutt-Ainé, Patricia, ed. and Librairie Au Service de la Culture. 1994. *Haiti: A Basic Reference Book: General Information on Haiti*. Miami: Librairie Au Service de la Culture.

Schild, Veronica. 1997. "The Hidden Politics of Neighborhood Organizations: Women and Local Participation in the Poblaciones of Chile." In *Community Power and Grassroots Democracy: The Transformation of Social Life*, edited by M. Kaufman and H. D. Alfonso, 126–48. London: Zed Books.

Schwartz-Bart, Simone. 1982. *The Bridge of Beyond*. Translated by B. Bray. Portsmouth, N.H.: Heinemann.

Scott, James C. 1985. *Weapons of the Weak: Everyday Forms of Peasant Resistance*. New Haven: Yale University Press.

———. 1990. *Domination and the Arts of Resistance: Hidden Transcripts*. New Haven: Yale University Press.

Shanin, Teodor. 1990. "Agendas of Peasant Studies and the Perception of Parallel Realities." In *Defining Peasants: Essays Concerning Rural Societies, Expolary Economics, and Learning from Them in the Contemporary World*, edited by T. Shanin. Cambridge, Mass.: Basil Blackwell.

Shiva, Vandana. 1988. *Staying Alive: Women, Ecology, and Development*. London: Zed Books.

Singer, Merrill. 1994. "Community-Centered Praxis: Toward an Alternative Non-dominative Applied Anthropology." *Human Organization* 53 (4): 336–44.

Smarth, Luc. 1997. "Popular Organizations and the Transition to Democracy in Haiti." In *Community Power and Grassroots Democracy: The Transformation of Social Life*, edited by M. Kaufman and H. D. Alfonso, 102–125. London: Zed Books.

Smith, Gavin. 1989. *Livelihood and Resistance: Peasants and the Politics of Land in Peru*. Berkeley: University of California Press.

———. 1991. "The Production of Local Culture in Rebellion." In *Golden Ages, Dark Ages: Imagining the Past in Anthropology and History*, edited by J. O'Brien and Wm. Roseberry, 180–207. Berkeley: University of California Press.

Smith, Jackie. 1998. "Global Civil Society? : Transnational Social Movement Organizations and Social Capital." *American Behavioral Scientist* 42 (1) : 93–107.

Smith, Jennie M. 1993. "Discourse, Domination and Contradiction: The Interdiction, Repatriation and Detention of Haitian Refugees—September 1991–May 1992." Master's thesis, University of North Carolina at Chapel Hill.

———. 1998. "Answering the *Lanbi* : Sociopolitical Discourses and Collective Initiatives of the Haitian Peasantry." Ph.D. dissertation, University of North Carolina at Chapel Hill.

Smucker, Glenn R. 1983. "Peasants and Development Politics: A Study In Haitian Class and Culture." Ph.D. dissertation, New School for Social Research.

———. 1986. "Peasant Councils and the Politics of Community." In *Politics, Projects, and People: Institutional Development in Haiti*, edited by D. Brinkerhoff and J. C. Garcia-Zamor, 93–113. New York: Praeger.

———. 1996. "Political Implications of Grass-Roots Organizations in Haiti." Paper prepared for the Haiti Project, Center for Latin American Studies, School of Foreign Service, Georgetown University, Washington, D.C. October.

Smucker, Glenn R., and Dathis Noriac. 1996. *Peasant Organizations in Haiti: Trends and*

Implications. Comité Haitien de Développement, Institut de Consultation, d'Evaluation et de Formation, Inter-American Foundation.

Smucker, Jacqueline Nowak. 1981. *The Role of Rural Haitian Women in Development.* Port-au-Prince: United States Agency for International Development.

Spivak, Gayatri Chakravorty. 1988. "Can the Subaltern Speak?" In *Marxism and the Interpretation of Culture,* edited by C. Nelson and L. Grossberg, 271–313. Urbana: University of Illinois Press.

Starn, Orin. 1992. " 'I Dreamed of Foxes and Hawks': Reflections on Peasant Protest, New Social Movements, and the *Rondas Campesinas* of Northern Peru." In *The Making of Social Movements in Latin America: Identity, Strategy, and Democracy,* edited by A. Escobar and S. E. Alvarez, 89–111. Boulder, Colo.: Westview Press.

Systèms Agraires Caribéens et Alternatives de Développement Université des Antilles et de la Guyane (S.A.C.A.D.) and Faculté d'Agronomie et de Médecine Vétérinaire Université d'Etat d'Haïti (F.A.M.V.). 1993. *Stratégies et Logiques Sociales. Paysans, Systèmes et Crise: Travaux sur l'Agraire Haïtien.* Vol. 2. Port-au-Prince: S.A.C.A.D. and F.A.M.V.

Targète, Jean, and Raphael G. Urciolo. 1993. *Haitian Creole-English Dictionary.* Kensington, Md.: Dunwoody Press.

Thompson, E. P. (Edward Palmer). 1978. "Eighteenth-Century English Society: Class Struggle without Class?" *Social History* 3 (2): 133–65.

——. 1991. *Customs in Common.* London: Merlin Press.

Tolstoy, Leo. 1939. *Anna Karenina.* Translated by Constance Garnett. New York: Random House.

Trouillot, Michel-Rolph. 1990. *Haiti—State Against Nation: The Origins and Legacy of Duvalierism.* New York: Monthly Review Press.

——. 1991. "Anthropology and the Savage Slot: The Poetics and Politics of Otherness." In *Recapturing Anthropology: Working in the Present,* edited by R. Fox, 17–44. Sante Fe, N.M.: School of American Research Press.

Underwood, Frances W. 1960. *The Marketing System in Peasant Haiti.* Yale University Publications in Anthropology No. 60. New Haven: Yale University Press.

United States Agency for International Development (USAID). 1985. *Haiti: Country Environmental Profile: A Field Study.* Port-au-Prince: USAID.

——. 1994–96. *Haiti: USAID Monitering Report/Rapport de Suivi d'USAID 3–6.* Port-au-Prince: USAID.

——. 1994. *USAID/Haiti Recovery Program (October Briefing Book).* Port-au-Prince: USAID.

Valdman, Albert. 1981. *Haitian Creole-English-French Dictionary.* Vols. 1 and 2. Bloomington: Indiana University Creole Institute.

Vallès, Marie-Thérèse. 1967. *Les Idéologies Coopérativistes et Leur Applicabilité en Haïti.* Paris: G.-P. Maisonneuve et Larose.

Vander Zaag, Raymond. 1999. " 'We Do Not Yet Have Development': Encounters of Development Knowledges, Identities and Practices in a NGO Program in Rural Haiti." Ph.D. dissertation, Carleton University, Ottawa, Ontario.

Various Artists. 1989. *Konbit: Burning Rhythms of Haiti.* Compiled by Jonathan Demme. A&M Records. CS 5281.1989. Cassette recording.

Verhelst, Thierry. 1990. *No Life without Roots: Culture and Development.* Translated by B. Cumming. London: Zed Books.

Vilsaint, Féquière. 1991. *Diksyonè Anglè-Kreyòl/English-Kreyòl Dictionary.* Temple Terrace, Fl.: Educa Vision.

Voices for Haiti Campaign for a Just U.S. Policy. 1995. *A Report on U.S. Elections Assistance to Haiti.* Washington, D.C.: Voices for Haiti.

Washington Office on Haiti (WOH). 1995. *October 27 Special Issue Report on the Rice Corporation of Haiti, S.A.* Washington, D.C.: WOH.

Washington Office on Haiti (WOH), with the Haitian Advocacy Platform for an Alternative Development (PAPDA). 1996. *The Haiti Economic Justice Campaign Information Packet.* Washington, D.C.: WOH.

White, Anderson. 1992. "Peasant Groups and Innovations in Soil Conservation in Haiti." Master's Thesis, University of Minnesota.

———. 1993. *Study on the Role of Women in Agriculture, the Socio-economic Status of Women, and the Status of SCF-Supported "Groupment" and Women's Clubs in Maissade, Haiti.* Report prepared for Save the Children Federation, Port-au-Prince, Haiti.

———. 1994. "Collective Action for Watershed Management: Lessons from Haiti." Ph.D. dissertation, University of Minnesota.

White, Robert. 1997. *Haiti: Democrats vs. Democracy. International Policy Report.* Washington, D.C.: Center for International Policy.

Wilentz, Amy. 1989. *The Rainy Season: Haiti since Duvalier.* New York: Simon and Schuster.

Willis, Paul. 1977. *Learning to Labor: How Working Class Kids Got Working Class Jobs.* New York: Columbia University Press.

———. 1981. "Cultural Production Is Different from Cultural Reproduction Is Different from Social Reproduction Is Different from Reproduction." *Interchange* 12 (2–3): 48–67.

Wirkus, Faustin, and Taney Dudley. 1931. *The White King of La Gonave.* Garden City, N.Y.: Doubleday, Doran and Co.

Woodson, Drexel. 1990. "'Tout Moun Se Moun Men Tout Moun Pa Menm': Microlevel Sociocultural Aspects of Land Tenure in a Northern Haitian Locality." Ph.D. dissertation, University of Chicago.

Index

CPSIA information can be obtained
at www.ICGtesting.com
Printed in the USA
LVHW02s0025100818
586508LV00004B/372/P

9 780801 486739